# SYMBOLS AND MEANINGS IN SCHOOL MATHEMATICS

*Symbols and Meanings in School Mathematics* explores the various uses and aspects of symbols in school mathematics and also examines the notion of mathematical meaning. It is concerned with the power of language which enables us to do mathematics, giving us the ability to name and rename, to transform names and to use names and descriptions to conjure, communicate and control our images. It is in the interplay between language, image and object that mathematics is created and can be communicated to others.

One theme which runs throughout the book is the core metaphor of manipulation. Practical apparatus in North America is known as 'manipulatives', some recent computer software is known as a 'symbolic manipulator' and we are taught to manipulate numbers, algebraic expressions, and geometric figures and images. What does the omnipresence of this term describing the doing of mathematics tell us about the two fundamental metaphors in English for understanding: touch and sight?

The book also addresses a set of questions of particular relevance to the last decade of the twentieth century, which arise due to the rapidly-increasing proliferation of machines offering mathematical functionings. What new light do such machines throw on age-old discussions of the teaching and learning of mathematics, in particular, the common tension between fluency and understanding? What new perspective is cast on the question not 'what is there is be known?' but rather 'what is worth knowing?' in mathematics?

**David Pimm** is senior lecturer in mathematics education at The Open University. He is the author of *Speaking Mathematically* (Routledge 1987).

# SYMBOLS AND MEANINGS IN SCHOOL MATHEMATICS

*David Pimm*

London and New York

First published 1995
by Routledge
11 New Fetter Lane, London EC4P 4EE

Transferred to Digital Printing 2004

Simultaneously published in the USA and Canada
by Routledge
29 West 35th Street, New York, NY 10001

© 1995 David Pimm

Typeset in Palatino by
Ponting–Green Publishing Services, Chesham, Bucks

*British Library Cataloguing in Publication Data*
A catalogue record for this book is available from
the British Library

*Library of Congress Cataloging in Publication Data*
A catalogue record for this book has been requested

ISBN 0–415–11384–9 (hbk)
ISBN 0–415–11385–7 (pbk)

For Birute, and for Dick,
without whom this book wouldn't

# CONTENTS

# IN ACKNOWLEDGEMENT: NAMING NAMES

There are many people who have contributed to the forming of this book: offering ideas, words, encouragement, criticism, faith, love. To all I express my sincere thanks and probably mutual relief that it is finally over once more. Most importantly I want to thank Eric Love (for many discussions and words, most evidently in relation to Chapters 2, 3 and 9), Birute Macijauskas (for ideas about art and photography, particularly for many enjoyable priority wrestles over mathematics and art) and Dick Tahta (for many discussions, ideas and words, particularly for pointing me at Ivins). I also wish to thank: my family, David Wheeler, Rosemary Clarke (for the breathing lessons), Robin Foster, Dave Hewitt, Lesley Lee, Richard Noss, Eileen Phillips, Jaclyn Phillips, and all of my colleagues at the Centre for Mathematics Education, particularly Christine Shiu, John Mason, Alan Graham and Heather Cooke, for suggestions and textual improvements.

*Photographic credits:*
David Pimm (p. x); C. K. Cooke, reproduced by permission of the Head Teacher of Hillesley CEVA School, Glos, England (p. 15, top two); Purdue University News Service (1988), *Purdue Problem-Centered Mathematics Project*. West Lafayette, IN: Purdue University (p. 15, lower left); David Pimm (p. 15, lower right); Julia Musgrave (p. 34); Birute Macijauskas (p. 60); The Museum of Fine Arts, Houston, Texas: *Church Interior*, Josef Sudek (p. 78); Birute Macijauskas (p. 112, both); the estate of Harold St Gray (p. 113); Alison Cave (p. 114 and p. 115, bottom two); image uncredited, from *To Heal a Nation*, J. C. Scruggs and J. L. Swerdlow (Harper & Row, 1985) (p. 115, top); David Pimm (p. 116); Birute Macijauskas (p. 123); The Museum of the History of Science, Oxford: *The Measurers*, Hendrik van Balen (p. 136).

*Textual credits:*
I am most grateful to The Open University for permission to reuse substantial portions of the monograph entitled *Mathematics: Symbols and Meanings* which I wrote for the course EM236 *Learning and Teaching Mathematics* (1992).

Lines from 'Description Without Place' (p. 126) and 'Bouquet of Roses in Sunlight' (p. 191), *The Collected Poems of Wallace Stevens*, are reproduced with the kind permission of Faber and Faber Ltd and Random House Inc.

Every reasonable effort has been made to clear copyright permissions with the holders of materials reproduced in this book, but in some instances this has proved to be impossible.

# AN IDIOSYNCRATIC PREFACE

Some of the main themes of this book are what they are as a consequence of my having taken up the tenor saxophone at the age of thirty-eight, with little prior musical training. It had been a long time since I had attempted to learn something that would take a great deal of my attention and a very long time to master. But more relevantly here, I was confronted with:

- having to contend with a relatively new notation and my occasional symbol blindness;
- coming to grips with different naming systems for referring to notes (positional on a stave, letter names, tonic sol-fa, interval relations) and to relate all of these to fingerings and sounds, yet with the explicit goal of automation;
- musical theory, and being offered precepts like 'to find the relative minor of a major key go down a minor third', or 'Jazz is all II–V–I, while pop music is all I–IV–V';
- being offered images such as the mouth acting as a gasket not a clamp, or trying to swallow and yawn at the same time: until I discovered I was doing something that I wasn't aware I was doing (and that it could therefore be done otherwise), I could make no sense of this latter suggestion;
- striving for a physical fluency and finding on occasions that my fingers were in advance of my conscious brain – also, that letting go of wanting to 'understand' and having to be in conscious control sometimes allowed interesting things to happen;
- systematic practice, and its sometimes complex relation to perceived improvement.

Later discussions with a singing teacher added the following parallel. A hundred years ago, she claimed, professional singers were trained predominantly by being asked to listen intently and to copy closely, without asking why. Developments in twentieth-century understanding of human vocal and other anatomy, among other things, led to a new tradition of explaining why and linking the how and the why – and in the process of change something got lost. The historical switch seems to have been from how can *I* do what they are doing to how do *they* do it. (The focus is different, and it is not clear how my detailed understanding of the physical operation of certain parts of my body will allow me to achieve what certain others can achieve.) Young children learning to speak, despite being described as copying, do not look inside others' mouths in order to ascertain physically what they ought to be doing in order to imitate it. They work on their own vocal sound production and use their ears.

Sometimes, while learning to play, I found myself thinking about mathematics teaching and learning, about similarities and differences, and about genuine and false parallels. Some corresponding questions for mathematics education are: what is named and what power resides in one system of naming over another? Do we ever work on anything other than the notation? Why do we offer and generate images for mathematical practices? What relations are there between fluency and understanding as twin, conflicting(?), complementary(?), independent(?) aims for mathematics teaching?

Work in mathematics education frequently presumes a currency and topicality of issues unmatched by actual practitioner discussion, whose concerns may be quite different. Discussion of issues of symbol manipulation, fluency and practice, memorising tables and other manifestations of so-called 'rote' learning are not commonly to be found in mathematics education books and articles published in the early 1990s. But they have not gone away. And my struggles with the saxophone put me back into direct contact with some of them.

### The name of the rose by any other name

baptism is neither explanation, nor description, nor definition. Baptism, the giving of a name, is merely the tying together in association of a particular object or quality and a particular word.

(Ivins, 1969, p. 52)

Of the questions listed above, I was particularly struck by the phenomenon of naming. I had encountered oddities about naming and the thing named as a young adolescent engaged in the pursuit of plane spotting. It is the registration serial (the aircraft's *name* in some important sense), and not the object labelled, that is the main focus of attention and source of desire. As the same aeroplane (as an object) is bought and sold, it can have many different names over time, and sometimes more than one serial can be found on the same plane at the same time. As with fractions rather than rational numbers, for instance, it is often actual symbols rather than the referents that provide the focus of interest.

A similar situation recurs with car licence plates. In Britain, they used to be unique identifiers, and if the car were destroyed, so was the plate, never to reappear. The tie between symbol and object was strong and complete – one of those ties that bind. Later, the strength of the link between object and name lessened and cars could (legitimately) have different plates over time and conversely, plates could endure across different cars. With so-called vanity plates in particular, there is an interesting shift of field and ground, in that it is the plates that get traded as valuable or desirable objects, while the car becomes merely the symbolic holder for them.

'What's in a name?' is a question that has been frequently asked. Richard Feynman, in a much-quoted anecdote, recalls his father telling him:

> "You can know the name of that bird in all the languages of the world, but when you're finished, you'll know absolutely nothing about the bird. You'll only know about humans in different places and what they call the bird. So let's look at the bird and see what it's *doing* – that's what counts." (I learned very early the difference between knowing the name of something and knowing something.)
>
> (1988, p. 14)

I think the view expressed in this anecdote is fundamentally wrong, in the following sense. Naming is done for a reason; naming is seldom 'mere'; naming is almost never arbitrary in the sense of unthought about. Baptism usually takes place against a backdrop of existing names, knowledge and perceptions, reflected in the relevant category of names. Names stress and ignore. Naming structures frequently convey much information, provided that access to the system can be gained. Nowhere is this truer than in mathematics. (For example, what information is conveyed by various conic sections being called *parabolas, ellipses* and *hyperbolae*?)

It is a common task in geometry to be asked to name things. Much of what comes under the English National Curriculum heading of 'Shape and Space' actually concerns naming knowledge. Naming allows you to talk about things you can see – you can use language to point. Naming also allows classification – and use of the same name invites pupils to look for similarities between things. However, naming *per se* is not the point of the exercise. In its worst form, the purposes behind geometrical naming get lost and the process degenerates into a sort of feeble natural history for shapes.

One aspect of geometry that is frequently missing is any sense of purpose in the classification. Why bother distinguishing rhombuses from kites, squares from rectangles, among all possible quadrilaterals? One important reason is that there are 'nice' results to be declared about particular collections of figures. Frequently, classes of shapes are brought into existence because they are precisely those objects that answer a particular question in geometry. (For more, see Mason, 1990b.)

There is a strong tendency to assume that if two things have the same name, or if the same symbol is used, such as '+' or '=', then they refer to the same object. Conversely, if they have different names, such as 'square' and 'rectangle', then they are surely necessarily different things, for otherwise they *would* have the same name. This assumption can have positive benefits in mathematics, where it is quite common for the same word or symbol to be used in contexts where the things referred to seem quite different, by hinting at underlying connections.

There is also always the possibility of confusion between symbol and object, particularly when mathematicians exploit such links between properties of the symbols and those of the objects in order to reduce the memory load when doing calculations. ('To multiply by ten, add a 0' or 'An even number is one that ends in a 2, 4, 6, 8, or 0'.) One teacher recalled being good at maths as a child and being very pleased with a question he had thought up when he was ten: why do two minuses make a plus and not an equals? He was understanding *make* to mean 'constitute' and two '−' could equally well be used to form the '=' sign as a '+' sign. He reported finding it hard to comprehend why his teacher wasn't very pleased with his question.

Most importantly, naming is one of the fundamental activities of mathematics. It is far from passive; on the contrary, it allows mathematics to be done. Names form part of both a cultural and an individual psychic context, attracting layers of meaning and serving as triggers calling forth responses at many levels. When the focus is on symbolising for naming alone, you may use different criteria from when invoking symbols for manipulation.

A very familiar tension in teaching mathematics at whatever level is between wanting symbols to be 'iconic', that is readily transparent with respect to their meaning or reference while yet, for fluency and automation, more compact, opaque symbols are frequently more efficient. There is a frequent trade-off: the more transparent a symbolism, the less compact, and hence the less easily manipulated. This is a theme that I shall come back to time and again.

The mathematical uses of language are not fundamentally different from other cultural uses, and the same questions of identity, form and function, of object and symbol, of purpose and meaning, are key elements in any account of teaching, learning and doing mathematics. This book is my attempt at a systematic exploration in the context of those mathematical 'objects', ideas, techniques, processes, and forms that are commonly invoked in schools.

# 1

# INTRODUCTION

Before anyone can reach spoken speech, he must already have access to meanings or he could retain nothing. No object has a name *per se*, and the name of an object means only something in the code (the language) that one has accpeted. But an object, name aside, has a meaning of its own, and all of us have had the good sense from our crib and later on, even without speech, to recognize meaning, to gain access to meaning. And once we have a general access to meaning, then we can put different labels on it, and the labels will stick to the meaning. Speech can come only after we have grasped the existence of meanings.

(Gattegno, 1970, pp. 17–18)

I begin with an anecdote. I was visiting friends in America and it had been some years since I had seen them. In the intervening space of time, their daughter, Lynn, had been born: she was now nearly two. My plane was delayed, so I arrived after Lynn was in bed, although she knew I was coming. The next morning, I awoke and, from the next room, I heard Lynn calling: "Mummy, Daddy, David, David, David. David, come here, come here now, I want you". I was summoned; I could only obey! I went into her room and saw a little girl standing up in her cot, half-excited and half-frightened by my image, an image she had conjured up by the use of language, and by the use of names in particular. Naming gives you a certain power over the external world.

This is a book about mathematics and language. It is the power of language in enabling us to do mathematics which I have chosen to focus on: a power we all share to a greater or lesser extent by having access to the resources of our native tongues. Having recourse to a language affords a power to name and rename, to transform names, to use names and descriptions to conjure, communicate and control our images, our mental worlds. Caleb Gattegno has written: "We live in our images and in this sense there is no reality that is not human" (cited in Beeney *et al.* 1982, p. 4). Images are also a major part of the stuff of mathematics, and consequently images as well as names will be in focus during the course of this book.

It is in the interplay among and substitution between language (including those designating words that name), image (including illustrative drawings that represent) and thing, between symbol and referent, that mathematics is created and can be communicated to others. The artist René Magritte wrote: "Sometimes the name of an object takes the place of an image. A word can take the place of an object in reality. An image can take the place of a word in a proposition" (cited in Foucault 1983, p. 38). Although not talking specifically about mathematics, he could very well have been. Zoltan Dienes (1963, p. 163) has provocatively claimed: "The process of connecting symbolism to imagery is at the heart of mathematics learning. It can be done by means of 'cover stories' or embodiments." Dienes' claim seems to imply there is no means by which this fusion can be made directly. We shall see.

But 'cover stories', those accounts we tell ourselves and others about what we are doing, as well as physical embodiments (often called 'manipulatives' in North America), will also be brought into play, offering vivid mementos and sometimes meaning by embedding accounts of what is to be done in everyday objects and practices. In algebra, talk of apples and oranges among pupils is common. With negative number operations, discussion might involve debits and credits, temperatures, or even time running forwards and backwards. Bob Davis's ingeniously contrived story of people jumping into (positive) and out of a pool combined with running the film forwards (positive) and backwards as the two operations, does indeed predict that running the film backwards of someone jumping out shows someone jumping in ('a minus times a minus makes a plus').

Despite the ingenuity of this account, however, it seems unclear to me whether this adds to a pupil's understanding or store of meanings for multiplication of negative numbers. It is more as if the vivid story serves as a mnemonic device for recalling (or possibly reconstructing) what happens, rather than explaining or accounting for it.[1] These examples make me wonder about the images offered for mathematical processes and the terms in which accounts are given for justifying why certain things are as they are.

Certain images deliberately offered or unwittingly invoked when talking about what we are doing in mathematics can be quite curious. When subtracting, the operation of 'carrying' is sometimes talked about in terms of milk bottles and 'paying back on the doorstep' or 'borrowing' from the 'next door' or 'neighbouring' column as one might a bowl of sugar. Do these classroom ways of speaking sometimes get the better of us? Why do we continue to use them?

Mathematics educators also make use of cover stories, those conventional terms and language patterns for discussing the teaching and learning of mathematics in schools. These, too, are worthy of more than a passing glance, though I only do this systematically in the penultimate chapter. But two key terms in this lexicon are unquestionably 'understanding' and 'meaning'.

What we variously understand by 'understanding' and mean by 'meaning' is far from obvious or clear, despite these being two central terms in any discussion of the learning and teaching of mathematics at whatever level. Understanding can arise from the creative use of language (particularly metaphor), and from images offering sudden illumination. Meaning seems, in part at least, to be more concerned with reference, hence more specific, more local; understanding seems less concerned with such particularities. Yet meaning can also come about from associations and connections (such as that between the last number said when counting and the number of objects in a set, or, going to extremes, the play on words which links 'pie' charts to 'pi'), as well as from a more direct sense of reference, of knowing 'what the fraction 2/7 refers to' in some particular context. As the linguist Paul Zipf has claimed: "Meaning is slippery stuff".

One continuing source of difficulty in learning mathematics comes from confusion of senses of words and other symbols which have particular and (often) variant meanings. Within mathematical language itself, there are questions about the choices of particular words that are conventionally employed. Why do we use the same word, 'multiplication', for quite different operations: between whole numbers, between negative numbers, between fractions and between matrices? Why do we call the first three of these 'numbers', but not the last?

In many cases, however, confusion has to do with a word having two or more senses in different contexts, and one sense being stronger. There are also instances where the word is similar in sound or spelling to another and gets absorbed into it, despite the meanings having no apparent connection. (If the same word is used in two different settings, it is usually possible to find some connection, over and above the fact that the same word symbol has been used.) Valerie Walkerdine (1982, p. 152) cites the example of a child in an infant class where, when asked what they were doing, replied, "You have to colour all the evil numbers in. First you have to write it up to a hundred and then you colour all the evil numbers in". Hassler Whitney (1973) has remarked on the closeness of the words 'fraction' and 'fracture' and suggests a possible sliding connection at the verbal level and a consequent accretion of senses. Many young children will have heard over and over the story of *The Gingerbread Boy*. This too may contribute to their sense of fraction.

He [the fox] tossed the Gingerbread Boy into the air. The fox opened his mouth and *snap* went his teeth. 'Oh dear', said the little Gingerbread Boy, 'I am one-quarter gone'. Then he cried, 'I am half gone'.

Then he cried, 'I am three-quarters gone'. And after that, the little Gingerbread Boy said nothing more, at all.

The connections pupils make in mathematics, when the teacher may only be aware of the customary mathematical sense of a particular word or phrase, can be fascinating. An instance of such connections surfacing came from a class exercise where a researcher invited twelve-year-old pupils with whom he had been working to write about their favourite fraction and to say why (Kieren, 1991). One pupil wrote:

My favourite fraction is 4/5. This is my favourite fraction because it gives me a lot of things to remember. Because there are five people in my family and only four of them are living in my house. My mom is the fifth person. She's the one that is gone.[2]

As my title suggests, this book is concerned with various uses and aspects of symbols in school mathematics, and also looks at the notion of mathematical meaning. The opening quotation from Gattegno makes a claim that meanings somehow exist prior to their being named. I have certainly had the experience of being in a foreign country and because I understood the situation could attend to the language to find out how to say what I already knew how to do. Margaret Donaldson's work (1979) on the greater sophistication of thinking exhibited by young children when offered versions of Piagetian tasks embedded in situations that made what she terms 'human sense' is also consonant with this.

However, I additionally wish to explore how names and other symbols can also bring meanings into being, reversing that sense of antecedent priority. At times, the form of the words can give rise to meaning, to understanding, making links across the symbolic gulf in the reverse direction. This is particularly so in mathematics, when the symbols may at the very least mediate our contact with the 'objects', and at times provide the primary experience. Stravinsky once insisted that it was words not meanings that he needed, when queried about his use of an obscure Russian poem as a vocal text. Mathematics too can, at times, need symbols not meanings.

The mathematician René Thom (1973, p. 202) has claimed: "The real problem that confronts mathematics teaching is . . . the development of "meaning", of the "existence" of mathematical objects". In addition to looking at the nature and role of symbols in mathematics (of which words form an important part), one general question I shall explore is: what are some of the central sources of mathematical meaning and what roles do symbols play in its generation?

Augmenting this diversity of sources, while being closely allied to it, is therefore the uneasy, complex set of relations ('the intolerable wrestle') between mathematical symbols and their meanings. Of all the school subjects, mathematics is the one where the interplay of symbols and meanings is intentionally the loosest. Much creative work is done by means of using the 'same' symbol for different things (for instance, the variety of operations that are indicated by '×' and consistently referred to as 'multiplication'), under the pseudo-implication 'same word, so same object'. This process, which in psychology goes by the name of *condensation*, may be variously seen as a source of confusion and conflict or a potential site of richness and powerful connection.

Conversely, but in a similar vein, how can 'square' and 'diamond' be the same thing: they have different names? Names reveal – they often indicate a stance with respect to the thing named. But names, including number names, can also conceal. Multiplicity of names, often deemed equivalent for our purposes (such as $2(x + 1)$ and $2x + 2$), is a core phenomenon in mathematics. The belief that 'a rose by any other name would smell as sweet' misses a central part of the experience of 'doing' mathematics, that of using the variability of name and form as both a thinking tool and a strategic aid: formulae are about forms. By slipping from one form to another we move away from our starting point: *displacement*, too, is a psychological process, one complementary to condensation.[3] Bill Higginson has mentioned to me that to rename is frequently to re-mean, not least because of the connotations that all words and other symbols accrete. And Yves Chevallard (1990, p. 8) has perceptively proposed: "Mathematics is a perfect example on which a *celebration of ambiguity* could be founded".

Very early on, we learn to use words. Words are symbols too, whether spoken sounds or written marks, but are frequently so familiar to us as adults that we fail to notice them as symbols. We are so 'at home' with them that, as we speak and write, 'the words don't get in the way'. Anyone who has struggled to generate expressions or sentences in a foreign language in which they are not very fluent will appreciate the reverse situation. It is said that playwright Samuel Beckett preferred writing in his second language, French, since this forced him into greater precision than using English, his native tongue.

No symbol is truly empty, devoid of connections. To be recognised as a symbol, it needs to have a stable, repeatable form: to function successfully as one, my attention cannot be on how to form it. Italo Calvino (1988, p. 29) writes of the literary value of lightness, claiming of something that "the fuller it is, the less it will be able to fly". The lightness of symbols allows transformations that the things themselves would discourage or prevent. For instance, I believe if we fail to offer pupils the transformative power of algebra, we prevent them from flying.

Symbols are often contrasted with objects. The actual objects may be a long way away (e.g. the moon), too large or small (e.g. a bacterium) or not physical at all (e.g. an idea, such as a number or a triangle). All of the 'objects' of mathematics (such as numbers, equations, functions, circles) are not part of the physical world and therefore cannot be directly manipulated physically. Yet mathematics seems to be portrayed as a very active subject, something you *do*. For instance, we talk about certain individuals being able to 'handle numbers', yet how do we 'manipulate' numbers in order to perform computations? We symbolise them, either with materials, using Smarties or counters, perhaps Dienes apparatus or Unifix cubes, or by marks on paper, in order that we may see to 'get our hands on them'.

One linking theme throughout this book, then, is provided by the core metaphor for doing mathematics, that of 'manipulation' in its various incarnations. Practical apparatus in North America is known as 'manipulatives', some recent computer software is called a 'symbolic manipulator'. We are taught to manipulate numbers (or is it figures that we actually rearrange – do we actually move anything?), to manipulate algebraic expressions and also, though less commonly, to manipulate geometric figures and images. Lurking behind all this is the negative connotation of 'manipulation of others' with its sense of imposition of another's will and control. There has also been recent unease expressed about the role mathematics can play in 'formatting' our society, (see Skovsmose 1992, p. 6) even to the point where discussions of thinking and even rationality itself are conducted in terms of mathematical thought and activity (see Chapter 8).

I shall also be exploring a related set of questions of particular relevance to the last decade of the twentieth century, ones which arise due to the rapidly increasing proliferation of machines offering mathematical functionings. What are some of the new features that symbolic manipulation technology offers us? What new constraints, what new vistas and at what cost – and most interestingly, what new light do such machines throw on age-old discussions of the teaching and learning of mathematics? What new senses, for example, do the terms 'efficiency' and 'automation' acquire, as well as what new perspective is cast on the question not of 'what is there to be known?', but of 'what is worth knowing?' in mathematics?

It is becoming clearer daily that the incursion of technology (particularly calculators and computers, and the considerable blurring of boundaries between these two devices) is markedly changing our relation to symbols and operating with/through them. Exploration of issues arising from electronic symbolic technology are distributed and discussed throughout the book, rather than singled out for specific consideration in one chapter.

In some sense, we have been here before, as history has recorded: one earlier 'technological' instance is the long transitional watershed between abacus computations and written numerical methods in Western Europe, and another the introduction of the slide-rule (both discussed in

Chapter 4). Yet, as the novelist Fay Weldon (1989, p. 2) reminds us: "We take lessons from history that we shouldn't. 'Can't do that!' we say. 'Look what happened last time.' But now is never quite the same as then."

This is not a book solely or even primarily about the role of new technology. But in all of its other discussions – whether about fluency or understanding, manipulation or practice, algebra or geometry – the context of available technology and the metaphors developed or extended all command our attention. The ways of seeing they offer inform the here-and-now, and through it, the near future. This uncomfortable domain is that fleeting, mutating context which young people[4] inhabit as they pass through our educational systems.

Before providing a chapter-by-chapter description of the rest of the book, I want to introduce one final theme: that of touch and sight, of tangibility and visibility, in relation to mathematics. There is an increasing modern tendency away from doing things 'by hand', resulting in a lack of direct manipulative experience. Our experience of the world in all its senses is becoming more and more mediated by means of machines, which of necessity shape and filter that experience. Tools often extend the powers of sight and touch – but never neutrally. It is possible to 'look' with the hand as well as the eye – in both cases we are really 'looking' with our attentive minds. Nowhere is this more true than with computers and Tom O'Shea (1993) notes the irony implicit in referring to 'hands-on' experience with a machine. Computers enormously privilege sight over touch, yet the increasing involvement of the computer mouse in what John Mason has called 'mouse mathematics' (see Mason 1990b, p. 44) suggests it is not total.

Touch is about direct contact, sight about indirect contact. I have already mentioned the ubiquitous word 'manipulate', which has its origin very firmly in the tactile, relying on the human ability to grasp. Mathematical symbols, particularly pencil-and-paper ones, although usually formed with the hand, are predominantly visual stimuli. Touch and sight are the two root metaphors in English for 'understand'.

## ABOUT THE BOOK

Following this introductory chapter, Chapter 2 explores the use of physical materials and apparatus in the service of the teaching and learning of mathematics. Chapter 3 explores the diversity of *images* (and the imagination) as a particular and powerful source of meaning in geometry.

Chapters 4 and 5 look at *manipulations* as a source of meaning (without claiming it to be the only one) in the areas of number and algebra respectively. This focus is offered, in part, because the outright rejection of 'rote' methods in mathematics teaching has resulted, I feel, in the devaluing and loss of some beneficial ways of working. The nature of numerical calculators and the recent appearance of symbolic manipulation devices are also discussed. Algebra particularly seems to demand the dual aims of fluent 'handling' of the symbol system and deep understanding allowing meaningful connection and application.

Chapter 6 explores the range of graphic representations (both static and dynamic, involving computers) that are increasingly offered in mathematics as images to think with. Graphs are frequently thought of as pictures to be merely 'seen' rather than as symbolic artifacts as much in need of interpretation as other symbolisms. The notion of 'measure' provides the theme for Chapter 7, both of material-world objects and mathematical entities such as squares and circles, while Chapter 8 looks at material-world *contexts* as a source of meaning for many mathematical problems, the texts of which frequently have peculiar and interesting characteristics of their own.

Before a brief, concluding Chapter 10 on the core metaphor of 'manipulation', Chapter 9 offers a somewhat different focus from the preceding ones. Instead of examining a mathematical device or area, it looks instead at some of the conflicting and confusing ideas and terms employed in discussions of mathematics education: terms such as 'fluency', 'understanding' and 'tradition'. My intent is that the earlier discussions of the interrelations between symbols and meanings in school mathematics will inform my attempts in this chapter to subject these notions to scrutiny. I offer a brief foretaste here.

There is a current tension in discussions of the teaching of mathematics, which has been polarised into a conflict between 'understanding' (adopting a so-called 'meaningful' approach) on the one hand, and obtaining automation and fluency at 'doing' on the other (using what are often pejoratively and undiscriminatingly labelled 'rote' methods). One view currently in circulation is that pupils should always understand *before* being asked to do a task or carry out a calculation. Another is that 'rote' methods require uniformity and regimentation, which is frequently seen as an anathema. However, it is possible to change the frame and see some so-called 'rote' methods, including group speaking and chanting, as expressly corporate and tribal *rituals* and hence as very powerful techniques.

The opening sentence of Mary Douglas's (1978, p. 19) first chapter entitled 'Away from ritual', in her book *Natural Symbols*, reads: "One of the gravest problems of our day is the lack of commitment to common symbols", adding: "Ritual is become a bad word, signifying empty conformity. We are witnessing a revolt against formalism, even against form". I indicate in Chapter 5 that I believe this to be true of attempts to teach algebra.

Later she writes: "I shall take ritualism to signify heightened appreciation for symbolic action. This will be manifested in two ways: belief in the efficacy of instituted signs, sensitivity to condensed symbols" (p. 26) and adds (p. 28): "Ritualism is taken to be a concern that efficacious symbols be correctly manipulated and that the right words be pronounced in the right order".[5]

Although her interest is primarily with comparative religious rites, she could be speaking directly to mathematicians! I find her comments resonate particularly strongly in relation to algebra. When in French someone speaks of two people sharing a common religion, the phrase *suivre le même rite* is used. Similarly, we need to be taught to follow the same rites of algebra. 'Conversion' and 'belief' are not over-strong words to describe what is required to accept the effects of algebraic manipulation as convincing.

Douglas concludes (p. 30): "Implicitly I find myself returning to Robertson Smith's idea that rites are prior and myths secondary in the study of religion". In mathematics education, meaning myths go by the name 'cover stories'. One prime concern of Douglas is that ritual is being forced out by the rational; mine, that the pressure of the doctrine of 'always understanding before doing' results in pupils missing out on what ritual can offer. At times, we need to encourage along Diderot's lines: "Allez en avant, la foi [compréhension] vous viendra."

Such a rejection of so-called 'rote' methods is very understandable, in response to a history of mathematics teaching in schools which has resulted in distressed, sometimes frantic, pupils on the one hand and in concerns about the level of mathematics learned on the other. However, one question which the 'meaningful' view leaves unanswered is how to work at gaining fluency in handling mathematical symbols, because until very recently pupils were required to do calculations quickly and effectively. How can pupils automate, and consequently 'forget' what they are doing, so that their conscious attention can be freed up for places or occasions where it will be needed in the future?

> We do not pay enough attention to the actual techniques involved in helping people gain facility in the handling of mathematical symbols. . . . In some contexts, what is required – eventually – is a fluency with mathematical symbols that is independent of any awareness of concurrent 'external' meaning.
>
> (Tahta, 1985, p. 49)

Into this discussion now comes modern technology. Eric Love has posed the question of what fluency might look like as a goal for mathematics education in the age of electronic computation devices, including most recently, the advent of 'symbolic manipulators'. Does the appearance of these devices mean that the tension between fluency of 'doing mathematics' and 'understanding it' is finally dissolved and that there is now a single uniform goal towards which teachers may aspire? I believe, instead, it has brought a sharper focus to questions of fluent functioning in relation to mathematical understanding.

## WHY TEACH MATHEMATICS?

Form is the external expression of inner meaning.

(Paul Klee)

Perceptions of mathematics and mathematical activity that are held by individual pupils, teachers and mathematicians, as well as by other members of the public and 'society' at large, are influential both in helping determine *what* gets taught in our schools and *how* it is taught. Justifications for the compulsory teaching of mathematics (up to age sixteen in the United Kingdom) vary widely both within and between cultures, and reflect both a range of purposes and also stated positions about symbols, about meaning, and about use. One somewhat prosaic claim can be found in the UK Cockcroft report on the teaching and learning of school mathematics.

> If we ask why this should be so [that mathematics has a privileged position within the school curriculum], one of the reasons which is frequently given is that mathematics is 'useful'; . . . For many it is seen in terms of the arithmetic skills which are needed for use at home or in the office or workshop; some see mathematics as the basis of scientific development and modern technology; some emphasise the increasing use of mathematical techniques as a management tool in commerce and industry.
>
> (DES, 1982, p. 1)

In the UK document *Mathematics for Ages 5 to 16*, the following explanation is offered.

> In the broadest sense, mathematics provides a means for organising, communicating and manipulating information. The language of mathematics consists of diagrams and symbols, with associated conventions and theorems. The special power of mathematics lies in its capacity not just to describe and explain but also to predict – to suggest possible answers to practical problems. The power and pervasiveness of mathematics accounts for its pre-eminent position, alongside English, in the school curriculum.
>
> (DES/WO, 1988, p. 3)

In the US, the *Curriculum and Evaluation Standards* (NCTM, 1989) and the National Research Council document *Everybody Counts* (NRC, 1989) provide similar utilitarian sentiments. A quite different possibility was offered during the second world conference on Islamic education held in Mecca over a decade ago, justifying the study of mathematics in the following terms.

The objective [of teaching mathematics] is to make students implicitly able to formulate and understand abstractions and be steeped into the area of symbols. It is good training for the mind so that they [the students] may move from the concrete to the abstract, from sense experience to ideation and from matter-of-factness to symbolisation. It makes them prepare for a much better understanding of how the Universe which appears to be concrete and matter of fact, is actually *ayatullah* signs of God – a symbol of reality.[6]

(Second World Conference, 1980, pp. 9–10)

My sympathy lies much more with this final justification. A mathematician, David Henderson, once said to me, "I do mathematics to find out about myself". Caleb Gattegno has written of algebra in terms of it involving an awareness of inner life (see Gattegno 1983, p. 34). And in an enticing passage, George Spencer Brown (1977, p. xix) writes of his sense of congruence between mathematical and psychoanalytical activity.

In arriving at proofs, I have often been struck by the apparent alignment of mathematics with psycho-analytic theory. In each discipline we attempt to find out, by a mixture of contemplation, symbolic representation, communion, and communication, what it is we already know. In mathematics, as in other forms of self-analysis, we do not have to go exploring the physical world to find what we are looking for.

To the extent that, through schooling, pupils are enabled to think like mathematicians, this possibility is made available for them. One further reason for teaching mathematics may then be so that our pupils can develop this means of finding out about themselves, in addition to our offering them access to a shared inheritance of mathematical images and ideas, language and symbolism, and the uses for mathematics which humans have so far developed. I like to express this possibility in terms of mathematics deriving from both inner and outer experiences, and meaning as being generated in the overlapping, transitional space between these two powerful and sometimes competing arenas.

# 2

# MANIPULATIVES
# AS SYMBOLS

Concrete action is by its nature slow, whereas the swiftness of vision
is very close to that of thought.

(Gattegno, 1963a, p. 11)

The use of the word 'manipulative' may be unfamiliar to some readers,
though it denotes roughly the same thing as 'physical' or 'practical'
apparatus. The noun 'manipulative' is used in North America to refer to
certain equipment used in the service of the teaching and learning of
mathematics. But any choice of word indicates a particular emphasis.
'Manipulatives' sound as if they are to be manipulated, that this is their
sole *raison d'être*. 'Apparatus' (whether in a gymnasium, a laboratory or a
classroom), on the other hand, perhaps forms part of the setting, and hence
may be seen as more neutral with regard to whether or how it is to be used.

Whichever term is the more familiar, what examples come to mind in
the context of school mathematics? Toffees and counters? Mirrors and
compasses? Cuisenaire rods and Dienes multibase arithmetic blocks?
Cardboard coins doing duty for other objects (including 'real' coins) as
well as coins standing in for circles? Or perhaps railway timetables and
direct measuring tasks in the playground or laboratory? What about the
construction of physical models – perhaps the making of the Platonic
solids using pipe cleaners and drinking straws? What about using students' own bodies as elements to be acted upon, transformed or manipulated – not least their fingers? Are pictures or diagrams drawn on paper
to be thought of as apparatus? Finally, are the abacus, calculator or
computer helpfully to be seen as 'manipulatives'? It can be hard to make
clear distinctions among these possible instances.

Different chapters pick up on some of these varied foci for mathematical activity and thought. Primarily for organisational reasons, I
shall not discuss either computers or calculators[1] now, nor pictures or
diagrams. Wherever the boundaries are deemed to lie, however, the main
issues I wish to explore here are what roles (including symbolic ones)
such materials can be expected to play and to what extent and in what

ways teacher expectations and intentions can be communicated to their students.

A common current belief seems to be that mathematical concepts can be more easily grasped if they are 'represented by' or 'embodied in'[2] physical objects. Need a teacher only provide the right apparatus for mathematics to be present? Is mathematics somehow *in* the equipment? If so, handling it alone may be sufficient to allow for learning to occur, by osmosis perhaps.

Notions of manipulatives and physical action are closely linked. It seems important that these materials are themselves both *tangible* and *graspable* – and that 'grasp' forms one central metaphor for understanding. Underlying all of these claims is the key physical sense of *touch* as an important source of knowledge. A common adult experience is to project our understanding into the object, and thereby assume it is readily available for all. This can result in being unable to comprehend why someone else cannot do something with it or see something about it: surely, they just have to look.

Physical apparatus does not offer unmediated mathematical experience: in itself, it can neither contain nor generate mathematics. Only people can do this, with their minds, and it is a central part of a teacher's role as teacher to help pupils to become able to do this for themselves. But talking about *where* mathematics is to be found or located is generally problematic, not least with the advent of computers.[3]

In addition, if the activity generated by the task[4] itself engages *all* the attention of the pupils working on it, the teacher's purpose in setting up the situation as a potentially *mathematical* experience may become diluted or even lost. Pupils may end up *just* manipulating the equipment. What for the teacher is one of a class of particular situations may for the pupil be the entire focus of their attention. Using manipulatives for teaching mathematics is always a means to an end and never an end in itself. T.S. Eliot writes of the possibility of having the experience, but missing the meaning – a situation that may well abound in mathematics classrooms. Whether or not the objects are the central *focus* of the pupil activity, the desired *meaning* is elsewhere.

Mathematics is fundamentally concerned with generality and any apparatus is particular (with its own specific physical properties and characteristics). Any object or device can only be in one state at a time, and thus some form of recording needs to be invoked in order to recall or regenerate earlier states. It is important to be aware that some possible situations may be missed. Being systematic when faced with the apparatus alone may be quite difficult. It is also possible to go from the notation in order to produce previously unachieved states. Another advantage to finding ways of recording possibilities is that it may later be possible to work with the symbolic representations alone.

13

It is also possible to mark the device directly: for instance, to use Blu-tack to indicate which faces of a constructed Polydron shape have been counted. Ironically, this can result in not having to attend to the counting mathematically. Such marking prevents double-counting or losing count (where the counting becomes divorced from the count), but also militates against counting-with-an-eye-on-the-pattern, a prerequisite for any move from the particular to the general. Attending to how you draw a figure or construct a shape can show how to construct or count in general, rather than separating these two processes into make first and then count afterwards.

In the first section below, I offer a brief analysis of particular apparatus use, before turning in the next to examine some of the terminology used for talking about this area. I try to tease out some of the senses behind different words, looking in particular at the various functions the apparatus is claimed to be performing. At the end of the chapter, I turn to an examination of some symbolic issues connected with touch and understanding. An undercurrent of this final discussion will be the question of whether the objects are to be seen as they are in some sense, or as pointing to or representing something else (a symbolic function). The notion of objects serving as substitute physical symbols will also come to the fore.

## OBJECT LESSONS: EQUIPMENT IN THE CLASSROOM

> It is possible that students may be so active that they fail to reflect and thus do not learn.
>
> (Wheatley, 1992, p. 536)

Apart from our own bodies, almost all of the apparatus I discuss here is *artifactual*, in the sense that it has been specifically designed and manufactured for classroom use, and does not have an independent existence outside of the school setting. Below, I give some capsule examples of different manipulatives in use. Instead of starting with traditional arithmetic apparatus and 'understanding' as a goal, I turn first to our physical selves as the prime manipulative and explore some images involved. The English language has the metaphor of 'getting a sense of'[5] something: in the course of this book, I want to pay attention to the actual physical senses at work at different points. My main reason for this, and its connection with understanding, is discussed at the end of this chapter.

### Our own physical apparatus

It is easy to forget how much, for young children, the world is primarily a world of touch. There is a useful adage: 'My fingers are an extension of my brain'. But even with the involvement of fingers in counting, finger use can be complex and sophisticated. There are both similarities and differences among:

- counting fingers;
- counting *with* fingers;
- counting *on* fingers (there are two senses here).

If I am counting fingers, then they are to be treated as objects like any others susceptible of being counted. I can also use them to 'show' numbers such as eight or five. Conventional ways of displaying numbers with fingers can produce both visual and tactile (felt) images.

If I am counting *with* my fingers, then they are serving quite a different purpose: they are part of my counting mechanism, helping to guide my attention in assisting the process of 'attaching' number names to objects, temporarily baptising them. (So I might initially be counting some of my fingers with others of my fingers. I have seen a video of a young child working on number tasks and using his nose as an extra 'finger' to provide tactile sensory information, when both hands were taken up with 'holding' numbers.) I mark the objects, in a way, by my fingerprint. In this sense, counting is initially most importantly about touch (much as games of 'tag' are), prior to it becoming 'touch' by sight, by attentive glance alone.

Finally, and contrastingly, if I am counting *on* my fingers, as well as the implied reliance on them (how odd the phrase "I am counting on you" is!), I am using them as placeholders for whatever number names I choose. (For instance, I might label each finger '-ty' and count in tens.) They are serving as dynamic physical symbols for the process of numeration itself, as I move around the number-name sequence.

Caleb Gattegno's (1974) intensive and inventive work with young children forming number complements on their hands draws extensively on precisely this dynamic control over folding fingers up and down. But what are the fingers doing in this case? Are they acting as substitutes of some sort. For what?

Whatever else, forming complements is something that children can *do*. They can work with their fingers, and at the same time encounter multiplicity and equivalence (the myriad ways of showing four or seven, for instance), the reciprocal nature of stressing and ignoring (turning fingers up into fingers down and conversely produces the complement), the condensation of number naming as well as its uniformity (choose a unit for the fingers). It also offers an image for number which can be internalised through the digits.

A different technique, known in the US as Fingermath (see Lieberthal, 1979), offers an alternative system of number attribution. Unlike with Gattegno complementation, the digits have absolute values (and particular digits at that) – but also different values. Using 1s and 5 (right-hand fingers and thumb respectively), 10s and 50 (left hand similarly) allows 1 to 99 to be displayed, exactly as on an abacus, provided certain conventions are adhered to, such as the placing and leaving placed of fingers in an invariant order. So, as with Roman numerals, the system is partly transparent with regard to numerosity and partly representational. The fingers offer an external means to produce and store totals dynamically.

Occasional associations with conventional notation are referred to: tens are to the left of ones, and 'so' we use the left hand for tens and right hand for the units; showing eleven 'looks like' 11. Because of the different valuings, some visual configurations conflict with conventional images derived from counting fingers. To call the various manual finger movements 'manipulations' is exactly accurate. Although techniques are offered for all four operations, they become more complex and counter-intuitive, in part because they are intended to stay close to the conventional pencil-and-paper algorithms and written format. For instance, the absence of uniformity leads to the need for digit swaps (called 'carryover') between two hands to model place value. In addition, the need to handle procedural complexity seems to outweigh the advantages of the system: the claims for comprehension I also find curious.

One fundamental source of *geometric* images can also be our own bodies: from our eyes coordinating with muscles, giving rise to notions of straight, vertical, solid, stable, balanced; from our elbows, and the rotating of other joints, images of turning and angles. There is a great deal of knowledge produced from and stored in the body (to which access can be gained) that can be helpful for mathematical work and thought.

It is not uncommon for younger pupils to be invited to exploit their own physical activity for mathematical ends. Janet Ainley (1988b) writes of a range of tasks and games which utilise links between mathematics and movement in the primary school – muscle memory, rhythm and counting, moving into shapes. Although less widely used, similar resources do exist for mathematical tasks at secondary school level (e.g. ATM, 1985; Bloomfield, 1990). One instance involved two children representing fixed points and the rest of the class being asked to place themselves twice as far from one of the 'points' as from the other. In doing this, some pupils commented they could *feel* the constraints inside themselves.

Irene Jones, a teacher of eleven to twelve-year-olds spent a class with pupils working on describing images they had seen in a complex geometric poster; towards the end of the lesson she had them choose and fix their minds on one single image from among those they had seen. They then worked in groups of three to five in order to depict it (for the rest of the class) physically and collectively using their bodies. The teacher reported being surprised at how comfortably and easily the groups worked together on this task.

However, such activity can be threatening for some adolescents. An experienced secondary teacher, Anne Watson, in a review of Bloomfield's book, commented on her experiences:

> I was attracted to the title [*People Maths*] because I feel the need for people to be involved in mathematics, not just intellectually but with a range of senses and in situations which fit in with other aspects of their lives. . . . So why don't I use physical games as much as I could? My excuse is that youngsters of 13+ are often too embarrassed to move if they are not used to it. They are also heavily conditioned about what is, or is not mathematics. I have to work hard to get them to trust me and sometimes I do not get there. It depends what has gone on before.
>
> (Watson, 1991, p. 28)

This connects to Papert's notion (1980) of 'body syntonicity' from the context of working with the computer language Logo (specifically turtle graphics), where 'playing turtle' encourages the bringing to consciousness of such awarenesses already in our physical selves.[6] When 'playing turtle', children walk through what the screen turtle needs to do in order to achieve the required path. Provided they can attend to their actions while in the midst of carrying them out, they may well be better able to decide what to do next at the keyboard.

With all of these physical possibilities, the fact that the 'object to think with' is part of the person doing the thinking can provide particularly direct access to the experience. But if the student's attention is not on the mathematical possibilities, this can also be *not* noticed more easily, because much physical action is smoothly and hence normally unawarely integrated into general functioning. Nor will such physical experience necessarily be available when faced with other mathematically related situations, but ones which do not call for physical movement.

### Some geometric apparatus

In many primary schools, three-dimensional wooden or plastic geometric shapes are available. One means of getting attention to certain properties of geometric forms involves focusing on the *tangibility* of these shaped objects through use of a Feely box (DIME, 1985). Such a box can be made from cardboard and has two holes for the arms of the person using it and an open back. Anyone can see in the back, with the exception of the person whose arms are through the holes.

But that person can *feel* the shapes that are placed there. Users try to describe the solid shapes they can feel with their hands and perhaps identify them by name: having a reference set of possibilities on display may aid identification. (A similar task setting involves a bag with wooden shapes in it, where *no one* can see which shape is being handled and described.) What do pupils focus on in their descriptions? What are the aspects of shapes that are most *tangible*? What descriptive language do they use? Can they identify an object from its feel alone? (See further Mason, 1990a.)

This challenge has a number of elements that can be widely used in designing classroom tasks. The first is focusing artificially on one of the senses – here, touch – by excluding another, sight, thereby producing a heightened sensitivity resulting from throwing out the normal sense balance. This offers quite a useful principle for developing mathematical tasks intended to focus attention on particular facilities. Variants might be: sitting back-to-back or using a telephone to describe something to another person, who then has to recreate it; describing something while sitting on your hands; saying what you have seen in a picture under the rules of no pointing and no touching.[7] Provided these constraints are taken on by the children as "the rules of the game", and there is feedback and comparison, there is the opportunity for them to practise using language to point.

This changed perspective may highlight differences: for instance, the most salient *feeling* of a shape may not be the most salient sight. How does a touch triangle differ from a sight one? Lastly, having to use words alone may focus attention on the need and usefulness of having words for certain characteristics of a shape, allowing a teacher to seed the discussion with them, without the words themselves necessarily being the main focus of the class.

A secondary-level lesson on angles involved each pupil using a pair of straws joined with a pipe-cleaner to represent angles. This improvised physical apparatus afforded tangibility, movement, and continuous change. When asked to draw certain angles, some pupils laid the straws on their books as if to help them visualise the required diagram. Just as with work on their own bodies, there remains the same uncertainty of whether memories of the direct manipulation of the straws would be available later to pupils when working only on a static, written representation on paper.

There is considerable material devised specifically for classroom use to help foster the development of geometrical images: plastic cubes, mirrors, geostrips, tiles. Among this range of material, geoboards are a particularly fruitful source.

What are some of the things such boards offer? They allow shapes to be made and unmade both quickly and with an accuracy which cannot be easily achieved in a drawing. Shapes made from different-coloured elastic bands can be compared directly on the same board, and those made on different boards are easy to juxtapose sufficiently for comparison to be made. As well as offering the pupil physical control over the shapes created, geoboards can allow a certain dynamic element to enter into the generation and transformation of shapes. But the dynamic sense is interrupted. When a triangle is made using three pins and the elastic band is moved from one of these to a new pin, there is a sense of 'in-between' triangles, but these images are quickly lost. Only certain privileged stages of the motion can be 'frozen' into relative permanence allowing further examination.

Geoboards provide temporary physical records which are portable and can be shared with others. They 'hold' images the user has made (providing a trace of the past) rather than proffer them from the outset, somewhat akin to the way an abacus can be made to 'hold' numbers.

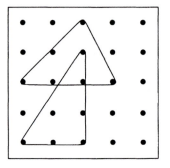

Nonetheless, geoboards structure space systematically and render it discrete. Much of the power for evoking imagery is created by the structure of the pins and lines on the board, which suggest new possibilities before they are actually realised. Thus, although at the end of the day, the geoboard is like a counting board or a calculator that has been cleared, in that there are no external records or traces left of what has been done, bodily (kinaesthetic) and visual memories may well remain. Geoboards can both increase personal stores of images and help develop the ability to create images.

### Some numerical apparatus

Not all mathematical images are associated with geometry. Other physical materials, for example a number track, or certain stylised configurations such as patterns on dice, dominoes or playing cards, may help to generate images for number. A number line offers an image to think with, but also provides a stable referent external to ourselves to help keep track.

But certain other equipment is intended to offer illumination: images and processes to think *with* rather than *about*. Cuisenaire rods model certain numerical and algebraic relations by ones of length; Dienes multibase arithmetic blocks are claimed to embody and make tangible aspects of the numeration system. Both present physical objects to handle and manipulate. Cuisenaire rods allow arithmetic computations to be worked out, but as Madeleine Goutard (1964, p. 3) is at pains to emphasise, they are not intended primarily as a tool to help pupils find numerical answers: "What is important is that the material be used in order to find out what makes such operations easy to perform mentally". Grouping or exchanging Dienes blocks is to be done in ways which echo the 'handling' of numerals in pencil-and-paper arithmetic. Iconic representations of blocks can also be found recorded in exercise books, alongside more symbolic records.

This is the first appearance of my interest in the nature and purpose of symbolic records. An iconic link between the written records and the apparatus can help to connect the experiences, provided that the link is not achieved at the expense of distortion. A group of primary pupils were working on addition of three-digit numbers. They were asked to work out 389 + 144 by means of laying out Dienes base-ten material (flats, longs and singles), to combine the material, exchanging where necessary, and then to write down their answer from the resulting configuration. The teacher's intent was for them to work on the notion of place value.

These wooden materials embody similar mutual relations with regard to length and area[8] as the numerical relations of the familiar base-ten notation for whole numbers. The apparatus can 'hold' some of the features of the situation, so the user can concentrate on other aspects (e.g. forget the numerosity and concentrate on the operation of combination). This is a similar strength to a functioning written notation. But the blocks also offer 'touch' imagery. (An example in Chapter 4 distinguishes the mathematical worth of the tactile images arising from the Japanese *soroban* (a form of abacus) and those deriving from the buttons of an electronic calculator.)

But the blocks are being made to serve as physical symbols for the symbolic property of place value embodied in our numeration (number naming) system. The rationale for 'exchanging' only makes sense within the numeration system which has no digit past 9. The way this latter system works forces an interpretation of activity with the blocks, and often a specific type of grouping and recording, whose rationale comes from outside the material itself. We use Dienes blocks in particular ways because we want them to mimic the operation of the decimal counting system. They are symbolising the way the notational system works, and not the other way round.

Amassing each type of block in columns (increasing strictly from left to right) and recording the number in each as a digit 0–9 (and 'exchanging' if there are more) is a teacher-mediated action to *force* Dienes blocks to signify in a comparable manner to the conventional decimal numeration system. In fact, Dienes apparatus better fits the spoken English system of numeration, where each power of ten has a different name ('thousand', 'hundred', '-ty') and any spoken number is composed by saying how many of each.

Children frequently go from written numerals to the blocks by working from left to right, matching the time order of appearance as the numeral is spoken (for instance, first producing six longs for 'sixty' and then four singles for 'four', in response to 64), and also carry out block algorithms that way too. Dienes' material 'holds' value independently of how or in what order it is manipulated.

Certain ancient, *non*-place-value numeration systems (such as the Egyptian one) involved an encoding process identical to Dienes blocks, albeit at a written level. Their symbols for hundreds, tens and units were independent of one another, resulting in a preservation of value irrespective of position.

| = 1

∩ = 10

⌐⌐ = 100

So ⌐⌐∩∩∩||||

was 234.

But mixing up the symbols did not change or destroy the number. So

∩⌐∩⌐|||∩|

was still 234.

So, for an Egyptian, writing down an addition sum and moving the symbols together constituted the answer, which could be 'tidied' by using an 'exchanging' principle. The same symbols provided at one and the same time both the objects to manipulate and the 'name' of the result. This is one important reason why place value as a mathematical idea cannot be *in* Dienes' apparatus, because the material fits a non-place-value numeration system at least as closely as ours.

Numbers are not blocks of wood. Place value is not a property of numbers, but a property of *some* numeration systems. Consequently, Dienes blocks do not offer direct access to properties of the numeration system.[9] But they can be made to model the desired manipulation of numerals, which are themselves substitutes for numbers. Certainly, with suitable teacher guidance, the blocks can be turned into a graspable focus for the 'actions' of arithmetic.

As with Cuisenaire rods, Dienes apparatus is not there to solve the arithmetic problem, though it can be so used. It is not primarily a calculating aid. For the teacher, such material represents something else: for the student, the material's status with regard to anything outside of itself is unclear.

### Algebraic apparatus

Algebra is particularly intangible. Unlike geometric objects, and to some extent unlike numbers in arithmetic, it is unclear what an algebraic object might be, as algebra is so much to do with transformation. It is consequently hard to offer algebraic manipulatives, as an algebraic focus is usually on relationships *between* objects, rather than on the objects themselves. Algebra arises from the structure of possible manipulations, rather than any given one.

The Rubik cube is not an algebraic object, despite providing an interesting mathematical phenomenon some years ago. As with finger complements, it provides a physical challenge involving manual dexterity and something complex to do with the mind. It also offers something to be practised to mastery, involving high levels of speed and efficiency. Shortcuts and other practices were commonly traded.

From a mathematical perspective, the 'objects' of attention are transformations of the state of the physical object – the cube. If a cube is in one state, it cannot be in any other in order to effect a direct comparison. What are children aware of (if not the algebra of the transformations) that allows them to 'do' the cube? The operations are tangible even if the effect is only discernible visibly. How are we to turn operations into things so that we can study their structure and possible combinations?

If I hold a Rubik cube in my hand, it is different from seeing one being manipulated by someone else or on a computer screen. One difference is with developing what might be called the 'knowing hand'; that is, part of the 'knowledge' is kinaesthetic, somehow distributed or located in the hand itself rather than in the head. Further manipulation and deliberate attention to what is being done may be required in order to gain confidence and the ability to recreate certain situations at will – in short, to gain a certain fluency with the apparatus. The dynamic nature of the transformations usually means the eradication of previous positions, so some separate form of recording may be required to preserve experience for reflection or to recreate a past sequence. The reverse is also possible: the notation can precede action, generating something that has not been done before rather than describing something that has.

One part of algebra deals with working with the unknown as if it were known, and techniques for doing this regularly involve use of the letter '$x$'. The question of the meaning of $x$ often arises, and attempts have been made to provide a physical referent for $x$ in order to permit direct physical manipulations, again mirroring the 'manipulations' of the symbols, which is what is actually to be learned.

Morelli (1992) has written about using a cube and counters as material for enacting 'think-of-a-number' problems. In her description, every verbal instruction has a physical action counterpart – and the manipulatives provide something to act on. Objects always offer a basis for an iconic written representation which may evoke previous experience. Where her proposal gets into particular difficulty for me is with the attempt to offer a sense of variable by allowing different numbers of counters to be placed in the cube. I explore this move from algebra to arithmetic further in Chapter 5.

As with Dienes apparatus, there are a number of places where the logic of the *mathematics* determines what is to be done with the apparatus; for someone who does not have prior access to it, such requirements could well seem arbitrary. The task may well move over to become: what do I have to do with these objects?

Dienes has proposed use of his material in an algebraic context, offering images and actions for manipulating whole-number-coefficient algebraic expressions into equivalent ones: a flat becomes $x^2$, and a long $x$, and a single 1. Certainly as a manipulable image for 'completing the square', as well as maintaining the difference among unlike terms, this proposal has something to offer. But some of the particularity of the material comes into play quite quickly: for instance, $x$ seems to be a fixed length (number) in terms of relations among the physical symbols themselves, and $x$ is an unsigned quantity. For this material to be used symbolically for algebra, we need count nouns, not measure nouns.

I do not wish here to present an extensive discussion of Cuisenaire rods and their underlying algebra: see, for instance, Gattegno (1974). But I think this work offers the most plausible account for physical material used in particular ways helping give access to algebraic awarenesses. Gattegno comments (1974, p. 45n) about Cuisenaire rods (which he sometimes called *algebricks*): "length and area are spatial or geometrical properties; the rods act as an *algebraic* model only when we put the stress on operating, changing, transforming, etc." So he is making clear that it is only as a result of employing particular attention that algebra can be perceived in operations with the rods.

Finally, there is a different sense in which algebraic manipulatives may be created, arising from making the algebraic symbols themselves into physical entities. It is possible to create symbols which allow pupils direct physical manipulation. By this, I do not mean physical 'manipulatives' such as Cuisenaire rods, where the rods are offered as counterparts of mathematical entities. Rather, I intend physical versions of conventional symbols to manipulate and internalise operations, to activate and operationalise the metaphor of 'manipulation' of symbols.

In a secondary classroom, pupils were asked to look at a felt board together with card symbols (e.g. numerals, operation signs, brackets, equal signs), each backed with Velcro tabs. Pupils were encouraged to make equations on the felt (such as $4(2(x) + 3)/7 = 6$) and then time was spent on inverting each operation in order to find a numerical expression for $x$.

The teacher, Matthew Fitzpatrick, commented to me, "It helps that they can actually see the symbols being moved by hand, and that each symbol appears only once, so there isn't the confusion that happens with working on the board when the '3', for instance, is on both sides for a time". He also distinguished two sorts of transformation of the symbols: 'move-ments', where an operation was being inverted, and 'tidyings-up', which had to do with the 'look' of the equation, spacing between symbols, relative position of the '$x$' to the '$=$', and so on. In other words, it was also important that the equation should look right.

When working in their books, the pupils produced their own set of manipulable symbols and started making and rearranging equations. Subsequently, they wrote equations and some pupils then matched the symbols on top of the page to work them out, and later, conversely, wrote down the result of symbolic manipulations in their books to have a record. On occasion, it seemed to me as if the symbols were soaking into the paper.

One general question (one that has arisen with most of the foregoing classroom accounts) is to what extent the tangible, and hence graspable and movable, properties of the card symbols remained once they had been transformed into their pencil-and-paper equivalents, where it is only in a pupil's mind's eye that they can be directly moved.

The challenge offers pupils physical actions to carry out, with the teacher intent of enabling them to be able to *do* something. The lesson allows physical movement to be put in – what might be called an attempt to make manifest the *virtual* movement of symbols – as a temporary substitute for what pupils have to be able to do eventually in their minds and on paper. It offers yet another device or story, embodying a way of talking about what is to be done.

Actions guide understanding and understanding in turn guides action. Eventually, many things can be carried out virtually, in the mind, with no action in actuality at all. We can certainly gain muscular knowledge from actions and manipulations, and then let it seep into our imaginations, and even down into our unconscious.

## DESCRIPTIONS AND PURPOSES

Below is a short list[10] of some of the mathematical purposes I see for using apparatus of whatever form. No single actual classroom situation is likely to be purely one or other of these types – but the objectives accessible from these uses are different. While the list is not exhaustive, I believe the main reasons (signalled by the verbs *illustrate, generate* and *represent*[11]) are included here:

- a means of illustrating something mathematical;
- a concrete representation of an abstract concept;
- a tangible means of generating and exploring mathematical ideas.

All of these propose physical activity which allows pupils to generate mathematics. In each, the question needs to be asked: what is the apparatus *for*?

*The Oxford English Dictionary* pairs the words 'symbolise' and 'represent', and also connects the word 'exemplify' with that of 'illustrate'. It can be difficult at times to distinguish the notions of representation and illustration, but one partial criterion for illustration may be that the material setting has some independent existence of its own. Bell-ringing can illustrate ideas about permutations, exemplifying them by means of the sequence of the bells. The ringing of the bells is not an embodiment or representation of permutations as such.

Illustrations can help, but if the context of the illustration is unfamiliar, pupils are faced with two new challenges: understanding the illustrative situation on its own terms, and endeavouring to make links between this and whatever mathematics it was they were actually engaged in coming to grips with. (It is not only with respect to manipulatives that this peculiarly pedagogic paradox arises: it occurs with mnemonics, with substitute images, with many other devices which are purportedly to help ease the overall burden on memory – by apparently *increasing* the load!)

Some, for instance, write of square dancing as a *representation* of certain transformation groups, whereas for me it is actually an illustration. Mathematics frequently involves substitute action on representations. One further distinction is that it is much harder to work directly from illustrations than representations in order to gain an appreciation of the *mathematical* idea – far more stressing and ignoring is required. When representing something by something else, the representative is acting as a symbol.

As with solely being caught up by the action, there is the possibility of becoming absorbed in the detail of the illustration at the expense of attention to what it is supposedly illustrating. Bell ringing and square dancing can be found fascinating in their own right and may leave permutations and transformation groups out in the cold!

A different form of representation occurs when a pupil chooses some physical material to represent aspects of a problem they are working on. The use here is directly representational, though the constraints of the physical may emphasise or prevent certain possibilities from being considered.

The third role for practical apparatus may be in raising or generating mathematical ideas or questions (such as hinges, mazes for routes, the Rubik cube for combinations of rotations to produce a particular effect, or other models, such as of the Platonic solids). Here, more than with the other two uses, the pupil's focus is much more directly on the physical material or setting itself. Mathematical thinking is to be used to find out more about it initially, even though the same questions and ideas may well be used subsequently in a broader exploration away from the original setting. I shall say little about this possibility here.

One of each of the following contrastive pairs of terms are often used for indicating purported properties of mathematical work with physical apparatus:

practical/theoretical
concrete/abstract
tangible/intangible

'Practical' when contrasted with 'theoretical' usually means of immediate use and relevance. The term 'practical apparatus' offers connotations of utility and convenience, whether to students personally or to society at large. One often misguided assumption behind valuing something as 'practical' is the presumption that it will therefore appear relevant to students. This is in contrast to offering them the possibility of productive engagement or involvement which seems to me to be a far more important requirement. 'Practical' may actually be referring to pupils finding meaning and purpose and being willing to submit to the task at hand – often as a result of perceiving a worthwhile challenge.

The adjectives 'tangible' and 'concrete' are commonly used in this context, conjuring up an image of practical objects which exist in the physical world, which can be touched, moved about, and generally manipulated with the hands. 'Tangible' (from the Latin verb *tango*, meaning "I touch") means that it has some material form that I can engage with using my physical self. (More generally, the word 'perceptible' means that I can experience it with one of my five senses.) Calling something tangible tends to imply it is real, that it is there. Concrete materials (echoed in the mistranslation of Piaget's third stage as 'concrete operations'), it is claimed, may help the user to contend with the abstract with which they are usually contrasted with the expectation of the 'concrete' being easier to comprehend.

However, the mathematician Jacques Hadamard has offered the maxim: "The concrete is the abstract made familiar by time". He is suggesting that concreteness is relative to our past experiences, rather than being an attribute of certain things in themselves. On the other hand, one consequence of this divisive split has been a contempt for practical knowledge. Formal/abstract knowledge is often considered the highest form of thought, and mathematics its representative. In mathematics, as in many other subjects, I think it is important to 'have a good pair of hands'. But what that means in terms of developing 'knowing hands' for doing mathematics is a subtle thing.

Physical manipulation alone is seldom enough: teachers also encourage pupils to talk about what they are doing, as well as taking steps to encourage them to internalise the substitute images that the apparatus provides. Through talking, the teacher can better ascertain what they are attending to among the myriad possibilities. After a period of unrestricted access and use, one sequence of steps might be to do work with the apparatus both present and visible, but impose a rule of no touching. Then, move to the material being initially present but then covered over, before finally merely invoking images and memories of the material verbally.

Georges Cuisenaire proposed such a three-stage consecutive approach, starting with using his coloured rods, followed by use of comparably colour-coded cards and finally conventional written notation. Caleb Gattegno, who developed, publicised and worked extensively with Cuisenaire's invention, commented:

> Cuisenaire's own pupils, and those who are using his method, are equally skilled with the rods, the cards (which bear the same colours as the rods, but are no longer capable of being manipulated), and the ordinary written signs.
>
> (1963a, p. 13)

Thus, it would seem that Gattegno is using the term 'manipulated' literally in order to contrast use of the actual rods with the cards as substitutes. These associated counterparts nonetheless retain certain links with the originals (most importantly, colour), while no longer allowing other actions to be performed upon them (in particular, direct comparison of lengths, as all cards are the same size). He claims:

> the pupil acquires a wealth of mathematically correct experience in fractions offered by no other method. It is both abstract and concrete; it shows what is invariant in situations and shows clearly and simply what the variables are.
>
> (1963a, p. 4)

The artist Paul Klee talked about art in terms of rendering the invisible visible.[12] By making visible that which cannot be seen, greater attention can be drawn to what was previously imperceptible. In the sense discussed in this chapter, accessing mathematics through manipulatives involves rendering the tangible intangible, though it is usually thought of as the reverse process (namely 'embodying' mathematics in the objects). Such objects never shed their physicality, but this materiality can be suppressed by the pupil attending to something else. Manipulatives can be both matter-of-fact actual and evocative of something else at the same time. They can be both symbol and object at the same time, but not usually the one for the other.

I see no inherent value in using apparatus for its own sake. In addition, there is always the difficulty of indicating to the pupil what you are attending to, so the risk is always there that the students will believe that the object itself is what should be focused on. When ideas are too abstract or confused to hold entirely in your mind, it can help to have some physical object to hold or in view, on which to focus. So one key function of apparatus is as a stabilising focus for the mind, a place to attend. It need not necessarily be a physical object – a picture or a diagram may on occasion serve the same purpose. But *feeling* the apparatus may provide a reassuring (if illusory) sense of the tangible materiality of the apparent object of our mathematical attention.

## TOUCH AND UNDERSTANDING

Man's reach should exceed his grasp, or what's a Heaven for?

(Robert Browning)

I mentioned in the Introduction that one of the common metaphors for understanding something is to 'grasp' it. If I don't understand something, then it is 'beyond my grasp'. I may also experience a need to feel 'in touch' with what I am doing. To be 'out of touch' is considered an undesirable state.

'Grasping' something is often related to possession of it, though the term can also be used derogatively of someone whose need to have things within reach overrides other social sensibilities. Are there intellectually 'grasping' individuals who have a burning desire to grasp, to understand? It was the mathematician David Hilbert who said of mathematics: "We will know, we *must* know".

One of the primary and fundamental means of young children encountering and exploring the physical world is with the hands (and then usually the mouth, but that is another story[13]). Although it was cited in the specific context of counting on fingers (which are often the first manipulatives), the claim 'my fingers are an extension of my brain' can serve as a more general indicator of the importance of touch. A theme I shall take up in Chapter 10 is that the domination of 'manipulation' in all its richness as the metaphor for doing mathematics suggests, rightly or wrongly, that the human sense of touch, and not that of sight, is still perhaps the most important mathematical sense.

I find little distinction is made in much mathematics education writing between visual and tangible aspects of manipulatives (for instance, Morelli's article is called 'A visual approach to algebra concepts'). Yet, they offer different supports. The one may be necessary at the outset, the other sufficient after a while. Is it the image that is to be internalised (if so, that suggests certain things to be done in the process of distancing or softening the support), or is it the feel, the gestural movements, the knowing in the hands that is deemed important (which suggests others)?

This chapter has discussed the physical interaction between individuals and physical materials in the service of mathematics. The term 'manipulation' often seems appropriate for describing the nature of this interaction. Humans *acting on* this material also offers a fitting description. But

29

Newton's third law of motion, that every action has an equal and opposite reaction, encourages us also to see the objects acting upon us at the same time. The Russian psychologist El'konin puts it this way:

> An educational task differs fundamentally from other types of problems in that its goal and its result consist of a change in the acting subject himself, not in a change in the objects on which the subject acts.
>
> (cited in Davydov and Markova, 1983, pp. 60–1)

But what makes these actions mathematical in some way? Is there something that distinguishes them from other actions on material objects, such as getting dressed or eating food?

Gattegno (1963a) has made much of the distinction between *actual* (or *real*) and *virtual* actions. In particular, he claims that perception (and with it the dynamics of the mind) is implicit in performing virtual actions, and virtual actions extend the range of corresponding real actions, while still reflecting certain constraints inherent in the original. He offers the following example:

> For instance, stringing beads is an action, while to imagine oneself doing this is, at first, to evoke the movement without actually carrying it out; to become aware of it as a possible action that can recur indefinitely is the virtual action which will serve as basis for the indefinite extension of addition of units.
>
> (1963a, p. 52)

But more particularly here, he proposes an interesting characterisation of what it is to act as a mathematician, one which I find illuminating of the difficulty of using 'manipulatives' to work on mathematical ideas:

> All those, then, who are capable of replacing actual actions with actions that are virtual and of contemplating the structures contained therein, act, when they do these things, as mathematicians.
>
> (*ibid.*, p. 53)

This is one sense in which mathematics is necessarily of the mind, in that Gattegno identifies awareness of the structure of virtual actions as characterising the mathematician. Students can be observed manipulating physical objects: how can we possibly observe them performing virtual actions, let alone ascertain whether or not they are *awarely* contemplating the inherent structures of those potential actions? But much of the equipment discussed in this chapter has been employed to substitute actual actions on material objects for virtual actions on 'mental objects' or symbolic representations thereof.

This chapter has offered an exploration of the main roles for physical objects in teaching mathematics, in terms of offering substitute objects for direct manipulation and, along the way, referents for some symbolic processes. I also discussed some of the variety of teaching functions such equipment is expected to perform. In later chapters, I argue that it is for precisely this reason that the metaphor of manipulation has been applied to symbols of various sorts. Symbols can come to act as the 'manipulatives' of mathematics, referring at times to the virtual actions of human beings acting as mathematicians at whatever level.

# 3

# GEOMETRIC IMAGES
# AND SYMBOLS

What will be the future of the individual imagination in what is
usually called the "civilization of the image"? Will the power of
evoking images of things that are *not there* continue to develop in
a human race increasingly inundated by a flood of pre-fabricated
images? . . . we run [a danger of] losing a basic human faculty: the
power of bringing visions into focus with our eyes shut, of bringing
forth forms and colours from the lines of black letters on a white page,
and in fact of *thinking* in terms of images.

(Calvino, 1988, pp. 91–2)

Geometrical drawings have been made as least as long as written records,
and physical objects created in geometric forms for just as long (see,
for example, Tahta, 1981a). Authentic ancient Babylonian tablets and
Egyptian papyri include geometric drawings; megalithic 'circles' litter
Britain and France. Straight lines and circles, traces of the two fundamental, elemental sources of motion (straight ahead or with steady
constant turning), have always played a central role in the attention of
those interested in mathematics and form. Different methods have been
found at different times to resolve questions about them, but these 'objects'
have remained in focus for some 4000 years at least.

We might speculate about the provenance of such figures and why these
shapes and not others came to be used: straight and circular forms rarely
occur naturally, and then only imperfectly. We do, however, 'read'
geometrical forms into the natural environment around us, offering a
converse interpretation to Stevens' (1967, p. 492) observation that: "The
world images for the beholder". Thus, straightness can be perceived *in*
tree trunks, *in* the fall of a drop of water, *in* paths of shortest distance.
Circularity, although even rarer in the natural environment, can be seen
*in* cross-sections of trees or *in* a full moon.

These shapes, forms, images are constituted mentally, enabling us to
create physical objects 'in their image', converted or pressed into objects
(through specific design). Many objects and processes humans make

suggest straightness: sticks, pins, edges, folds, cuts and stretched strings. Flatness is mirrored in walls, floors, ceilings, boxes, tables, and so on. Once the wheel was invented, many circular objects appeared: tables, manhole covers and coins provide present-day instances. Geometrical shapes have also been used to decorate other human artifacts since the earliest times, and continue to do so in pottery motifs or clothing patterns.

Certain geometrical figures such as the circle have been used culturally as symbols of beauty and perfection – though the perfection of the circle is only 'graspable with the mind's eye', to mix sensory metaphors. We can imagine a circle with no thickness that is perfectly round, but we can never create one by drawing freehand or even with a pair of compasses. Using the computer language Logo to get the turtle to draw a circle (e.g. forward a bit, right a bit, lots of times) brings us up against the difference between an image on a screen and a 'real' circle. But the development of our geometric perception also allows us to see these traces *as* circles. Seeing *as* is a very important part of geometry – it allows us to 'read' objects and images in a geometrical way.

One view of mathematics has the world being mathematical and so the mathematics is 'out there' waiting to be perceived: 'mathematics is all around us.' You apparently just have to look. Galileo proclaimed: "The book of the world is written in the language of geometry". An alternative view holds that mathematics is human and hence only inside our minds. We therefore need to place it onto the world, rather than finding it there. Curiously, Euclid, besides being a Greek geometer, also developed a theory of vision, according to which light rays emanated *from* the eye, striking the object, and that was how we were able to see them. Seeing involves projection.

Paralleling this highly mathematical view of vision, it is in this same active sense that we *see* mathematics in the world, namely that we project mathematical forms onto it. But either way, the result is we see geometric shapes in the environment and naming them can help direct attention to particular aspects or features.

Geometry is strongly linked to the human sense of *sight* (in contrast to touch, highlighted in the previous chapter) and the visual perception of form. It is closely connected with the action of drawing, with the creation of shapes, the conjuring of images. But geometry also invokes their dynamic manipulation. There are various sorts and sources of images: hand-drawn images, which differ from screen images, which are different again from mental images.

Among the questions that geometers ask are: what are the properties of certain figures? What relationships hold among parts of a particular figure? What do certain situations have in common? (See Mason, 1991.) Geometric language is often seen as a language of description. Mathematical points are imagined with no thickness or area, with no other intent than acting as a focus of attention. There is a close link between the action of pointing and the mathematical notion of *point*. Points get called into existence through the action of pointing.[1]

Nowhere is this more apparent than with modern geometrical software packages such as *Cabri-géomètre* or *Geometer's Sketchpad*, where a 'mouse' is used to point, but also, most innovatively, to 'grab' and 'drag' screen objects. A new emphasis can be on transforming, *manipulating*, what you have constructed with the aid of the machine. These programs do not offer drawing tools in the same way that Logo's turtle graphics can be used. The computer's general role in offering dynamic, seemingly graspable images is explored in the third section of this chapter. I say 'seemingly graspable' because they appear to be presented directly to us – we just have to summon them by name from a menu – certainly in comparison with algebraic means of naming and hence control. Yet screen images are not directly tangible.

There is something very spare and stark about geometric images, when compared with other scenes conjurable in the imagination. In his poem *The common life*, Wallace Stevens writes of Euclid's 'absent shadows' and 'one-sided forms'. Yet that very paucity of detail, the absence of cluttering particularity, enables us to focus so directly on the relationships between geometrical forms and among their parts. It is one source of the power of geometric images. But there are others.

Tahta, in his discussion of *Cabri-géomètre* from a curricular perspective, draws attention to the fact that it is always incidence properties of configurations that are in view: points, lines, circles and the facts of contact and crossing, where and how.

> That points lie on lines or circles, that circles touch lines or other circles, and so on, are important and worthwhile notions, not only because they lead to the life-enhancing achievements of builders and engineers, or of artists and designers, but also – and, in my opinion, more crucially – because they are reflections of psychic incidences. Geometry matters – for various reasons, but also because points, lines and circles are symbols of what I lie on, pass through or touch.
>
> (1992, p. 39)

Thus, Tahta suggests powerful and emotive perceptions can arise from inside too, as well as alluding to some of the psychic condensations that may exist around such fundamental elements.[2] So even these apparently direct images may have further symbolic residues. One of our earliest experiences was that of being 'inside' our mothers, in the (topologically) spherical container that marked the limit of our early worlds. This closed boundary offers an important primitive sense of inside and outside. One universal source for geometry that may be being echoed here ('mixing memory and desire', based on 'lucid souvenirs of the past') is that of our ante-natal, three-dimensional existence. Perhaps we attend to and see what we see on the outside because we are projecting from the inside – from *inscape*, as it has been termed, onto landscape.[3]

## SOURCES OF STATIC AND DYNAMIC IMAGES

> Images develop an autonomous status, they become great summarizers of action.
>
> (Bruner, 1966, p. 13)

Human beings are natural image-makers and geometry springs from particular kinds of images. There are a number of sources that are particularly fruitful in giving rise to geometric images. The ones that will be explored in this section are: the material world, animations on video and computer screens, and words which can serve to evoke images in the mind.

School mathematical tasks may involve movement of one's own body, manipulating cubes or rods, cutting paper with scissors, folding card. But, however absorbing the activity may be, activity is not the end in itself. Mathematics in general – and in this, geometry is no exception – involves focusing on relationships between parts and wholes, exploring change and constancy, stressing this and ignoring that. Mathematical activity is the means to an end, to encountering some idea or some property, to seeing or realising that something *must* happen or *cannot* happen. Very young children are capable of mental imagery, just as sixth-formers can work with paper and scissors to mathematical ends.

Frequently, such activity can stimulate an image, an ideal, a goal towards which the action is focused, as well as enabling feedback between what is achieved and intended. One way of achieving control over geometric images comes about through language, through describing what you see or want to see, and from others talking about what they see. Language can also be used to generate new images, ones which have never been thought about by humans before. Computers can also play a part in this imaginative generation of novelty, as the recent work on the beautiful pictures of fractals attests.

In *Speaking Mathematically*, I wrote:

> When a baby wishes to operate on the world to achieve its various ends, its first contact is direct and physical. The development of spoken language permits certain goals to be achieved indirectly, e.g. by asking for or demanding them. Further control of written language again broadens the range of possibilities which are now 'within reach'.... Knowledge of a computer language affords control over various 'screen objects' for instance, but this control is also very much one of action at a distance. The desire to be able to interact with these screen objects provides a strong and genuine motivation for struggling with the syntactic complexities of a computer language.
>
> (1987, p. 6)

Young children also produce mental images, shaped by their visual contact with the external world, but also conjured from within, by the imagination.

An individual's images are as private (but also no more private) than thoughts. We share basic images as we share many words, though of course what they *signify* for each of us can and does differ widely, depending in part on the interaction between inner and outer meanings. Images get objectified, partly through being impressed into objects, partly through being named, and as result are rendered far more static. With stasis comes particularity, as they can no longer partake of the dynamic which links them. Geometric objects both come from these sources and are returned to them: material objects, actions and images – not following that slavish order, but deriving from any one of these human possibilities.

Almost any physical object, whether naturally occurring or manufactured, can be a source of images, and visual representations, proliferating owing to modern reprographic techniques, have become an immense source of images, including photographs and posters. There are also many quasi-geometric signs in our culture: two familiar ones may be the radiation hazard symbol and the Mitsubishi logo.

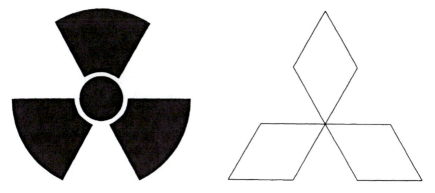

These are very close to geometrical figures, but are not usually seen as such. Their meaning is in what they signify as a gestalt, an icon, not in the relations observable among the elements of the figure. Nevertheless, they are chosen partly for their spareness which makes them visually memorable. We can look at and analyse them with a geometrical eye.

By contrast with such static sources, moving pictures on film, video and television screens offer dynamic images. But one aspect all these media have in common is that the images or sequences of images themselves are planned and determined in advance, which places the viewer in a subordinate relation to them. Indeed, this is one point of any film (as indeed, of any book) and is essential in presenting a narrative. This applies equally to geometrical animations on film where the intent is to focus attention on particular configurations in motion.

Other possibilities are also available. One of the recent changes in the way images can be created, offered and manipulated in a mathematical context has been through the microcomputer. It is now possible for the pupil herself to conjure and control dynamic screen images in fundamentally new ways. The level of interaction varies with computer software, which offers a range of modes of control from a computer language such as Logo, through choice from menus, to use of the mouse. Some of the best software gives the user a level of control similar to that with the geoboard (discussed in Chapter 2), but with a degree of animation similar to that achieved on a film or video. As with the geoboard, such software makes a version of private mental images available for public scrutiny, comparison and discussion.

But as with any change, there are gains and losses. The freedom given by having control over the generation of images allows children to create ones that are appropriate for themselves, but lack of constraints can mean that children may not be brought into contact with some important kinds of geometrical experiences. There is a continuing debate about the use of Logo's turtle graphics concerning the balance to be achieved between having children set their own tasks and projects and providing them with more teacher-focused tasks: for instance, offering challenge images, primitives or programs for exploration. (See, for example, Ainley and Goldstein, 1988.)

Finally, one of the most effective ways of creating images can be through the use of words alone – for instance, an imagining task such as 'Think-of-a-picture'. One might begin thus.

> Close your eyes. Imagine a square. Stretch it, shrink it, rotate it, move it around in your mind to get a sense of all the squares it might be. Bring it back now to the centre of your 'mental screen' and arrange it to be 'square' to the picture, with a top, bottom and two vertical sides.

A group of teachers have provided classroom accounts of mental geometry activity resulting from working with words into images (Beeney *et al.*, 1982). The extract below is from writings by nine- and ten-year-olds about their 'inner pictures'.

> My point was the tip of a triangle. The light from it seemed to start in the middle when it was blue. Then it went outward a little and became red. . . . My triangle started off in complete darkness; then suddenly it seemed to be a kind of lawn with a path on it . . . It was funny but I seemed to be the triangle and yet I saw it with my own eyes.
>
> I saw a big square that went all the way round the picture. It was not a real square, some of the lines were not straight. The square was red and it moved a little bit at a time. In the square was lots of more lines going across and going down. There were all different kinds of colours. All of these lines made lots of little lines. Then the little square began to get filled in.
>
> *(ibid.,* p. 11)

As the images are described with words, the pictures evolve with a narrative thread and are generated by a linear syntax. Although words can serve to conjure images, as mental images are inherently private and personal, there is no direct way of offering them to others.

## WORKING ON STATIC IMAGES

Each of the sources mentioned in the previous section offers certain possibilities for pupils to work mathematically on images. Because of the remarkable shift in public, dynamic imaging possibilities introduced by the potentialities of film and video and, most importantly, of computers, I devote the third section to these sources alone. Particular accounts of ways of working with paper, on a poster, and on a diagram, are given here.

## Working with paper

A piece of paper can simulate and substitute for working with pure surface. Although different weight paper has different properties, it can prove quite a flexible medium, providing numerous opportunities for constructing images while working with geometric possibilities. Folding paper circles can generate lines across circles. One task might then be to see what shapes are possible whose sides are fold lines; overlapping circles and exploring the possible resultant shapes is another possibility.

For instance, children can be asked to fold a piece of paper twice and then cut off a corner, then sit on the folded paper. They can then be challenged to predict what the shape will be when it is unfolded, and prompted to visualise the unfolding and the resultant shape. This task can be extended to thinking about what different possible shapes might be obtained with *two* cuts, and how many sides the final shape could have.[4] Here, images are needed to act as templates of target shapes.

There are a number of general mathematical purposes for such work. One is to predict the effects of actions *before* they are realised: this is in order to have a stake in the outcome, to have to develop an expectation to be confirmed or confounded. A second is to be able to 'say what you see' in order to develop the ability to 'point' with words, so as to communicate with others and to describe and analyse complexity.

In mathematics, there is always movement back and forth between the potential (the possible) and the actual. The question of alternative possibilities can be partially explored by looking at particular cases, but one important mathematical challenge lies in identifying *all* possibilities, eliminating impossibilities and convincing others that all cases have been considered.

There is a tension between reflection and immediacy. The instruction to 'sit on the folded paper' is one device for interrupting the physical immediacy of the situation, in order to encourage prediction and thought. Cutting and unfolding as quickly as possible is the *simplest* way of finding out what the shape will be in this particular case, but if the teacher's intention were to encourage geometric thought, then there would need to be a force towards trying to slow things down and intervene in the pupil's process in order to ensure time for reflection.

In this situation, as in many others, teacher and pupils are partial antagonists. The pupils (consciously or not) want to close down the task, bringing it to an end as quickly as possible. Teachers want to prolong the imaginative exploration of the possible at the expense of the actual as long as is feasible, and often without indicating that that is what they are doing. For this will provide them with the most opportunities for teaching.

## Working on a poster

When shown a picture or a poster, and asked to say what has been seen, it is common to use a combination of words and gestures (perhaps pointing or touching or using direction of gaze) to direct the questioner's attention. Within the context of a mathematics lesson, different criteria may be involved in order to accentuate the mathematical potential of the task. Part of learning to speak like a mathematician is to be able to use language both to conjure and control personal mathematical images, as well as to convey them to others.

One means for achieving these ends has been developed where the class sits in front of a photograph or picture. Pupils then take it in turn to come out to a 'hot-seat' at the front and 'say what they see' to the rest of the class. The task requires 'no pointing and no touching' rules to be strictly adhered to, in order to force attention onto the adequacy or otherwise of the description given. The focus on the poster and/or the speaker allows the teacher to escape from the limelight, and encourages the communication to go from pupil to class, rather than from pupil to teacher. Questions can be asked and pupils have to work on refining command of mathematical language, in order to convey their desired meaning.

There are a number of interesting aspects of this task. The first is that it is quite artificial. In everyday life, if you want or need to explain to someone something you have seen, it is normal and efficient to gesture as well as describe. The constraints imposed are part of what gives the lesson potential as a site for learning. The focus is on the use of spoken language itself to point, to stand on its own, aside from accompanying gestures. Provided the pupils take on the 'game' aspect (in the sense of a rule-governed task with a particular goal), then they are able to practise certain linguistic skills. These include, for the speakers, precision in describing what they see and, for the listeners, ability in evoking images from words. (An account of such a lesson, with a middle-school class and a complex, multi-coloured poster as geometrical focus, is given in Jaworski, 1985.)

The task also encourages the perception of projective seeing. When I was working with a group of teachers on a particular poster, one remarked on her language patterns shifting from, "You can see . . ." to "I can see . . . . Can you?" The pronoun shift indicated a considerable move in her self-awareness that something she had unthinkingly assumed was 'taken-as-shared' was, in fact, quite possibly not. The statement 'I can see a cube' is subtly but importantly different from 'You can see a cube', or even 'It's a cube' or 'There is a cube in the picture'.

Finally, this task also connects to the power of naming. If someone asserts that they cannot see any cube at all, then what the speaker knows about that object can be brought into play in her descriptions, until the others can see what was invisible to them before. This can cause pupils to realise that what is going on in their heads is hidden from others, and that language is a powerful means of communicating such thoughts and images. Because the teacher also has to visualise from the words being used by the pupils, there is more scope for 'genuine' questions (see Ainley, 1988a). The teacher desires to find out the answer because she does not know and, in some fundamental sense, *cannot* find out in any other way.

### Working on a diagram

Diagrams are commonplace in mathematics textbooks and a widespread element of heuristic problem-solving advice is the invocation to 'draw a diagram'. One intent of providing a diagram is to stabilise thought, a role shared by other symbols, as well as to provide a focus for attention. Yet, because diagrams seem so iconic, so transparent, it is easy to forget that they too need to be 'read' rather than merely beheld. Here are three diagrams:

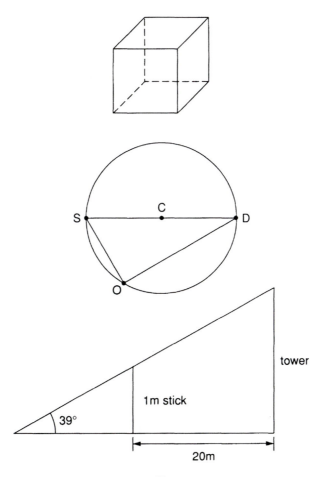

The first of these is intended as a two-dimensional representation of a three-dimensional object. Interpreting such drawings can present difficulties, especially for younger children. The conventions of the drawing do not allow us to decide, for example, whether it represents a complete cube or one hollowed out at the back.

The second diagram is a static representation, yet it can be seen to 'point' to a range of generality. It is a particular configuration, but it can be seen to 'speak' about more than one situation at a time. In this sense, the diagram can also be seen as a symbol as well as a particular picture (with its particular shape, size, location and orientation).

The third appears to be a scale drawing, but the 'actual' angle in the picture, although marked 39°, is nearer to 29°. The task associated with this diagram was to make a scale drawing of the situation in order to produce an estimate of the tower's height, and then to use trigonometry in order to compare the result. The actual angle needed to be 'wrong', as otherwise there would be no need for the pupil to make a scale drawing – merely directly measuring the 'tower' in the picture and scaling the result would suffice. (Here the diagram is 'standing for' a real-world situation.)

Yet it seems peculiar nonetheless that an angle of one size is labelled as being another. Part of the rubric in some examinations includes a disclaimer statement that the angles shown in the diagrams do not represent the actual angles – thereby drawing attention to the symbolic rather than iconic nature of the geometric diagrams. For instance, the Graduate Record Examination booklet proclaims:

> Figures that accompany questions are intended to provide information useful in answering the questions. However, unless a note states that a figure is drawn to scale, you should solve these problems not by estimating sizes by sight or by measurement, but by your knowledge of mathematics.
>
> (GRE, 1993, p. 25)

It later reiterates: 'Comparisons should be made based on a knowledge of mathematics rather than appearance' (*ibid.*, p. 27).

One of their questions is as follows:

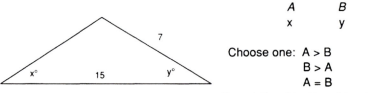

$$
\begin{array}{cc}
A & B \\
x & y
\end{array}
$$

Choose one: A > B
B > A
A = B
the relationship cannot be determined

I was unable to ascertain by direct measuring that this was not an isosceles triangle, despite the 'actual' picture being considerably different from this. A common expectation of sketch diagrams is their being generic or in general position (so that a small perturbation of any measurement does not alter the 'type'). The word 'sketch' is often used to indicate its approximate depiction, whereas diagrams are usually there to be relied upon.

In addition, there seems a possible confusion between the task that produces scale drawings, such as geometrical (often called technical or engineering) drawing, and the one giving rise to diagrams for doing geometry with. In the former, accuracy is crucial, often so that measurements can be made directly from such drawings – a task resulting in diagrams acting as counterparts for the actual thing (somewhat like navigation charts). The representations need to be as accurate as they can be made – because the substituted drawing *is* the object you are measuring. Even in certain artistic representations, for instance, the pressure for accuracy comes from aesthetic considerations, of wanting a drawing that 'looks right'.

A geometric diagram can be more like a sketch map. With geometric diagrams, accuracy of measurement is far less important, as no measurements are made directly on the figure, though it can help to be suggestive if it is approximately accurate. The second diagram on p. 41 is typical of those found in many older geometry books. Although it might be showing a particular configuration, it can also be interpreted as a still frame from a sequence of moving images, where one or more of the points are moving round the circle. It can thus be read as a particular standing for the general – a generic image.

What could it mean to work on a diagram? One possibility for the first diagram is to discuss possible solids that it could be representing. This is similar to the kind of discussion about ways of seeing that could arise in the task with the poster discussed in the previous sub-section.

One further way of working on such diagrams, in order to indicate some possible meanings it could have, is to introduce a dynamic element into how pupils are to see it. In the poster, there is no dynamic – only flips in perception from one static image to a different interpretation. A task based on the second diagram might be as follows:

Imagine that O moves round the circle. What happens inside your head? What do you see? What do you notice? What changes and what stays the same? What are some extreme positions?

Another starting point for such mental activity might be:

J is the centre of the circle

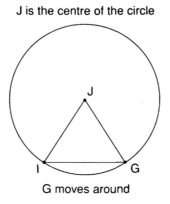

G moves around

Mental manipulations of this sort can draw pupils' attention to the continuity possible through the dynamics of the mind. They may even become aware of how, in some sense, the diagram does speak about all of these situations at once. The difficulty of one triangle in a geometric diagram 'standing for' *all* triangles in some sense is widespread. The static representation (even two or three examples) suggests that there are a lot of isolated, static triangles. An alternative possibility is to use moving images in order to try to capture the generality.

Geometric figures are often presented in standard orientations: triangles with the longest side horizontal to the bottom of the page, squares 'square' to the page, and so on. Remember too the radiation hazard logo, which is also recognised in one standard orientation. All of these configurations are 'stable', as if gravity were operating on a page. One difficulty can arise with pupils not knowing which aspects they are to stress and which to ignore about the particular examples they have been presented with. Richard Skemp recounts an anecdote of a pupil being taught Pythagoras' theorem and being asked to construct 'the square on the hypotenuse' and producing the following diagram:

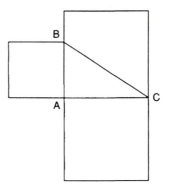

A plausible conjecture is that the boy had only ever come across squares 'square' to the page. Stories such as these can act as reminders that we can never know what pupils are seeing in what we or they draw.

I often read that geometric figures should be presented in various orientations in order to emphasise what remains constant. But lying behind this injunction is a belief that these are the *same* figure, rather than different but related figures. There are also some verbal ambiguities involved in referring to transformations. Sometimes it is useful to call upon other squares, rather than stretching 'it'. So all squares are present and we move from one to another, highlighting ('calling into being') with our attention (either continuously or disjointedly). Motion in film or the imagination may be considered as such – as in transformation geometry or Euclidean congruence proofs – or the figure may be conceived (more symbolically perhaps) as an icon pointing to generality, i.e. representing an equivalence class of shapes, and usually an infinite class at that.[5]

## WORKING ON DYNAMIC IMAGES

One important distinction among geometric images is whether they are static (and therefore single and isolated in some sense) – such as a poster – or dynamic (and therefore multiple and connected) – such as in a video. A poster can support a range of images, depending on how it is seen, and can encourage a certain dynamic when switching between them. Furthermore, an individual diagram can be seen as a snapshot taken from a dynamic sequence. Constructing 'flickabooks' from a series of separate snapshots can produce an effect similar to a film and help to bridge the gap between the two. Thus, it is not a hard-and-fast distinction, because film or television images themselves form a discrete sequence, running usually at the rate of twenty-four every second, and therefore only simulate continuity of motion. Nevertheless, this animated simulation produces effects far closer to the seamless dynamics of mental images in the mind.

### Working on an animation

I finished the previous discussion by suggesting that a diagram could be used as a means of invoking a dynamic sequence. With an animation, there is the possibility of working directly and mathematically on moving images. One possibility is to offer a complex geometrical film for reconstruction.

In contrast to the static poster, the dynamic element introduced by the sequential time aspect allows a 'story' to be created, as well as interpretations to be made about what was happening or why.[6] Below is a brief and partial description of a short Nicolet film.

A red circle appears and moves around the screen, growing and shrinking in a smooth and continuous way. A point appears and eventually the circle passes through the point and is 'captured' by it, and from then on, it passes through that point. A second point appears and 'captures' the circle from the first point, then both points capture the circle, and finally the circle gets larger and larger.

In a book such as this, I cannot provide you with direct experience of this film. I can only offer you words – which you might use to generate your own images – or a sequence of drawn 'stills' (perhaps of key transitions) that suggest the motion, the chronological sequence. Words are quite different from images. The above story is my story: a familiar mixture of description and interpretation. I could instead have given a structuring overview: for instance, this film is about circles and constraints, first none, then one, then two.

Of course, other accounts are possible in response to the same short sequence. For instance, is it the 'camera' that is moving and 'actually' the circle is remaining the same? Is it the circle that captures the point, or *vice versa*? More subtly, was it one circle changing size and position, or was it a whole sequence of different circles being illuminated in turn, one per frame, which brings us back to another key feature of geometry, namely continuity.

With a circle that is moving continuously around the screen and shrinking and growing, for example, there are at least two different ways of seeing what is going on: one circle moving and changing size and position, or the picking out of a (large) selection from an infinite set of all possible circles. Random (rather than continuous) illumination of possibilities can help to suggest the latter perception. The above account is very brief, yet it can be used to generate a complex sequence of images – a word here being worth a thousand images.

In a group discussion of this film at a conference, someone later remarked, "I never actually *saw* a family of circles superimposed at once on the screen. It was only over time – things stayed in my head." Someone else asked, "Why did we read this film as mathematical?" A third commented, "Moving images have multiplicity. With words, it is hard to attend to what is *not* being said, whereas the unsaid, the undemonstrated, can be present and functioning with images."

The time sequence allows it to be read as a story, and the continuity of image (the close proximity of circle size and position in adjacent frames) invites a reading of a single circle (one *object*) changing, rather than a succession of distinct circles being attended to in turn. For that to be initially the more salient, a sense of discontinuity (jerky, flashing movement) may be required. The plane can be viewed as being empty until a circle is placed there, or it can be viewed as made up of all possible circles permanently present, from which one can be singled out and brought to our attention. Curiously, words can invoke continuity directly, whereas the discrete nature of film images can only invite it.

A lesson based on the use of another three-minute silent, animated film, this time of conic sections, is shown in the video *Working Mathematically on Film with Sixth Formers* (Love, 1987). In the lesson mentioned, after being allowed time to fix certain key images in their minds, pupils were invited to start to reconstruct the film as a group account, each contributing their recollections and their uncertainties.

Comments and questions by the teacher, Eric Love, included, "Nobody expects you to remember all that", "What was the first thing that happened?", "Is this right?", "You have no recollection of this", "And then what happened?" In this way, focused attention can be brought to bear on memories of the stream of images, as well as identifying quite precisely points of unease or lack of clarity that can provide places for close attention when the film is eventually shown for a second time. Love later commented, "If I keep showing them the film, they'll think it is about remembering. I ask them to reconstruct the film communally. There are always things you don't remember, but others do, that can start your images moving again."

Using *silent* films allows the viewer's attention to be captured by the screen images, rather than waiting for the commentary to direct them where to look. What can follow after showing the film is a conversation about personal images, using spoken words and gestures. The words and gestures are impermanent and the only trace left may well be the mental images generated. A considerable amount of work is needed to create, develop and refine the use of language to describe and re-conjure images, both for oneself and others.

A further comment by Love concerned the generality of what was shown:

> The film creates the sense of generality, of large numbers of pos-
> sibilities that you can work with. It is not a *single* ellipse on the paper
> as it would be in an ordinary lesson based around textbook ideas. So
> it is the dynamic range of possibilities that is the central thing that
> comes from the film.

It is also possible to show extreme cases (circles expanding to become straight lines, for example), which in static diagrams would not be regarded as representative or perhaps even related.

One factor which makes working on such an animation into a mathematical event is that it is not a film of particular circles and ellipses in the same sense that a film of birds in flight is, indeed must be, of a given flock. (I explore this further in Chapter 6.) Every frame of the film is symbolic, and needs to be carefully read and its potential meaning and significance discussed and possibly agreed upon. Geometry arises when these images are internalised and worked on by pupils.

## Working on computer screen images

Computers are rapidly developing the capability of producing sophisticated screen images of astonishing variety and detail. In exploring how the capabilities of these devices are being used in school mathematics education in geometry, I focus first on work using Logo's turtle graphics, before turning to contrast the use of pseudo-synthetic geometry packages: *Cabri-géomètre* or *Geometer's Sketchpad*.

In general, the computer allows you to focus on particular things, by doing some others for you, thereby easing the demands of the situation. This is true of all media that offer images. The range and type of interaction allowed by any program is one important part of this control.

### *Turtle graphic images*

I said earlier that computers offer quite new forms of encounters with dynamic geometric images; pupils take a very active role in their creation and manipulation. Much the most widespread geometrical work using computers has been with the subset of Logo known as turtle graphics (see, for example, Ainley and Goldstein, 1988; Hoyles and Sutherland, 1989). One of the most striking things about Logo in this context is that it becomes a language which *generates* and *controls* action, rather than merely *describing* it. Instead of looking at an image on the screen and then describing it in terms of the language, language is used generatively to *create* something on the screen. The computer code necessarily comes *before* action, and, as a consequence, the user is forced to focus on the language. Logo language statements are implemented on the screen, yet for the computer the screen phenomena are secondary effects.

Despite this, the screen is usually the focus of the pupil's interest and the language is, at best, relegated to the position of being a means to an end. For instance, spectacular effects can be produced by the REPEAT command, but concentration on these alone, perhaps by printing out the resulting screen images, may be reinforcing inattentive use of language. Teachers counteract this by not merely admiring a remarkable output, but by asking: *how* did you achieve that?

There have been numerous descriptions of how pupils wanted to do something on the screen with Logo, and then went about acquiring particular intellectual tools and mathematical knowledge towards achieving that end. It seems to be one of the strengths of Logo, related to its implementability of action, that pupils can generate for themselves, see on other pupils' screens or be tempted by a teacher offering an idea, image or procedure, something they want. They therefore create or take on some goal toward which they are willing to work, making use of whatever resources they can.

Another way of working on the language itself is for teachers to offer sophisticated programs to pupils as objects for exploration, as might be done with regard to certain, unfamiliar algorithms (such as one for finding square roots). Tom Kieren comments:

> One of the first primitives I had kids playing around with was something we found in *Byte* magazine. It was a procedure called 'Squiral'. It made interesting spiral shapes. . . . The turtle simply went forward a bit and turned an angle, went forward a bit further and turned the same angle, went forward a bit further, and etc. Although this seemed like a fairly harmless activity, the primitive carried with it three parameters which kids could play with. Because it had a lot of power, the kids came to see that there was much, much more to shape than they might've thought of previously – shape in a controlled sense, not shape in some random, non-replicable, drawing sense.
>
> (Kieren and Pimm, 1989, p. 26)

All of these different shapes came from the same procedure, thereby suggesting that these shapes which otherwise might have been seen as totally different, actually have something in common. The fact the shapes are all generated by the same procedure can also suggest that it is worth looking for commonalities across a wide range of different phenomena.

Such generating and processing of the visual by language plays an important part in work with turtle graphics, where pupils are encouraged to see shapes recurring in other shapes or as made up of other shapes, in order to allow the procedural power of this particular computer language to come into play. In the British government document *Mathematics from 5 to 16*, the following figure occurs, alongside the claim given on the next page:

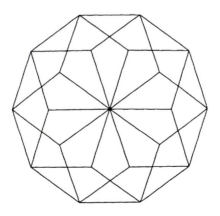

for example, using LOGO many children of infant age and many children of low ability in secondary schools can program a micro-computer to produce their own designs [such as this one.]

(HMI, 1985, p. 14)

Logo code can generate powerful and impressive effects on the screen that pupils can happen upon. If taken up and explored, these can provide an impetus towards understanding the effects of the code which resulted in the figure. If the picture is seen as consisting of rhombuses, then it is a very complex task to program this 'seeing'. If, however, it is seen as consisting of overlapping regular pentagons, then it is much simpler (using the REPEAT command) to program.

Multiple seeings form a very important part of mathematics, and the two seeings described above will be embodied in quite different computer programs, even though the screen effect will be identical. (Is the mathematical focus, indeed the goal, the drawing or the drawn?) Logo is not a neutral language with regard to the perceptions it encourages. Because of its structure, good programming style entails seeing figures in certain ways, valuing some seeings over others. Logo programming offers its own aesthetic, which at times has more to do with the machine than with the desires and aspirations of geometers.

In the everyday physical world of the child, she carries out her intentions by acting directly on things. It is one important constraint of educational value in the Logo environment that children *cannot* directly act on the screen turtle. It is not a manipulative in the sense discussed in Chapter 2. Even with a floor turtle, pupils are not encouraged just to pick the turtle up and move it around. In order to come to grips with some of the mathematical potential that the Logo turtle offers, pupils need deliberately to use language. Provided the pupil is willing to take on the constraints of the machine and software, then mathematical learning can take place.

In relation to mathematics, this emphasis on action is interesting. On the one hand, it is *initially* a very powerful device for showing some of the interpreted effects, in practice, of symbolic statements that can be written down. In mathematics classes, it is very easy to get tied up in the form of the language without paying much attention to the meaning of what is going on – in fact, pupils are often encouraged to do precisely that. This linking between one element of the form and the meaning (in the sense of the geometric effect it can produce) is a very powerful attribute that computers offer to us.

But in his work on pupils' developing notions of proof, Nicolas Balacheff (1988) argues that ultimately we should aim to take pupils away from action and have them look at the *form* of the argument as a whole. This suggests that perhaps the close tie-up in turtle graphics between Logo language and action might eventually be an *anti*-mathematical force.

The enticing implementability lures pupils into remaining in touch with the 'meaning' (in this case, the turtle-drawn pictures on the screen) at all times. In other symbolic work in mathematics, one of the important features is that meaning can be ignored, in order to work on similarities and links between the form of the symbols alone. I say more about this in Chapter 5.

### Geometry packages

While Logo is a programming language, other software, including sophisticated Euclidean geometry programs such as *Cabri-géomètre* or *Geometer's Sketchpad*,[7] involve quite different forms of control, seemingly offering direct 'manipulation' of screen images of geometric elements. They constitute powerful pieces of software for aiding exploring and conjecturing in the realm of Euclidean geometry, enabling geometry to be worked at dynamically (see, for example, for *Cabri-géomètre* ATM, 1992).

*Cabri-géomètre* can be used to render trivial certain currently-challenging geometric problems (such as many loci problems) which can enhance powers of imagining. But just as Cuisenaire rods are not primarily calculating devices, it is important to realise that such software is more like Dienes blocks than a calculator (in that it is unlikely to be found outside schools). Work in an educational setting must build in the importance of prior prediction and reflection, in order to have a stake in the outcome, precisely because it is so easy to use the software to 'do the geometry for you'.

In some ways, the contrast with the static, single images of geometry textbooks (from which the reader had to generalise) could not be more marked. Earlier in this chapter, I described imagining some parts of a static diagram moving. With *Cabri-géomètre* or *Geometer's Sketchpad*, the user can directly cause figures to move continuously and *see* what happens.

My colleague, Eric Love, reported one early experience with *Cabri-géomètre* as follows.

> I had chosen three points and named them A, B and C. I intended to explore how 'reflecting' a point (i.e. creating a new point, the same distance but on the opposite side) first in A, then that point in B and then the resulting one in C would continue if I continued reflecting in A then B then C. I found that this sequence of points eventually returned to my original starting-point.
>
> Would this happen with a different starting-point? I was about to choose a second particular starting-point, when I realised that I could 'move' my starting-point with the mouse – continuously – and that the whole sequence of reflected points would move with it and I could directly see the effect of changing the starting-point.

51

What you can do with *Cabri-géomètre* or *Geometer's Sketchpad* is to create a static picture and then cause it to move or deform: for instance, specify three points and then 'ask' for them to be joined up to form a triangle. The mouse allows you to 'pick up the triangle', and to change it – to *manipulate* it, in the language of Chapter 2. For instance, you can 'pick up' one corner of the triangle and move it by means of the hand-driven mouse – and the rest of the triangle follows. The screen cursor sometimes takes the form of an icon of a hand – not a hand that draws, but a hand that moves things about.[8]

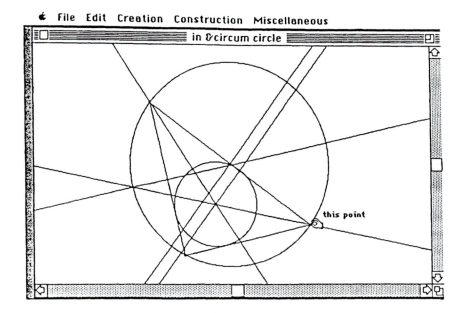

The implicit metaphoric invitation is to see the screen hand as my hand. At other times, the cursor is an icon of a pencil, as if a figure is being drawn. Thus, *Cabri-géomètre* distinguishes between what Brian Rotman (1987), in a numerical context, has contrastingly named as 'gestural' and 'graphical' possibilities.[9] Having invoked a construction, *Cabri-géomètre* also offers an arrow or hand as a pointer, accompanied by 'this point'. (See note 7.)

One of the most mathematical aspects of *Cabri-géomètre* involves the use of continuity of the movement of the mouse to instigate and control the continuity of movement of the screen images directly. The emerging language is that of physical contact with objects: points are 'picked up' and figures 'pulled', 'dragged' or 'moved around' the screen. By clicking on a point in a figure and then dragging with the mouse, the image changes, apparently continuously. Unlike with the geoboard, any 'in-between' figure can be frozen to become *the* screen image: there is no visible grid privileging some configurations over others.

The software preserves the relations among the points and lines of a figure (such as lines being perpendicular or bisecting one another, or points lying on a circle or being equidistant from two lines). *Cabri-géomètre* holds or remembers *relationships* for you, allowing concentration on other things. The machine preserves the specified relationships among the elements, enabling the current screen image to be seen and treated as a single, movable object, at once coherent yet unfixed. However, although both *Cabri-géomètre* and *Geometer's Sketchpad* allow loci to be produced on the screen, to date the locus cannot subsequently be manipulated as an object. Thus, loci do not yet have the same conceptual object status as other primitive geometric objects in the system, in contradistinction to newly-generated Logo procedures.

As with any technological substitution, *Cabri-géomètre* does not merely enhance perceptions, it also alters them. While there are various types of objects which can be conjured up (points, lines and circles) and various pre-programmed constructions that can be performed (such as joining two points, finding mid-points, drawing circles), there is a striking shift in how these 'constructions' can be employed, in terms of an object–tool distinction.[10]

Suppose I want to find the image of a point reflected in a line.[11] I could use the physical tools of geometry classes, a set square perhaps to draw a perpendicular line to the given line and a compass or pair of dividers to measure off an equal distance on the other side of the line.

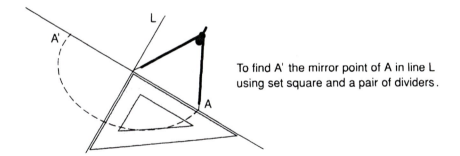

To find A' the mirror point of A in line L using set square and a pair of dividers.

Within *Cabri-géomètre*, a pre-set, primitive construction is to draw a line perpendicular to another through a given point, which could be used to construct a perpendicular bisector to the desired mirror line through the given point whose reflection is required. Following that, a circle can then be used to 'construct' the required image point. This involves a shift of thinking from seeing a circle as an object which itself can be constructed, into seeing a circle as a *tool* for constructing other points (usually requiring 'equal distance'; another tool use for a circle could be for checking parallelism). Tools are means to an end rather than ends in themselves.

A comparable situation existed in early Greek geometry where many curves (such as the conic sections) were first called into existence as constructive tools, rather than objects of study in their own right. The so-called *symptom* associated with a curve (the natural language description of how the points on the curve relate to one another[12]) later became its definition in a shift to definition by properties (see Pimm, 1993b). Software such as *Cabri-géomètre* may allow a renewed contact with an earlier, now-superseded geometrical tradition. However, as I shall now discuss, there are also some important differences.

### The drawing and the drawn

We regularly talk about *drawing* a diagram, but also about *drawings*. The word 'drawing' suggests the process rather than a result (that which is drawn), and drawings necessarily evolve in time. Watching how students actually draw diagrams can inform our understanding of how they are viewing the problem. What we are usually offered are completed drawings. What extra information is conveyed by knowing the temporal evolution of *how* diagrams are drawn in the solution of problems has been simply but elegantly explored by Nunokawa (1994).

Earlier, I mentioned that Logo engenders an aesthetic that gets embodied in the code: *Cabri-géomètre* likewise. To take the example of the animation described on p. 46, seeing the point as captured by the circle or the circle as captured by the point have to be constructed differently and thus set up different dependencies: order of construction matters. Thus, a *Cabri-géomètre* diagram carries its constructive history with it: the drawing still exists inside the drawn.

In a profound and stimulating paper, Colette Laborde (1993) identifies some distinctions between pencil-and-paper geometry and 'Cabri-geometry'.[13] She declares that the abstract *Cabri-géomètre* referents are not identical with conventional Euclidean ones: that is, the geometry arising from static drawn diagrams. Cabri-geometry, arising out of consideration of dynamic screen images, is therefore in an interesting sense, a non-Euclidean geometry. She also makes it clear that different constructions of the 'same' geometric object may have different drag properties and, even more strikingly, some theorems of Cabri-geometry depend (albeit not arbitrarily) on the decisions of the software designers.

Laborde makes use (though far from consistently in her paper) of Parzysz's (1988) distinction between 'figure' (*figure*) and 'drawing' (*dessin*) – an identical one to that between 'number' and 'numeral' respectively. She claims that creating geometric computer-screen images requires a refinement of this distinction, in that the stressing and ignoring that a mathematician can do (in order to see through drawings to figures) actually involves some mathematical understanding and knowledge, and this needs to be programmed into the computer tolerances. Laborde writes: "The referent attached to a drawing cannot be inferred only from the drawing but must be given by a text in a discursive way" (pp. 40–1).[14]

Laborde discusses what she calls 'black-box' situations:

> A Cabri-drawing is given to the pupils, they do not know how it was constructed and the facilities of the software giving access to the construction process are removed. The task for the pupils is to reconstruct the same Cabri-géomètre drawing, i.e. a drawing on the screen behaving in the same way as the given Cabri-géomètre drawing when it is dragged. . . . A discursive description of the figure must be given in addition to the figure.
>
> (1993, p. 47)

With black-box situations, the challenge is thus not just to make a static, visually indistinguishable screen image copy, but also to create a drawing that is *dynamically* identical as well. This is a mathematically new task, one that was not offerable prior to the development of such software environments.

William Ivins (1969, pp. 61–2), whose work I shall make much of in subsequent chapters, writes of the role of symbolism and syntax in the creation of hand-made images historically, contrasting what he calls 'visual statements' with collections of word symbols.

> Thus while there is very definitely a syntax in the putting together, the making, of visual images, once they are put together there is no syntax for the reading of their meaning. With rare exceptions, we see a picture first as a whole and only after having seen it as a whole do we analyse it into its component parts. . . . This leads me to wonder whether the constantly recurring philosophical discussion as to which comes first, the parts or the whole, is not merely a derivative of the different syntactical situations exemplified on the one hand by visual statements and on the other by the necessary arrangement of word symbols in a time order. Thus it may be that the points and lines of geometry are not things at all but merely syntactical dodges.

Any process of holding images must have a syntax: for instance, the grid of the geoboard.[15] Laborde makes clear that Cabri-drawings have the sequential temporal syntax of verbal statements, the product of the process of 'explicit description' which necessarily precedes their generation. Cabri-drawings have memories – their generational history forms part of the figure and the machine insists that they be 'read' this way. Thus, Cabri-drawings provide a new and mathematically important instance of Ivins' 'rare exception'.

In his discussion of *Cabri-géomètre*, Dick Tahta writes:

> it presents the user with direct images of the basic elements – points, lines, circles – of plane geometry. . . . I believe, however, that it is the direct manipulation of geometric images – whether on mental, video or computer screens – that should form the central core of any geometric curriculum.
>
> (1992, pp. 37, 39)

The screen images offered are undoubtedly 'direct', in the sense that there is an external source impinging on my retina. They are certainly direct when compared with the devices of traditional analytic geometry[16] or matrix transformation geometry. But they are not direct in the sense of being unmediated; geometric objects are not screen objects. The former are virtual, their genesis and location confused; the latter simulates certain features of material objects and drawings.

There is a powerful irony here. *Cabri-géomètre* is a fundamentally algebraic piece of software – at one level, merely because it is the solving of equations and extensive use of coordinates that generate and drive the screen effects, which to the user are primary, yet to the machine are quite secondary. The screen images are still symbolic. In a more fundamental sense, the associated Cabri-geometry is a 'descriptive' geometry only in a particular text-based sense: the necessary syntax of its drawings renders it algebraic. Tahta (1990a) has offered a mathematical formulation of a Taoist motto: 'the geometry that can be told is not geometry'. Cabri-geometry undoubtedly offers a tale worth the telling. But I wonder about its subtext concerning the nature of geometry itself.

## WHAT IS THE ROLE OF SYMBOLS IN GEOMETRY?

*Ceci n'est pas une pipe.*

(René Magritte)

The symbol for a circle is a circle.

(Dick Tahta)

At first sight, it might seem that there is very little in the way of symbolic activity in Euclidean geometry (other than perhaps the suggestive labelling of vertices for reference), in contrast with number or algebra. Geometric forms, properties and relations are surely directly perceived, without need of intermediate representations.

One background question for this chapter has been whether the *meanings* of geometry lie in images in the mind: if so, are the images images *of* something (but what?), or things in themselves? Ironically, perhaps, because the objects of geometry seem unproblematic, there is usually less questioning of reference, with what a circle or a triangle 'really' is. Are mental images what the 'facts' of geometry[17] (such as that the angles of a triangle always add up to 180 degrees, or the diagonals of a rectangle always cut each other in half, or all quadrilaterals tessellate) are referring to?

Thinking further about the nature of any geometric drawing or diagram (whether in a book, on the board, or on a screen) suggests that things are not straightforward. The status of the drawing and its use as an aid to geometric reasoning is ambiguous. Reynès (1990) poses the question of why an 'error' of drawing does not automatically result in an error of reasoning and cause problems in the same way that an error in an arithmetic or algebraic calculation can. One key difference, offering a partial resolution of this interesting question, will emerge in the next chapter with the discussion of the different symbolic functions of significa-tion and being a counterpart. The arithmetic/algebraic computations use the symbols as counterparts, whereas geometric diagrams are seldom so used (unless the task is one of technical drawing – see Sträßer, 1991).

The aim of using such diagrams is to see *through* the particularity of the diagram to grasp the generality of what the drawer is attempting to focus attention on. The diagram is symbolic to the extent that it is not the object the theorem is speaking about. Any physical or drawn square is not a square. When a teacher says, 'Draw a square – don't bother with your ruler', she is attempting to draw attention to the fact that what is wanted is a symbolic (albeit suggestive) representation on which to work: a sketch. Yet some pupils may be unwilling to draw a straight line without a ruler – unable or unwilling to stress and ignore with their minds what is in front of them to 'make' it into a straight line.

This section's opening quotation from the Belgian surrealist painter, Magritte, accompanies a direct and accurate pictorial representation of a pipe. The title[18] of the complete picture (including those painted words) is, however, *The Use of Words Number 1*. How are we supposed to make sense of the apparent claim that this is *not* a pipe? In the preface to a small book by Foucault on Magritte's paintings, James Harkness comments:

> After all, would anyone seriously argue that a word *is* what it represents – that the painting of a pipe is the pipe itself? Must we say rhetorically, with Foucault: "My God, how simpleminded!" Yet it is exactly from the commonsense vantage that, when asked to identify the painting, we reply "it's a pipe" – words we shall choke on the moment we try to light up.
>
> (Foucault, 1983, pp. 5–6)

And what about the diagram on the following page?

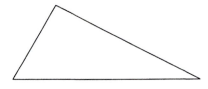

Does it make any sense to accompany it with the claim 'This is not a triangle'? A drawing of a triangle is not a triangle. OK, well and good. But another part of the confusion arises from a drawing seeming to assert the existence of the thing of which it is a drawing in the way a photograph does. (Foucault speaks of how a painting "independently establishes an invisible world that resembles itself" – p. 34.) In offering itself as a substitute for the thing, a diagram seems to imply that it is as good as the thing itself for our purposes. We speak metonymically of the drawing of a triangle as a triangle.

There is a further complication. Mathematicians *use* one diagram of a triangle on occasions to represent *all* triangles. This is reminiscent in algebra of the use of letters for *any* number, though one important difference is that a letter is not any particular number, whereas the drawn triangle used to represent all triangles can itself also be seen as a particular triangle.

Because all circles (and squares for that matter) are similar to one another, there is a strong sense in which a diagram reflecting what happens *in particular* is generic of what will happen no matter which circle is drawn, provided no particular length relations have been made use of. Not all triangles are similar to one another (it is not even true that all right-angled triangles are similar), and so there is much more required in order to 'see' that the construction or property of the drawing is indeed common to them all. Why don't geometric proofs thereby necessarily fall into 'cases', sets of similar configurations that partition all possible examples, for each case of which there is a generic proof?

Returning to the earlier discussion of *dessin* and *figure*, rather than 'figure', I prefer the term 'configuration' to refer to the equivalence class of diagrams, where the 'sameness' is that one could be mouse-dragged into another. Laborde (1993, p. 43) suggests: "In a sense, Cabri-géomètre offers a reification of the notion of geometrical figure". I believe, conversely, that we seem in a similar position to the situation with number where the action of drawing (rather than counting, as with number) is what brings geometric figures into existence – once again the symbol precedes the referent.

What is the status of a *Cabri-géomètre* screen image and an underlying configuration from the point of view of generality? A particular image is constructed by means of instantiating general constructions in sequence on chosen base objects. Deformation by means of the mouse results in a different image, but one belonging to the same configuration (an equivalence class determined by the mutual inter-relationships specified among the elements). A static diagram is both viewable as a particular and a representation of the general. With *Cabri-géomètre*, you can move from one particular to another so easily, that I wonder whether this has the effect of emphasising the particular status of a diagram at the expense of the general. Devices can change the relation between general and particular. With a dynamic, interactive medium which supports direct variation, where the dependencies survive direct manipulation, seeing the one *as* the many, rather than the one as one *among* many, may not be so valued a perception.

# 4

# WHAT COUNTS AS
# A NUMBER?

They said, 'Them as counts counts moren them as dont count'.

(Hoban, 1982, p. 18)

We talk about someone being good at 'handling' numbers, figures or calculations. How are we to get our hands on them that they may prove susceptible of being handled? One way is by means of numbered objects.

A trip to a delicatessen or a Chinese restaurant may produce a numbered object. You become the number on the ticket or disc. In some cases, order matters; in others, it is just a means of identification by association – "Number 15 please". But in either case, no distinction is made between the number and the token with that number on it. Playing cards and dominoes, too, are numbered objects, though using a predominantly iconic presentation rather than by means of Indian-Arabic numerals.

But these numbered objects are not too useful for reckoning with. Counting boards are about reckoning with counters, while pencil-and-paper algorithms are about reckoning with ciphers.[1] Any partial answer to the question of what numbers are (and there are several proposals) involves a substitution, a deflection, a looking-elsewhere. We can have no *direct* experience of numbers.

At home and in school, I might be equipped to think about and work with numbers by means of *physical* materials: counters, perhaps, or an abacus, Cuisenaire rods or Dienes arithmetic blocks, and the patterns they allow. The rods quietly assert that numbers are in some important way like lengths. Calling my voice into play, learning to produce certain sounds in fixed order, according to the particular language patterns of number words, also allows me some sense of conjuring and control. I could invoke my fingers and their movements: it is far less clear what this substitute offers – images perhaps, or a focus that allows something else to occur. I can also write words or numerals (the ciphers) and operate on them *as if* they were numbers: for some, numbers are inherently written. I might evoke metaphoric images such as 'a number is a point on the number line'. Finally, all of these somehow rest on the process of counting: without counting, there are no numbers. More strongly put, counting brings numbers into being.

Teachers can and do choose to offer pupils Cuisenaire rods, for instance, in order to supply a more tangible referent for number. Teachers can also offer abacus-based actions in order to suggest a more transparent calculational means. They also can and do choose to offer number-word games and rhymes, where there is no such appeal to physical materials, where the task is almost entirely linguistic. They regularly offer opaque Indian-Arabic numerals and the algorithms that this numeration system supports. Working at such algorithms can result in meaning in exchange for attention.

Teachers can and do provide electronic calculators, despite the fact that these are not pedagogic objects and are widely available in the outside world. Calculators can deflect attention from actual calculation – suggesting "you need not attend to this: it is being taken care of for you". The history of working with number is a history of means and physical/notational devices.

Despite regular claims to something being *the* way to teach number, classroom decisions are seldom an either/or. All of these resources (physical, gestural-graphical and linguistic) contribute to the meaning of numbers, and all can be made to 'hold' number and to carry out calculations in different ways. But all involve conventions: of form, of structure, of use. It is also far from obvious whether one should come before another.

I have used the words 'counting' and 'calculating'. What is a *counter*? A counter can be the *person* doing the counting – the one-who-counts. (The US TV programme *Sesame Street* has a counting character called The Count.) It can be a *device* that counts for me – like a revolution counter. A counter can be the substitute *object* that is counted with. (One stone for every sheep in the pen: counting the token, the tally, having made sure that they tally. The Latin word *calculus*, whence 'calculate', means "pebble".) Finally, a (shop) counter is sometimes the *place* where counting is to take place (along with the counting board, counting table and counting house).[2]

What of doing calculations? We are so used to computing *with* figures,[3] with the symbols that comprise our numbers, that it can be hard to conceive that for some cultures, the *holding* of numbers and *calculating* with numbers were distinct processes: for example, Roman numerals and counting boards or abacuses. The abacus outcome was recorded using the numerals, but there was no way of checking the outcome other than by repeating the actions. (It is possible to derive symbolic algorithms working on Roman numerals, but they are not simple, even without coping with the complexity added by the combined additive and subtractive principles.)

And what is a calculator? According to the *Random House College Dictionary*, a calculator is:

1. a person who calculates or computes;
2. also called calculating machine: a machine that performs mathematical operations;
3. a person who operates such a machine;
4. a set of tables that facilitates calculation.

(1979, p. 191)

The sense of myself as the calculator, as the one-who-calculates, is turning into the one-who-operates-the-calculator. With every calculating device, it is possible to ask the question: to what extent when I use this device can I still see *myself* as the one-who-calculates?[4] The shifting reference for the word 'calculator' mirrors the contemporary devolution of much of the responsibility for that-which-is-calculated onto the device. As a user, my focus then becomes: have I given the machine the correct things in the correct order to have it do what I want?

There is a sense of agency and agent in the electronic calculator itself that is almost absent in an abacus. The abacus merely holds numbers, while within the range of manipulations its design allows, it is completely indifferent to how things are carried out. As well as holding number symbols, the electronic calculator also holds *procedures*, over which I have no control or even access. The continuity between the electronic calculator and earlier computational aids, as well as the sense of singularity and rupture, is explored in the third section of this chapter.

What sense can I make of my actions with these devices? How scrutable is the device to an enquiry as to how and why it works? How transparent are the necessary actions? It is important to remember that unlike most manipulatives, no calculating aid is primarily a *pedagogic* device – though they all provide untaught lessons nevertheless. Cuisenaire rods and Dienes blocks are not calculating devices, in the sense that their primary intent is not to facilitate computations *per se*, but to aid their *comprehension*. To use these latter two (or similar) devices for enabling children to get their 'sums' right is to misunderstand fundamentally their purpose. There may also be a trade-off between transparency on the one hand, and fluency or efficiency on the other: and the former may be important if the device is used for an educational purpose. But before concerning myself with calculating means (including algorithms) and calculating devices, I return to the core notion of counting.

## ON COUNTING

Katie is three. She has learnt how to generate spoken number words, in order, up to a hundred. (She still looks to her mother for confirmation at certain decades, particularly forty and fifty.) In front of her is a board game from a book her mother has been reading to her, comprising a snaking path of squares numbered 1 to 46. Katie is able to say the English number words one at a time, coordinated with (or is it by?) touching the correspondingly numbered square. Does she have a sense of counting anything, or is her touching more like conducting, a way of keeping the rhythm going? Touch with fingers is manifestly involved in the striking complexity of these actions.

She can count small numbers of objects accurately and has just that day for the first time succeeded in systematically counting thirteen 'pies' depicted on a card, the image structured in alternating lines of two and three. Katie has some difficulty with the board game, which involves using a dice (yet another presentation of numbers), preferring finding the square bearing the numeral that goes with the configuration of dots shown on the dice face to counting on that many from where her counter was before. She announces that she does not need to use the dice, and hereafter decides herself where to move her counter to next.

I wonder whether the fact that she has previously gained spoken control over this key part of the number-naming sequence[5] means that she is free to attend to the numerals that she is making correspond by her fingering. Can she go directly from the written symbols to the number word when above ten? Not quite. (She is pretty fluent back and forth below ten, and nine is her favourite number – the largest with a non-composite

63

representation.)[6] All of this has to do with the complexity that is counting and number.

All aspects of counting contribute to the richness of meaning and use of numbers in our culture, and sense needs to be made of them by children. Each child will have particular connotations for certain numbers which play an important part in their lives. An extreme instance comes from the film *A World Apart*, in which teenager Molly Roth's mother is imprisoned in South Africa for ninety days. We see her with the numbers from 1 to 90 written in an exercise book, drawing a line through them one by one as the days pass. (Recall too the 4/5 anecdote from Chapter 1.)

While such particularities are important, they can get in the way of seeing general arithmetic relations. It can be hard to see pattern among small numbers, in part because of this particular luggage we all acquire – and some of it is unwanted baggage. These specific meanings do not help pupils acquire confidence and security in handling large numbers, the sense that 'all other hundreds are the same'.

When children are first learning to count, they are often asked 'Can you count?' What this usually means is not whether they can determine how many objects of a certain sort in a designated collection there might be, but whether they can generate correctly a certain set of spoken noises in order. Number words *are* words, but they are special in that they form an ordered and closely structured collection.

In English grammar, there is a distinction between transitive and intransitive verbs, which broadly separates verbs into two classes, those that have a direct object and those that do not. For example, the verb 'to describe' is transitive (I describe *something*), whereas 'to sleep' is not (I don't sleep *something*, I just sleep). But 'to count' can be used both transitively and intransitively: I can count things (e.g. counters, children in the room, minutes I have been alive) and I can also just count (say the counting words aloud in order).

'Just' counting – that is, counting intransitively – is often used by children to accompany games, as well as in number songs and as a thing to do in itself, to practise to mastery. Counting *transitively* for children involves saying the whole number words in order as they touch objects in turn – usually with the intent of answering the question 'How many?' In order successfully to count transitively, you have to know what *counts*; that is, which items are to be counted and which not. If unable to decide whether or not thumbs count as fingers, or how to tell a finger from a toe, you will not be able to count consistently or agree with the results of others.

It is striking to me that these two different activities do not go by separate names in English. Yet there are also important messages in this elision of difference. The same holds true for the fact that the English language names for the number symbols 0–9 are the same as for the concept named. Thus: what's that? A nine. What does it mean? It means nine (of something).

Intransitive counting is a linguistic ability, and is only possible because the number-word system in any language must be highly regular and structured. The English one is not completely regular, otherwise 'thirteen' would be 'onety-three' and 'twenty-five' would be 'twoty-five', and so on. But, in the main, it is systematic, otherwise there would be an impossible amount to remember – the number 'poem' would go on and on.[7]

In order to be able to count transitively, intransitive counting must be mastered, otherwise the reference set of sounds (words) against which the objects to be counted are being set would be a non-standard reference. And young children initially offer *countings* of collections of things: one, two, three, four, five. If asked how many there are, following a counting, they may well respond with the entire counting again (just as with an abacus computation). The question apparently triggers a procedure to be gone through. They have to learn the convention which says the counting process can be compressed into saying the last number alone: that 'five' is enough.[8]

How are whole numbers to be compared? I can claim that six is bigger than five because it is said *after* five in the ordinal sequence. I can claim six marbles are more than five marbles because after pairing there is one left over. We want to associate these observations, so that subsequently we can put our trust in the order of the names to 'carry' the physical – 'six thousand and forty marbles are more than six thousand and thirty-nine marbles, because six thousand and forty comes after six thousand and thirty-nine' – and there is no need (and it is pretty infeasible anyway) to carry out a one-to-one matching. Combining these two perceptions of comparison and relating them is part of what creation of number meaning entails.

A fruitful task with young children can be to challenge them to order numbered cards or discs (0–99) on a number board. The accessible ordering principle is that of the spoken names, rather than order of 'size'. They are all numbered objects of the same size, the frozen result of one particular counting. All the 'thirty-somethings' belong together; confusions of, say, 17 and 71 can be resolved.

In some important sense, counting *things* is a mere application of intransitive counting – albeit quite a hard one to master. Here are some categories of things that can 'go wrong' with young children (aged four to seven, say) counting transitively. The following examples draw in large part on an article by Jan van den Brink (1984).

- Infants frequently appear unsurprised that a second count of a collection of objects produces a different result from the first. Where does that sense of invariance arise from?

- Martha (aged four) stops on 'three' when counting on her fingers and, pointing to her middle finger, asks: "What's 'three' about that?" The counting of collections of objects can get confused with baptising individual objects in the course of a counting: van den Brink advocates pauses when counting objects, or 'stops' as he calls them, in order to direct the child's attention to the (cardinal) number of what has already been counted. When counting with fingers, others suggest indicating nested collections of fingers are being numbered by squeezing them together each time the next number word is said, so 'two' or 'three' labels a set, not an individual finger.
- Sometimes objects are inadvertently left out and therefore not counted (in some sense, they are deemed 'not to count'). This omission destroys the (transitive) counting. Yet in some counting games (e.g. Fizz-buzz), leaving out the saying of particular numbers is common.[9]
- Sometimes there are mismatches between the telling of the number words and the indication of the objects. This can occur either physically (e.g. the two processes of saying and touching not being synchronised with each other) or verbally (e.g. instead of counting with whole words, children sometimes count with syllables, 'se-ven' counting two objects and 'e-le-ven' three).

In summary, when counting *things*, the following must happen:

- the number-word sequence is inviolate: nothing must be omitted and the order must be exact;
- every object must be counted once and only once, all are equal with respect to the count. You also have to know what to count.

Whereas intransitive counting can:

- start anywhere in the sequence;
- take large or small steps (or even differently sized ones) as desired;
- include whatever sorts of number names suit the age and experience levels of pupils. For example:
  - start at ten and count on in tens;
  - start at seven and count back in fours;
  - start at six and count on alternately in threes, then twos;
  - start at minus five and count on in minus threes;
  - start at nought point one three and count back in nought point nought twos.

Such tasks can help pupils gain familiarity, fluency and mastery of the system of number words themselves, quite independently of the question of how these number words can be made to apply, through transitive counting, to the material world.

The difference between transitive and intransitive counting is an important one, and provides a further illustration of the distinction mentioned in the first chapter, between 'meaning' on the one hand and fluency on the other. Why do we insist that pupils have to 'understand' number first, by restricting them to numbers under ten, then twenty, then up to a hundred – as schemes or curricula often suggest? A comparable parallel might be to restrict pupils initially to only three-letter words in school. It raises questions about the presumed order in which certain ideas, techniques and 'know-hows' should be taught. Is the 'meaning' of counting, and hence number, to be found completely within counting things? Is that, then, where I *must* start? How can I become a fluent and confident counter?

By delaying the naming of 'large' numbers, the cardinal (how many?) sense has been given preference over the ordinal (what comes next in the spoken sequence?). An alternative approach could make the presumption that learning to name numbers in order is one way of constructing numbers themselves (i.e. the symbol can both precede and generate the object) and that this task is relatively independent of learning about the supposed 'hundred and twenty-twoness' of 122.

A pedagogical device for working on naming numbers is the 'tens table' (due to Caleb Gattegno). One version of it is given below.

| 1 | 2 | 3 | 4 | 5 | 6 | 7 | 8 | 9 |
|---|---|---|---|---|---|---|---|---|
| 10 | 20 | 30 | 40 | 50 | 60 | 70 | 80 | 90 |
| 100 | 200 | 300 | 400 | 500 | 600 | 700 | 800 | 900 |

Gattegno (1967) has described how he gave 'visual dictation', using a pointer to touch in turn up to three signs from the table (one per row, moving from bottom to top) to teach written and spoken decimal numeration to five- and six-year-olds. The table can also be extended in a number of ways and used with widely different ages: for example, adding more rows underneath to work on reading larger whole numbers, or putting a vertical bar at some point and masking everything to the right of it. This latter alteration (effectively restricting oneself to selecting entries from the first so-many columns) allows work on different number bases. Equivalently, for bases larger than ten, additional columns need to be added and given symbols such as *a b c* and *a*0 *b*0 *c*0, etc.

| 1 | 2 | 3 | 4 | 5 | 6 | 7 | 8 | 9 |
|---|---|---|---|---|---|---|---|---|
| 10 | 20 | 30 | 40 | 50 | 60 | 70 | 80 | 90 |
| 100 | 200 | 300 | 400 | 500 | 600 | 700 | 800 | 900 |

The tens table modified for base seven work

The table offers an image which reflects the structure of the spoken and written numeration system and the task works on how to pass from one to the other and back again. At no point is the cardinal (transitive) sense of counting activated. Consequently, this approach to the naming of numbers reveals its own constraints about how far to go, reflected in the number of rows used at any given time. Certainly, 'up to 20' is not a natural stopping place from this perspective, though 'up to 99' is. Saying '79' requires as little (or as much) energy and thought as saying '22'.

Recent work with calculators (see PrIME, 1991) has further indicated how easily young children can familiarise themselves with large numbers and learn how they are written and said. They are also able to think quite explicitly about them. Angela Walsh (1991, pp. 67–8), in an article about calculators and young children, cited a conversation between a group of eight- and nine-year-olds and their teacher about which is the largest number in the world. One said, "Nine thousand million . . . It starts with a nine, but it won't fit on my calculator". Another commented, "I do think it goes on and on, but the biggest number that I can find out is on the calculator". A third, Anna, made the observation that, "It stops at any number you can't count to", and when the teacher asked what she meant, added, "Like if you can only count to one hundred, it stops there for you". The power of being able to name plays an important role in bringing numbers into existence.

Questions about naming and counting are not only of concern in the primary years. For instance, the increasingly common habit of reading decimals as if they were two whole numbers separated by a 'point' (e.g. reading 10.36 as "ten point thirty-six") can lead to confusions with regard to magnitude and the ordering of decimals. One secondary teacher commented about a pupil:

> I asked him why he talked about 0.23 as "point twenty-three" and 0.104 as "point one hundred and four". He objected, "Decimals don't have names. 794 is seven hundred and ninety-four, but 0.794 is just supposed to be said point seven nine four", but he accepts that 0.23 is bigger than 0.104.

The place value indication is not commonly used in writing decimals. We write 12,345.333333333 and not 12,345.333,333,333. The space or the comma helps us to read large whole numbers. (This is not the case in Mandarin, where the spoken naming structure relies on grouping every four digits – see Powell, 1986.) But, as the pupil above observed, the saying of decimals usually involves a 'spelling' reading, one which does not convey any information about size. Other mathematical examples of this distinction include 'two over three' versus 'two-thirds' and '$dy$ over $dx$' versus 'the derivative of $y$ with respect to $x$'. One advantage of spelling readings is that they are frequently quicker to say (see Pimm, 1987, for more detail).

The tens table can be extended in the upwards direction to work directly on reading decimals.

| .01 | .02 | .03 | .04 | .05 | .06 | .07 | .08 | .09 |
|-----|-----|-----|-----|-----|-----|-----|-----|-----|
| .1 | .2 | .3 | .4 | .5 | .6 | .7 | .8 | .9 |
| 1 | 2 | 3 | 4 | 5 | 6 | 7 | 8 | 9 |
| 10 | 20 | 30 | 40 | 50 | 60 | 70 | 80 | 90 |
| 100 | 200 | 300 | 400 | 500 | 600 | 700 | 800 | 900 |

(from Brown, 1991, p. 23)

Certain research on children's learning of decimals (e.g. Swan, 1982) has pointed to common beliefs, such as not accepting that there are any numbers between, say, 3.12 and 3.13. Pedagogic devices like the tens table (with its implicit indefinite continuation) may help towards resolving such misconceptions by offering the power of naming to bring into existence.

## WAYS OF PROCEEDING

Civilisation advances by extending the number of important operations we can perform *without* thinking about them.
(Whitehead, 1925, p. 59; my emphasis)

Numbers are for calculating with, as well as for specification. Algorithms are about practice, about what to do, about how to proceed, as are routines and procedures. The term 'mechanical routine' is still commonly employed, even in an era where most devices are electronic, to mean something unresponsive to difference, something exactly repeatable, always to be done in the same way. If I *understand* a routine, I can then adapt it flexibly to a new situation, or if a detail is forgotten, it can be reconstructed. I may also need to convey to someone else what it is I am doing, how I think about it and why I do what I do. There are, thus, two separate aspects of algorithms, namely the 'what to do' and the 'why this is what we do' connected with awareness and inspectability of action. Fluent pencil-and-paper users want to be able to (con)fuse symbol and referent when calculating, because it is so much quicker and more efficient. To hold tight to the 'meaning' when, say, trying to divide two fractions, is pretty well guaranteed to bring disaster.

These terms suggest that there is a sameness across a range of situations ('You have a method when you notice yourself doing the same thing twice.'). They tend to be used interchangeably, although in some quarters, the word 'algorithm' gets restricted to mean "standard written algorithm". I shall not use it with that limited sense here. Common features of algorithms are that they are *explicit* in terms of what to do, and are *general* with regard to being applicable to a range of related situations (though the fact that the same algorithm can be applied can actually help *create* that sense of commonality).

Algorithms are about mathematical *practice* – about *what* to do, about definite procedures for solving problems (e.g. an algorithm is embodied in a formula for solving a quadratic equation). Algorithms are also about *not* discriminating – about treating everything as if it were the same. Finally, algorithms are about *not* having to think.

Unfortunately, one upshot of this can be that they are not valued. Stephen Brown (1974) complains that multiplication, for instance, is seldom allowed to become problematic for pupils. Pupils do not commonly have the experience of developing an algorithm, codifying their hard-won understanding of a situation and experiencing an increase in efficiency and speed, accompanied by a decrease in the level of attention required. They may never develop a sense of 'I've done this before', nor even of 'Not this again', if the method or algorithm is taught first.

One purpose of formulating an algorithm is to solidify a common response into a single entity, with the intent of making the thinking embedded in it more automatic, thereby increasing efficiency of functioning. One problem of pencil-and-paper algorithms is the way that the meaning and the algorithm get confused, so that the symbol for multiplication becomes a trigger to use the algorithm. Algorithms offer *a* way to carry out a procedure, not *the* way to carry it out. Yet can I understand the notion of, for example, square root deeply if I have no algorithm for its evaluation? In addition to the choice of different methods or algorithms to achieve the same end, there is always a choice of *means* of implementing any particular algorithm. Algorithms usually exploit particular features of the means.

Besides using a calculating device, there are three main means for performing numerical calculations: mental; with the aid of physical apparatus; with the aid of pencil and paper – though most commonly they will be used in some combination. Each means has different strengths and weaknesses, and any particular algorithm will be more or less suited to different means. (I postpone further discussion of mechanical or electronic devices until the next section, where I discuss how calculators embody both a *method* and a *means* of calculating, and whether both are accessible to the user.)

### Mental arithmetic

The term 'mental arithmetic' may conjure up an image of an archaic, whole-class setting in which pupils were pushed for speed and accuracy in table recall: arithmetic computation in a highly charged and competitive atmosphere. Here, I mean merely ways of calculating that can be done solely in the head without recourse to either physical devices or pencil and paper. At some point it moves from a way of solving *this* problem, to a method for solving a class of problems. In fact, they are frequently spoken methods, related to the spoken structure of the number-naming system.

Such methods can draw on particular strengths, such as I may happen to know my doubles, fives and tens better than some other combinations. So I can simplify a multiplication problem by splitting the numbers into parts I can do easily. Fluent and varied fragmentation of numbers seems an important component skill. However, mental methods come up against constraints of memory and functioning.

Mental methods can be shared, mental calculation sessions could include discussion and exploration and comparison of methods, and not solely practice. The form of mental methods often differs from that of codified written ones. Mental methods are frequently uneven, in that they work much better for certain numbers than others. When numbers are written down on paper, they seem to lose their connection to other things that are known. Too often, the production of mental methods disappears once algorithms are taught, and even mental imagery seems dominated by images of the pencil-and-paper format.

In a book suggestively entitled *Dead Reckoning: Calculating without Instruments*, Ronald Doerfler documents a range of techniques and methods (old, relatively recent and new) of computation and approximation of arithmetic operations and elementary functions (such as trigonometric ones and logarithms). He comments that the methods learnt at school were normally considered the only or the best ones, and adds:

> For mental calculations, they usually are not. An analogous situation occurred in the development of our pencil-and-paper methods of calculation that minimize erasures, supplanting the ancient sand reckoning methods in which digits were continuously and instantly erased and overwritten in the course of the calculations.
>
> (Doerfler, 1993, p. 2)

Although speed is certainly one concern, other criteria are employed and he offers certain algorithms as worthy items of mathematical interest. He proposes (for interested adults) a list of preferred characteristics for algorithms to be performed mentally. The details of his actual proposals are less relevant here than the mere notion of the importance of being aware of such criteria and using them to evaluate current algorithmic practice.

### Apparatus algorithms

In using the term 'apparatus algorithm', I have in mind methods for performing numerical calculations by means of physical apparatus such as Cuisenaire rods or Dienes blocks (despite, as I mentioned, this not being their primary function). While there is a sense in which an abacus can be thought of as an object which involves apparatus algorithms, I prefer to maintain the distinction between a calculation device (available and used in the outside world for that express purpose) and pedagogic apparatus being used for illustrative calculation purposes. I explore aspects of abacus use in the next section.

The first computational 'apparatus' used is unquestionably the fingers, both to hold the numbers and to count with. I discussed various involvements of fingers in Chapter 2, and it always strikes me when working with young children how orientated to the *tangible* they are: everything is to be acknowledged, taken into account, by means of touching. When working at 5 + 3, they may well count five fingers, then count three fingers, then count them all. Later, they may well be content to start with five and then count on.

Fingers are good for counting on, allowing as they do someone to be saying one thing while the fingers are keeping track of another thing at the same time (this dual processing obviously needs careful calibration). The next physical apparatus may be bundles of sticks, toothpicks, or other substitute tallies, in fives or tens, transparent with respect to their multiplicity. The substitution for the actual objects of interest has already taken place.

This seems a good point to start to make explicit a distinction that I will return to in later chapters – and one that has been hinted at in the foregoing whenever I have talked about substitutes. Robert Schmidt (1986), a historian of mathematics, makes a distinction between the functions of symbols serving as *signs* and serving as *counterparts*. A sign names or points to something else, but bears no necessary relation to the thing named. A counterpart stands for something else, but does not name or point to it (an indicative function): however, there is an actual relation, a resemblance or connection, between the object and its counterpart. These two functions can coalesce on the same symbol, but there may be confusion when this occurs.

Fingers can serve as counterparts (as can counters!), and the process of complementing described in Chapter 2 can generate fingers as referents for number names (so 'four' has a huge number of referents, all equivalent). Geometric diagrams are remarkably iconic signs – perhaps in some ways akin to photographs – for the abstract 'figure', that is the supposed 'object' of geometric study.

Schmidt uses the example of lines drawn on a nautical chart to illustrate the notion of a counterpart: a nautical chart in no way names what it stands for, but it allows computations and actions to be made upon it which can be directly transferred to actions on the actual object represented. Technical drawings, as opposed to geometric diagrams, are counterparts, though when teachers invite pupils to use rulers and protractors on geometric drawings they are shifting the drawing's status to that of a counterpart. Counterparts are to be acted on, and then the results interpreted via the connection. Counterpart forms can also provide substitute images. One instance might be 'symmetry' of algebraic form (such as $xy + yx$). It suggests a visual phenomenon: the *shape* of an expression.

Schmidt claims:

> It is also the nature of counterparts to draw attention to themselves, while it is in the nature of signs to lead our attention away from themselves and towards the thing signified.[10] . . . Furthermore, it is in the nature of counterparts to turn their object into themselves, while it is the nature of signs to disclose their objects.

> (*ibid.*, p. 1)

I see the signification and counterpart functions of symbols as complementary; neither one suffices for mathematics, yet they seem to conflict with one another, pulling in opposite directions. I shall say more about this distinction in the next chapter.

Manipulatives such as Cuisenaire rods or Dienes apparatus are undoubtedly offered as physical counterparts for numbers. Or is it that Cuisenaire is a counterpart for number, while Dienes blocks are actually confusingly used as a counterpart both for numbers and as a sign for the place-value numeration system? An important observation, arising from the discussion of Dienes apparatus in relation to place value in Chapter 2, is that written numerical algorithms are seldom identical either in form or structure to the 'corresponding' manipulations with the blocks, in part because the former frequently draw on specific properties of the decimal, place-value numeration system.

The apparatus allows or encourages certain ways of operation, and this needs to be transformed before the 'traditional' algorithm can come to be seen as a 'mere' record of operations with the apparatus. Thus, records can be seen as relics of actions. (It can be an interesting mathematical question as to whether the residue is sufficient to reconstruct the process.)

Ironically, in order to see connections, pupils must already understand to some degree that which the blocks are supposedly helping them to learn. The operations with the written symbols are what is to be learned and that is what is guiding the way the equipment is being used. Robin Foster has asked a key question: who is in control of the apparatus, and, in particular, who the interpretation of the meaning? This is one reason why there seems such a difference between asking about the 'meaning' of a geoboard and the 'meaning' of Dienes blocks. Once again, the danger is that the wrong thing is being seen as primary.[11]

The word 'recording' suggests it comes after the action, whereas the action is frequently being carried out 'on the record', which can be acting as a counterpart. A group of seven-year-olds were working on how many ways two same-coloured eggs could be placed in a six-egg carton. After a while, one pupil began working on his record alone to generate examples in pairs (one a reflection of another). The records were starting to be used as counterparts, and not solely as designating signs. Robin Foster has also remarked that recording is often the only evidence the teacher has that a child is using a method, and children may have little notion of what is important and what not. He cites a child who, when asked to subtract eighteen from a hundred, worked it out and then put in the relevant marks afterwards to 'show her working'.[12]

## Pencil-and-paper computations

we usually assume the mathematics curriculum in the first 8 years of school is about numbers, whereas the actual school work is mainly about a particular representation system for numbers – the base 10 placeholder system – and *its* properties and the representational systems [fractions and decimals] for rational numbers. The essence and power of numerical algorithms reside in the freedom to deal only with the *representations* of numbers without regard to the numbers they represent.

(Kaput, 1984, p. 20)

One practice that is the hallmark of mathematics occurs when symbols start being used *as if* they were the objects themselves, namely as counterparts. Most of primary school arithmetic involves acquiring familiarity and fluency with aspects of the decimal place-value numeration system, learning to operate with numerals alone, in order to carry out mathematical operations.

When calculating, the movements are virtual (the 1 is never actually 'carried down'), gestures summon the numbers, but they cannot be grasped or manipulated. They are not tokens, counters. Figures are not moved about on the page; they are repeated, or rubbed out or crossed through (made *not* to count).

Indian-Arabic number signs name numbers, they call numbers into being – but pencil-and-paper computations treat them as if they were counterparts. Young children commonly look for some counterpart relation between the symbol and the object: for example, counting the 'pointy bits' on the 3. The Roman symbol V is often linked with the hand and X, for ten, in terms of mutually inverted Vs, encouraging links between symbol and meaning suggestive of the counterpart function. One confusion is that there is no necessary link between the Indian-Arabic numeration system and numbers that allows the numerals to be perceived as counterparts.

In *The Mastery of Reason*, Valerie Walkerdine (1988) explores the complex significations that occur in relatively commonplace arithmetical terms and draws attention to the creation of meaning within practices. She attempts to document some of the subtle linguistic ways in which the teacher and pupil (by means of a combination of talk and gesture) *create* mathematical meanings in classroom settings, as well as pointing to experience with symbols as a necessary part of learning mathematics, even with the youngest children.

A key (general) question appears right at the beginning of her book (p. 3): "How do children come to read the myriad of arbitrary signifiers – the words, gestures, objects, etc. – with which they are surrounded, such that their arbitrariness is banished and they appear to have the meaning that is conventional?" In other words, how are these signifiers to function as signs, in the terminology of Schmidt. Nowhere is this question more pointed than with number signifiers.

In a chapter entitled 'The achievement of mastery', she offers an episode from a top infant class (of six- to seven-year-olds) where one pupil, Michael, comes to grips with the possibility of working with the signifiers alone (the numerals) when doing two-digit additions, despite the teacher using bundles of matchsticks as erstwhile signifieds (the offered counter-part) for the procedure.

What sort of discovery has Michael made? It is not about action with objects. His discovery is a linguistic one about the mathematical writing system, which allows him to operate with the symbols as if they were the objects of mathematics. This acting 'as if' is one of the powerful functioning practices of mathematicians. But there is always the invitation to confuse symbol and object, and hence to confound which is prior and which will predominate in our attention – an invitation which in some sense cannot be refused, and which also has its advantages when working at developing fluency.

The language of algorithms sounds like the language of action, of movement, of manipulation, as if physical objects were being moved around (and the language is focused on digits, not their place value interpretations). Thus, "You *put* a 1 here, and *carry* the 4". Algorithms are frequently described, explained and taught in terms of operations to be carried out on the symbols, sometimes with injunctions like 'to multiply by ten add a nought', 'take it over to the other side and change the sign' or 'to divide by a fraction, invert and multiply'. The sentences encapsulate 'what to do' into short precepts, appropriately couched in terms of manipulations of symbols.

At the level of *what* to do, this description is entirely appropriate as this is the level of action of a pencil-and-paper algorithm. The notation allows such clipped ways of speaking. It is when attempting to explain 'why' this is what is to be done, that arcane cover stories (some of which were mentioned in Chapter 1) get called into play, attempting to render the operations comprehensible and transparent by means of models generated in reverse. It may well be that some level of practice is required before it even makes sense to ask 'why?'

A key question remains: how are numerals like counters? Indian-Arabic numerals can be used both for holding number but also for direct computation, manipulating the marks *as if* they were counterparts. But what is the link? I return to this question in the final section, but before then I turn to look at calculating devices, which started out offering directly manipulable counterparts and end up offering rapid traceless computations ostensibly with Indian-Arabic numerals.

## CALCULATING DEVICES

Throughout history, various invented devices (such as mathematical tables, abacuses, slide-rules and mechanical or electronic calculators) have been devised to assist with the performing of calculations. With each one, there are practices and conventions to be learned concerned with how to *use* the device to implement an algorithm (such as when and how to move beads or change rows, or how to read off from the cursor, or which buttons to press and in which order). With each there are historical questions about rivalries and investments, both financial and of energy, about how one came to supersede another in particular circumstances.

In addition, with each device there are questions about what service they may be in *learning* mathematics directly (rather than merely helping it to be done). What images are offered implicit in the way numbers are represented; what understandings about operations or the numeration system do they support, as we become more fluent users; what sort of devices are they?

### Slide of hand

I start with neither an account of the abacus nor the electronic calculator, but with a brief look at the slide-rule. Costel Harnasz (1993) has produced a clear and illuminating account of its educational history, entitled 'Do you need to know how it works?', and relates his discussion to current concerns about the use of electronic calculators in schools.

In particular, he quotes Richard Delamain[13] (1630; cited in Cajori, 1916, p. 90):

> for no one to know the use of a Mathematical Instrument, except he knows the cause of its operation, is somewhat too strict, which would keep many from affecting the Art, because they see nothing but obscure propositions, and perplex and intricated demonstrations before their eyes.

and contrasts this with Delamain's rival Oughtred's concern that certain teachers' students were "only doers of tricks and as it were, jugglers". As Delamain made instruments, he had a certain vested economic interest in not restricting the allowed audience. The issue, once again, is practice over understanding. Being able to 'affect the Art' is precisely at the core of the current debate over calculators: the fear of apparent sophistication of performance unrooted in understanding, and the perennial desire of teachers to be able to read comprehension from successful practice (the latter having the advantage of being observable).

I wish to make some further observations based on Harnasz's description. First, it is clear that something is being measured by the slide-rule, and hence that there are inherent errors associated with measuring to contend with.[14] In some sense, it is a calculational device which *approximates*, rather than strictly calculates. How different was a slide-rule from a set of logarithm tables? Users may not have been aware of inherent inaccuracies in the latter, where the connection with measurement is not so in evidence. The specificity of entries in tables can offer the illusion of exactness.

Second, the slide-rule still exists in living memory, as its complete superseding by hand calculators is relatively recent, though the practices surrounding its operation may no longer be current. Third, this device draws on particular mathematics for its design; in this case, the idea of logarithms. As the device followed swiftly on the heels of Napier's account of logarithms, there was also initial uncertainty about an appropriate mathematical understanding. Such devices always involve a practice. Underpinning ideas of mathematics are always related to such devices, *combined with* the prescribed means of functioning, rather than just to the device alone. (This is as true of pedagogic devices as with solely calculational ones.)

Once the device exists, it can be used independently of the mathematical understanding used to create it. It may be possible to use the device with its prescribed means of functioning as a means of access to experience with and an understanding of logarithms themselves. Reflecting on the practice may thus provide some access to the 'embedded' mathematics; understanding the mathematics may allow the practice to be seen as 'obvious' or transparent, and hence not needing to be explicitly learnt. In either case, I am unclear whether the 'understanding' makes you a better user.

### On the abacus

With computing on an abacus or counting board, the movements are actual; physical substitute objects can be grasped, they have both tangible qualities and visible components. Addition is accumulation and subtraction returns beads to the realm of unselected possibilities, rather akin to fingers folded down with complements. An abacus offers physical counterparts for numbers.

The abacus uses single beads as holders of value, but also as representative units. The particular wire they are on takes care of the different powers of ten, without a need for this to be marked on the beads themselves or to have differentiated beads. I mentioned earlier the fact that the counting board was used to calculate with, but Roman numerals were used to record the results. This combined practice nicely separates the counterpart from the signification functions, though they were closely linked (it is easy to see Roman numerals directly as an abacus entry). We are so used to the coalescing of these two somewhat conflicting aspects of symbol use in our familiar use of Indian-Arabic numerals, that it can be hard to separate them at times.

In the tenth century AD, Indian-Arabic numerals were introduced to the Latin West by Gerbert (later Pope Sylvester II), grafted onto the abacus or counting board. Instead of numerals as direct counterparts, he offered *apices*,[15] counter objects numbered with symbols for 1–9, to be used within the counting board's structure in place of the traditional, uniform ones, as a variation of existing practice.

With apices, there are counters standing for a number of other counters (the ones now marked with 1), so not all counters are the same any more, the commonality has gone. This destroys one of the beauties of the counting board, where the individual counters were all equivalent to one another, and so only needed to be attended to in terms of their presence and whereabouts.

There was a substantial computational cost. This hybrid device required combinations and equivalences to be recognised and known, and then the equivalent disc found at every stage of a calculation. This was particularly problematic with multiplication and division, which involved many exchanges of counters. It also entailed translation back into Roman numerals rather than merely reading off the abacus. This variation of existing counting board practice was soon ignored,[16] and Indian-Arabic numerals reappeared independently as manipulable symbols on their own two centuries later. Just as with apparatus algorithms and Dienes blocks, the practice of apices on counting boards does not match the written practice: the key difference involves zero.

As with Dienes blocks, the abacus mirrors the Roman or Egyptian numeration systems in not requiring a zero. There is no corresponding action on the abacus to writing a zero – the empty row is not manipulated – and the structure of the device serves the realigning function of the role of zero in place value. Employing a written zero corresponds to the user's eye and hands shifting rows. It is thus a different sort of action, one which acknowledges the presence of the (human) calculator.

In his subtle and profound book, *Signifying Nothing*, Brian Rotman (1987) writes of the hostile reception of zero in mediaeval Europe in the thirteenth century: it was deemed both incomprehensible and unnecessary. It took some four hundred years for Roman numerals effectively to be replaced by Indian-Arabic ones. (One minor trace of this unease lies today in the requirement to write cheques using both words and figures.)

Rotman describes the dual nature of zero, at once a number among other numbers and a different sort of sign, one whose presence indicates an absence: "Zero is not the sign of a thing". There was no zero apex. Part of the power of the written system lies in 0 being accepted and used just like any other symbol, *as if* it were a number itself.[17] He identifies (p. 13) the crucial rule of the misunderstood zero in allowing the combining of the counterpart and signification functions:

> Finally, one can see that zero, by signifying the absence of signs, facilitates the lifting of calculations from the abacus onto paper; the shifting, that is, from 'counter-casting' with physical numerical tokens, to 'pen-reckoning' with the written Hindu numerals themselves.

Historically, abacuses (without apices) were widely used (and in some countries, for example Russia and Japan, still are), as were counting boards. Both these devices afforded direct physical manipulation of the 'counters', the substitute counterpart objects that encode numbers. We cannot get our hands on the figures in the graphical liquid display of a calculator: instead, we have to use the key-pad. These historical counting devices and associated practices provided a mental image of a computation.

In an article on the Japanese abacus, the *soroban*, Catherine Hoare remarks how, after gaining remarkable facility with the *soroban* in performing computations, the schoolchildren she saw (aged eight to eleven) were given mental arithmetic (six-digit) additions and subtractions.

> The pupils sat with their eyes shut or half-closed running their fingers an inch above the desk top as if the soroban were still there! At the end of each question just under half of the pupils had the correct answer, but all had attempted questions which would have been unthinkable within our conception of mental arithmetic. Their method consists of mentally visualising a soroban and working through the problem using standard techniques.
>
> (Hoare, 1990, pp. 13–14)

This account raises many questions. What range of images do pupils have when carrying out mental computations, and what support do these images offer? Are images of Dienes apparatus, for example, available to pupils who have worked intensively with it – are there physical motions in muscle memory (where the hands are doing the thinking) available to be drawn on? Hoare adds: "Through mechanisation of operation, therefore, the soroban becomes as automatic to the Japanese as the calculator has to the younger generation of English". Yet, as with the differences between numeration systems, the structural differences of these two devices are relevant to mathematics education.

## On the calculator

Modern electronic calculators are nowhere near as 'transparent' with regard to their functioning, and therefore do not offer much imagistic support: the input and output is Indian–Arabic numerals, the actual processing with electrical counterparts is completely invisible. A corresponding body sense to that of the *soroban* obtained from fluency on a calculator could only reflect the structural layout of the numerals on the key-pad, something which has little if any mathematical import. Certainly, the fact that on most key-pads the 3 is directly above the 6 and the 0 is in the middle at the bottom has no connection with useful or interesting properties of the decimal numeration system.

Numbers are entered from right to left, as when written down, which acts to 'move' the digit across each 'place'. It is an interesting and open question whether this relative absence of associated imagery with a calculator is a potential weakness – the mechanisms are opaque and therefore offer very little support – or a potential strength – leaving pupils free to form their own imagery – with regard to using such devices to help gain either numerical fluency or understanding.

But what about the numerical operations? With most calculators, there is no difference between any of the four arithmetic operations and taking powers or square roots (except possibly a slight time difference in operation). All are carried out by pressing a single operation key. With the *soroban*, the algorithm is accessible to view, implemented by the user, and can be internalised through repetition of hand movements. With the calculator, everything is inaccessible, invisible.

The calculator has single buttons that perform an increasing variety of mathematical functions. But with a calculator, you lose the sense of an algorithm for these operations, as there is no evidence of intermediate steps. Such single buttons become *primitives*, in the sense that no further interrogation of how they are being carried out is possible – they become inaccessible. What is different between a set of square-root tables and the square-root button on a calculator? Written tables may not provide much clue as to their genesis, but it is a single object open to inspection and analysis, complete with interpolation rules.

One contrast between abacuses and calculators, then, is the degree of

Based on a cartoon by John Johnson

transparency of their operation. In the case of the abacus, the physical symbols which are used to 'hold' the numbers are uniform and open to manipulation. In addition, the abacus is operated directly by the user's hands. In the case of the calculator, the user has no access whatsoever to the functioning of the device and so is in a far more passive position with respect to the device. (With hand-cranked adding machines, there was an illusion of surveyability, of openness to inspection, even though all the hand-cranking did was to provide the motive force for activating the mechanism.)

## Devices and desires[18]

> Thus, it is becoming increasingly hard to justify trying to teach students to become good symbol manipulators unless it can be shown – but no one yet has so shown – that such skills are required in order to develop an understanding of the underlying mathematics at whatever level such understanding is desired.
>
> (Churchhouse *et al.*, 1986, p. 35)

The history of number calculation has been a mixture of devices and desires, of notational possibilities and physical inventions, and of gestural and graphical movements. A belief in the need for the development of the individual to mirror that of the history of the species *in some form*, must also acknowledge that new developments, ideas or devices can short-circuit access to certain ends and offer previously undreamed-of facility.

There has been and continues to be concern, confusion and reticence over the use of hand-held numerical calculators, even some fifteen years after their introduction to primary schools. It is claimed that spending a lot of time teaching pupils procedures that can easily be automated on a machine comprises at best an irrelevant task and is at worst a damaging waste of pupil time and attention. As pupils no longer need to be able to compute unaided by an electronic calculating device, there is no point teaching them pencil-and-paper methods, or so the argument goes.

The ready availability of cheap numerical calculators has once again unleashed a rhetoric of concern about change and loss of established practice that any technology triggers, one which harks back to the Calvino quotation at the beginning of Chapter 3. Mathematician Michael Atiyah (1986, p. 50) echoes this much-voiced concern at the increasing incursion of computers in mathematics education: "any over-reliance on machines can lead to the atrophy of the human faculties involved". Atiyah also likens the computer 'revolution' of the latter part of this century to the industrial revolution of the last, though it is one where the labour of the brain rather than that of the hand is being automated by machine and thus rendered redundant.

I mentioned earlier the situation with the introduction of the slide-rule. Is this just another incarnation of the same struggle? Such a concerned response could arise solely from a lament by the old about new ways of doing things, and indicate a rearguard action to justify and preserve the investments *they* have made in the past? Or are there deeper concerns lurking? One fear is that as we turn our backs on tradition, we lose the experience of generations. I cited the work of Doerfler (1993) on mental methods of calculation earlier in this chapter. Most relevantly here, he argues that far from being an outdated task, made redundant by hand-held calculators, attention to mental methods of computation is actually timely for cultural reasons of history and diversity:

> the proliferation of electronic calculators and computers throughout our lives and educational systems are [sic] eliminating calculational techniques from our memory and from our children's education, threatening to dim our already narrow view of this rich field.
>
> (*ibid.*, p. 3)

With a functioning technology alone, there is less incentive to work at gaining an understanding. In the past, some, lacking the means to transform it, chose instead to try to understand it. One difference over the past is with the degree of inscrutability of the device. The theoretical justification for 'why' the device works is complex and opaque. Machines are offering more and more single-button primitives, which can mean that reflection on our own functioning in these areas is effectively blocked off as a means for increasing personal understanding.

With manipulatives, I denied that the mathematics was *in* the devices. With an electronic calculator, it can seem harder to argue that the mathematics is not *in* the device. What mathematics has been embedded in its construction and how easily available is it to a user? Richard Noss (1991) has written a challenging piece on the general relation of mathematics to technology, looking in particular at how mathematics is incorporated into computer technology. He develops the notions of *density* (how much mathematics is incorporated into a device) and *depth*: "a measure of how near the surface of that technology the mathematics is" (*ibid.*, p. 210). He goes on to write:

> A washing machine incorporates within its chips a surprising amount of mathematics. It is mathematically dense. But that mathematics is also deeply buried: to view that mathematics would be extremely difficult, even supposing that one had access to other technologies which would permit any kind of access to it at all.

Consequently, offering a washing machine as a pedagogic device for learning mathematics would be a poor choice. In addition, he points out that the tendency of evolving technology is to bury increasingly dense mathematics ever more deeply, and this is an important way in which people come to exercise less and less control over technology.

So, in the terminology of Noss, the mathematics is less deeply buried in a mechanical calculator than in an electronic one. Just how deeply buried in the latter case was discovered by Tom O'Shea's (1994) attempts to find out how the trigonometric functions were actually computed by familiar scientific calculators. His account is of industrial algorithmic secrets and obfuscations, as well as surprising mathematics that is programmed into particular machines. (For instance, O'Shea observes that most mathematically conversant people wrongly assume the values are calculated by means of truncated power series.)

This degree of opacity with regard to the method of functioning actually constitutes a shift away from even a calculational *aid* towards a complete substitution for calculation that is resistant to understanding at any but a very deep level. Slide-rules may require an understanding of logarithms in order to comprehend 'why' they allow multiplication to be modelled by addition of lengths, but as Doerfler comments:

> Newer algorithms, such as the Fast Fourier Transform (FFT) method of multiplication, often rely on internal architectures of micro-processors and their siblings, arrays of available memory locations, and/or inherent bit-shifting operations, none of which find analogy in our thought processes. Once again, a difference of degree becomes a difference of kind.
>
> (1993, p. 3)

It is important to recall that calculating devices are not specifically pedagogical devices. They exist in quantity in the world beyond schools. They have their own design criteria related to their perceived uses and forms of application. How they are useful in an educational setting is still a matter for exploration.

*Computational* devices are primarily concerned with automation and fluency of operation. *Pedagogical* devices are about illumination and understanding. Confusion of the two functions leads to crossed intentions and erroneous expectations, as well as missed opportunities. In addition, if the calculator is there, it determines the syllabus to an extent that may be far from desirable. We desire a lot of our school devices. We want machines that do the work, yet let us in on the processes involved. Arguably, you want shallow and transparent devices in schools for pedagogic purposes; what is the point of providing mathematically deep objects in schools for *mathematics* education?

## ABACISTS AND ALGORISTS

I mentioned in the last chapter Rotman's use of the terms 'gestural' and 'graphic' in relation to the abacus and pencil-and-paper calculations respectively. With the former device, the numbering objects are grasped by hand; with the latter, it is the pencil which conjures the symbols that are to be 'grasped'. Both of these computational practices involve the hand quite centrally, but what the knowing hand knows differs. In addition, both practices are equally calibrated by eye. To be able to read off the answer from either calculational means is an acquired skill.

Each practice offers imagery, each involves movements of hand and eye; both can be a source of reflection for augmented understanding, both can be practised to the unattended level of fluent implementation. (I recall coming across a delightful cartoon in the Soviet satirical magazine *Krokodil*. Two pictures side-by-side showed different production lines. By the side of the first, which manufactured abacuses, a checker stood using a calculator. And adjacent to the second, which produced calculators, a checker stood using an abacus.)

The woodcut above (dating from 1503) is quite frequently interpreted as showing a competition between computational practices, sometimes interpreted in terms of *The Spirit of Arithmetic*'s favour being bestowed on the new-to-Western-eyes computation by means of the numerals alone.

However, there is another way of interpreting the picture. *Arithmetic* may be granting favour to both of these practices, and is willing to embrace them within the realm of her dominion, the old and the new. She holds *both* texts, one in each hand, both arms outstretched, though I acknowledge that her direction of gaze suggests she is looking at the 'algorist'. That they are not competing, however, is suggested by the fact that they are carrying out quite different computations (unlike the IBM computer/abacus 'races' held in Japan in the 1970s). Also, both men seem turned the one towards the other, which could be read in terms of interchange of interest rather than competition. It suggests to me that *both* practices may be of interest and of use in school settings, offering different things.

Computational practices must overlap to the extent that they enable certain common core tasks to be carried out. To that extent there must be a competing. Until one has supplanted the other, however, questions of gain and loss can be hard to address. When one is familiar, it is natural to attempt to understand one in terms of the other. This is the message for me of Gerbert's apices. In moving from being an abacist to an algorist, zero becomes the stumbling block: the different status of the signs is reflected in the physical device. As Tahta[19] (1991, p. 227) comments: "The rivalry between the algorist and the abacist was not so much about notation as about how you calculated".

The unity that came from using Indian-Arabic numerals for both storing numbers and calculating can be seen as an economy. But it also confuses the signification and counterpart functions which pull in different directions. When I look *through* Indian-Arabic notation, I see numbers. When I start carrying out pencil-and-paper operations on them, they become opaque counterpart objects, drawing attention to themselves and I temporarily lose sight of the notion of numerical value.

To the extent that understanding arises from reflection on the practice, particular hard-won understandings may differ. The novelist Vladimir Nabokov writes of "transparent things through which the past shines". One loss with the new numerals may have been access to the past, and with it a sense of perspective on contemporary practices.

As I write, an issue of the (UK) Association of Teachers of Mathematics' journal, *Micromath* 9(3), has just appeared on my desk, bearing a contemporary parody of Reisch's picture (*The Spirit of Arithmetic*). Two aspects in particular struck me in relation to my concerns in this chapter. The first is that the name of the person at the counting board, *Pythagoras*, has been changed to *Mathematica*, the name of a computer algebra system (so the girl is framed as the one-who-uses-*Mathematica*). The second is that it was the abacus user rather than the pencil-and-paper user that the computer has replaced, creating a different juxtaposition and hence an alternative tension. Is the calculating device offering a comparably different practice, or should the significant comparison, sense against absence, be between the abacus as a device and the computer as a device?

On this latter point, Tahta comments wryly:

It is ironic that it is now the skilled algorist who claims that people will not understand what they are now doing when they merely push buttons on a calculator. Both then and now, the innovators claim that the new technique offers greater accuracy and that understanding will develop from confident and successful use. The issues continue to be discussed in schools and in the market place.

(1991, p. 236)

In summary, are these practices of the abacist and the algorist currently competing from an educational point of view? Ironically perhaps, both have been superseded at the level of non-educational practice by the electronic calculator. Consequently, solely from the point of view of access to a means of functioning computation alone, *neither* practice need form part of a school education. Looked at from a less functional perspective, however, because functionality and instrumentality are not my primary reasons for offering an educational mathematics curriculum, *both* can be used in order to offer some insight into mathematical possibilities behind such electronic devices, arithmetic possibilities for humans to engage with.

# 5

# ALGEBRA
# TRANSFORMING

> Some secret center became vitalized in those hours of silent practice
> in the arts of transformation.
>
> (Richards, 1989, p. 20)

Algebra as an activity precedes algebra as an area of mathematical study, both historically and in school. Algebra is about form and about transformation. Algebra, right back to its origins, seems to be fundamentally dynamic, operating on or transforming forms. It is also about equivalence: something is preserved despite apparent change.

In mathematics, two important contrastive focuses occur, interact and recur. One is the nature of the objects about which generalisations are made and the other is the nature of the language used for their generation and 'manipulation' (as with geometric images, algebraic forms need to be both conjured and controlled). In the last chapter, I discussed the symbolic functions of counterpart and signification. More than with arithmetic or geometry, and despite its abstract air, 'doing' seems to be central to algebra. In the process, attention is moved away from what, if anything, is being 'manipulated'. With algebra,[1] 'manipulation' comes into its own, with symbols as counterparts very much to the fore; the 'true' nature of the algebraic object becomes ever more confused.

Fluent users report two awarenesses when working with algebraic expressions: being able to see them as structured strings of symbols (and hence symbolic objects in their own right) *and* seeing them as descriptions connected with some 'reality' or situation they are concerned with. Maintaining this dual perspective, of substituting counterpart and indicating sign, is of central concern when working on mathematical symbols at whatever level, and places a heavy burden on novices. As Schmidt (1986) points out, algebra offers both a calculus and a language.

Transformation is a key power of algebra, the most important means for gaining knowledge. Operation symbols in algebra are virtual and not actual as they seem to be in arithmetic. What is transformed is the expressions, viewed as counterparts and not just as descriptions, and different forms reveal different aspects. Algebra invokes forces that transform: algebraic expressions are shape-shifters. But what else is being transformed as I manipulate the symbols? Counterpart algebra involves an echo, a shadow.

Boero (1993) observes that every algebraic manipulation contains an anticipatory element, a sense of where you might be heading, a sense of what the desired form might be like. Intensive student practice of standard transformations does not by itself develop anticipation, but equally it is hard to improve anticipation without a certain facility at transformation. Successful manipulation may also involve fitting templates (into which certain often-repeated transformations become objectified) to forms, such as 'the difference of two squares', though there may be some preliminary shape-shifting required until familiar algebraic 'seeings' such as this one can be applied. Developing this sense of anticipation can provide, in part, an alternative to 'blind' manipulation, and provide more support for a conversation with pupils about symbolic manipulation.

There are familiar cover stories offered to novices in order to try to inculcate the desired practice.[2] 'Take it over to the other side and change the sign' is a succinct counterpart formulation suggesting physical movement of an object, whereas 'subtract the same thing from both sides' invokes a mathematical operation which can be carried out actually on numbers or virtually on expressions.

In going from $2x + 7 = \pi$ to $2x = \pi - 7$, a second equation has been written after (usually underneath) the first. The textual implication of coherence suggests that it is in some way associated with the first, but it is not current common practice to indicate how or why they are related. Both verbal formulations in the previous paragraph attempt to express the *relationship* between two successive statements. In the new mathematics texts of the 1960s, there were some attempts to write in brackets what the transformations were, and why the two equations were 'the same' or 'equivalent'. Nonetheless, it remains the desired practice to be able to write sequences of equations, whose connection with one another is unmarked on paper.

We all have difficulty symbolising transformations as such.[3] What is written in an algebraic demonstration are not the actions but the *results* of actions: sequences of equations show the results of transformations, not the transformations themselves. Hence, the algebra takes place *between* the successive written statements and is not the statements themselves.

One resource of algebra is a rich plurality of symbolic forms; one core notion that of equivalence. Equivalence and transformation are linked notions, indicating sameness perceived in difference for some purposes, or indifference with respect to others. The existence of multiple expressions 'for the same thing' (highlighting 'naming') can suggest the very possibility of transforming expressions directly to get from one to another, without necessarily going back to the particular 'seeings' of the original situation that gave rise to them. Increased fluency in manipulation of algebraic expressions can thereby go hand-in-hand with decreasing regard for the 'meanings' of the symbols or the context from which the expressions originally were derived. Algebra therefore firmly presents itself for exploration in any discussion of understanding and fluency as mutually desired goals for mathematics education.

At bottom lies the following question: what is $x$? As with zero, the presence of $x$ speaks of another absence. At different times, $x$ is both a name that points to something else, and a counterpart that is more resistant to being 'seen through'. A move to letters can provoke a sense of real loss. Particularly in algebra, the relation of the sign to the thing signified is weakened, perhaps deliberately destroyed.

> Algebra is powerful – but it can also be frightening. It demands a shift of attention from signified to signifiers. It can then become a game in which signifiers are exchanged with other signifiers. . . . Algebra creates an alternative world which may be under our control, but in which some people feel that nothing is real.
>
> (Tahta, 1990b, p. 58)

With algebra, there seem to be two clearly identified alternative emphases in terms of where our attention is to be placed. To sharpen the distinction, on the one hand – and putting it succinctly – we can work with symbols as counterpart objects, components in a language-game without much explicit reference to what they may 'mean' or 'represent'. (This, of course, does not mean that each individual does not attach meaning or reference – whether privately or publicly – to the elements of the game.) The language is *generative*. The emphasis is more on what you do with algebraic expressions once you have them.

On the other hand, we can offer reference objects (but what?), and particular actions upon them, and then – through ordinary language initially about a situation – code these with symbols. The language is *descriptive*, coming after the actions on the objects themselves, and the context of description is very near the surface. The sense of structure of expressions that allow their manipulation may not be strongly present. Here, the emphasis is on the process by which some generality is expressed.

There is a trade-off, similar to the one mentioned for numeration systems in the last chapter, between the relative transparency of expressions on the one hand, and compactness and efficiency when it comes to their manipulation on the other. Natural language versions can be more transparent with respect to what the expression is intended to say. When there is the possibility of manipulating expressions of generality, however, transforming one into another, then the criterion of compactness comes into its own. This provides another instance of the theme of greater comprehension suggesting one preferred solution, while developing fluency at manipulation invites another.

The relations between form and meaning in algebra are complex and important. Among the contributors are:

- the fact that multiple equivalent expressions are possible, yet each may be related to a particular 'seeing' of the situation;
- the fact that symbols can be manipulated without recourse to meanings and this can be efficient: yet possible meanings can also be explored for the manipulations carried out;
- the tension between holding on to (thereby enriching) particular meaning and fluent use arising from *not* attending to the meaning;
- the fact that after a certain point, some people can come to rely on the symbols, and are content to and convinced by working with them alone. "To a high degree the language of formulae can be handled autonomously, independent of the understanding of the content" (Freudenthal, 1973, p. 310).

## 'MANIPULATING' SYMBOLS AND EXPRESSIONS

In this section, I shall try to illuminate the above by means of discussion and description of two pairs of algebra lessons (taught by Dave Hewitt). I can only give a brief outline here of what are very complex lessons; unattributed comments come from an interview I carried out with him afterwards.[4]

The first pair of lessons relates to think-of-a-number tasks with a class of fourteen-year-olds, and invokes the sense of 'doing the opposite' as a way of undoing or unwrapping linear equations. His focus is on the process of inverting operations, rather than finding the 'correct' number. In the second pair, called 'rulers', with a class of thirteen-year-olds, he develops algebraic expressions initially as traces of moves around an imagined grid. A notation is developed first to record sequences of moves (the language is primarily descriptive at this stage) and later to produce them (the language is generative now).

### Think-of-a-number

At the outset, Hewitt focuses orally on the doing (the wrapping-up process where a sequence of operations is carried out on 'the number I am thinking of' to produce an equation) and has them verbally produce the undoing. (Thus, "I think of a number, I add 3, I multiply by 2 and I get 14" evokes "I take 14, I divide by 2, I subtract 3 and that is the number you were thinking of".) The facts of mutual pairs of inverse operations and dealing with the numbers in the reverse order from that of the doing are quickly established. Far more complex written instances are soon offered (involving all four arithmetic operations), though his focus is still on the pupils' language determining the actions on the written forms.

As the lessons progress, he stops part-way through an unwrapping and makes observations about what has been done and what has yet to be done; various mid-stage situations in equation-solving are exemplified. The 'answer' contains all the structure (inverted) of the original. (He could have asked them to reverse the 'answer', using the same notions of undoing, to reconstruct the original encoding of the actions.) The algebraic task was self-contained: no 'real-world' context or 'motivation' from the external world was offered or required. What was provided was a challenge to engage with, that successfully captured his pupils' interest and attention.

Towards the end of the second lesson, he has them generate an equation for which he is acting as scribe at the board for them all to work with. (An unspoken message is that because nothing is pre-arranged, *any* equation can be dealt with likewise.) When they offer him particular numbers, at times he writes alpha or gamma ("that's what I heard, wasn't it?"), while at the same time supporting them: "I'll let you know what that is later." The pupils quite happily solve this equation too.

On many occasions, Hewitt employs (different) audible noises for each of the various arithmetic operations when working in front of the class at the board. His intent is to draw attention to a particular thing, enclosing an expression in brackets perhaps, or the need for alignment of symbols. As he said afterwards, "At one point, it is the fact that after a division has taken place, the +2 is lined up at the level of the division symbol. There is no reason for this, so I do not try to give one; it is a convention." I am struck by the harsh simplicity of this comment. Everything doesn't have to have a meaning, a rationalisation, a cover story. Some things just are.

There were a pair of strands that were being tied together. The first was the connection of the action to a story offering a certain meaning, namely 'Think-of-a-number', where the various equations produced were frozen snapshots in the wrapping and unwrapping process. As I shall describe shortly, he also took subtle steps to undermine this meaning. To some extent, pupils were being subtly encouraged to 'let go' of the meaning and work on the symbols themselves.

Although 'Think-of-a-number' was providing the ostensible goal, opportunities were being offered for recognising patterns in expressions and equations. These patterns were structural, brought about by attending to the nested, sequential aspect of operations:

> They know what it is they want to do and now they are forced to work on the challenge of finding my number. The notation is learnt by subordinating it to the challenge; the notation becomes the vehicle through which they can engage with it.

Secondly, there was the force of consistency in the symbolism itself: when something was said, there was always a written equivalent. Hewitt believes in the importance of presenting a consistent set of notations for arithmetic (and later algebraic) operations, so there is always something to write for each spoken term. Brackets can be included as a written version of 'times' or 'multiplied by', and hence remove questions about this notational device having to be 'taught' explicitly and separately. Conventional irregularities can be worried about later, for example, replacing 6(x) by 6x. His approach involves refining a functioning and consistent notation into the one that is conventionally employed, rather than striving for the fully-fledged, conventional one from the outset.

### Rulers

The first lesson introduces an imagined number line running round the room, with the teacher hitting the wall successively with a large ruler and the pupils naming the next number. The line is relativised by Hewitt announcing a locating number with each first hit ("That's seventeen"). He then combines moves (perhaps three to the right and two to the left) and focuses first on where he is now, and then shifts very deliberately to "What did I do?" to get there. He remarks that, at the outset:

> the numbers are explicit and the operations are implicit. As I chose this activity to work on algebra, at some point I wanted to change the focus of attention onto the operations. Arithmetic is concerned with getting an answer, algebra is concerned with how you might get there.

This shift from where I am now to what I did to get there reverses the implicit and explicit focuses of attention. The lesson continues with developing statements of what has been done, now starting from $x$. When first introducing $x$, pupil attention is firmly on the actions, the operations (in this case, adding four and taking away one, written on the board as $+ 4 - 1$). He asks them, "What number did I start with?", and a pupil replies, "You didn't say." He draws a linear grid and marks in $x$.

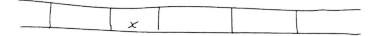

So he writes an $x$ in front to produce $x + 4 - 1$, and remarks, "I'll let you know what it is later, OK. But whatever number I started with, I'm going to add four and take away one. I'll let you know what that number is later."

*x* is the written form associated with the spoken 'whatever number I started with'.

Hewitt now says to the pupils, "I'd like to start here [writes *y*] and I'd like to end up there [indicating a box two to the left]. By the way, what is that?" [Pupil offers "*y* take two".] The structure of an expression can also tell you how you got to where you are from the previous location. There is also the notion of the simplest expression in terms of 'what's the quickest way of ending up there?', of going directly.

Moves can be made and the algebraic notation developed to record the new state at each stage. There is a similar structure – state, then operation, giving rise to a new state – to ordinary arithmetic expressions. $6 + 7 = 13$ can be interpreted as state (start with 6), then do something (add 7) to give a new state (13). Consequently, it is possible in rulers, for instance, to write $y + 4 = y + 4$ as a result worth recording: namely, start at the box labelled *y*, go on four squares, resulting in you being at the box labelled $y + 4$.

Later on he introduces a second row, the double of the one above it, so the vertically downward movement is 'multiply by two' and upwards is 'divide by two'. This introduces the operations of multiplication and division as additional possibilities. Clearly, further rows are also available for extension.

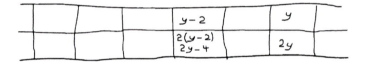

Two equivalent routes from *y* to the same square

Expressions name specific squares, but also tell you what to do to get from one privileged location (*x* or *y*, or whatever) to the one named by the expression. They create 'story-telling' expressions, so before any simplification or tidying up, they bear the traces of their generation (as *Cabri-géomètre* diagrams do – see Chapter 3). There is a deliberate blurring in the situation about whether the algebraic expressions developed are names of locations or instructions about how to move (though when going from expressions to moves, they clearly have to be interpretable as moves), and both are exploited.

It is possible to take different routes and end up at the same place, thereby generating different expressions which *must* be equivalent, because they 'name' the same place. This is similar to the fact mentioned above that finding multiple expressions, arising from different 'seeings', suggests the possibility of algebraic transformations. One aim of the task is to offer pupils experience of generating equivalent expressions, yet as it is being carried out, the overt focus is not those expressions themselves. The key algebraic elements of '$x$' and '$=$' are introduced almost without comment, "as the written language through which we record what we have just said to each other".

In general, Hewitt deliberately focuses their attention on certain things (what is to be done and why), and works on developing algebraic notation by avowedly pointing elsewhere. He commented to me, "Because the focus is on what we are doing, it is not the answer that matters but how we are getting there. It doesn't matter what number we start with, I can still say what we have to do."

Again there are attention-grabbing noises (the ruler hitting the walls or blackboard) and big gestures: the ruler gets handed over to pupils as soon as the way he wishes them to act is clear. The single bangs originally get associated with add or subtract one, but once the second row is introduced, they can also mean add or subtract two: more attention needs to be paid to context. As I mentioned, addition of the second row also brings in multiplication and division and it is only due to the fact that multiplication is being discussed that brackets appear. These brackets are linked with large hugging gestures: associations are established and strengthened by simultaneous juxtaposition and repetition. Finally, the teacher's movements, gestures and sounds bind them all together, combining speech, writing and actions to produce the symbols in a quite specific way.

There are a number of shifts of focus as the lesson progresses: from counting and naming the position reached to what was done to achieve the effect; from associating name with location ("That is five"), first to relativising the location (where he can announce where he is), and then to an unspecified location (no matter where I am, this describes/generates the actions). In this final state, the message is: 'I am starting somewhere – we are not lost – but I'll let you know where later.' He is 'holding' the uncertainty for them. Because the link between number and position is relative, it is possible to generalise and not work with particular numbers (and hence actually performable arithmetic operations), but rather to use some non-specific name for the number in order to act as a trace of the sequence of virtual operations.

### What is going on?

All of the above discussion may alert us to the ways we talk about what we are doing when working algebraically with symbols, and whether we miscue pupils by the language we use. In order to get away from concern with the things, pupils need to have something else in view. Hewitt comments:

The appearance of $x$ can be puzzling and disturbing for children. I choose to introduce it at a time when the starting number is not the focus of attention; it is the journeys that are being made explicit. . . . In fact, $x$ can only appear because of the fact that the particular number is no longer of importance. If this shift of attention had not already been made in the activity, I would not have considered introducing the $x$.

The focus offered is actions and movements, and the mathematical language is connected to them. The philosopher Alfred Whitehead has written:

Algebra is one chapter in the larger technique, which is language. . . . It is true that language strives to embody some aspects of [its] meanings in its very structure. . . . In fact, the art of literature, vocal or written, is to adjust the language so that it embodies what it indicates.

(1947, p. 107)

All symbols have forms when seen as objects in their own right. I see at least two instances in these lessons of attempting 'to adjust the language so that it embodies what it indicates'. The first is through the noises. They have little *conceptually* to do with the mathematical operations, but become associated with them by deliberate juxtaposition. The particular sounds chosen do, however, partly reflect characteristics of the symbols themselves (a repeated sound for the symbol 'plus', for instance, one as each line of the symbol is drawn). Hewitt's pupils on occasion make the same noises themselves when writing, as if the auditory image helps them to recall how things are written. By their striking nature, as well as calling for attention, they may help to provide part of the developing 'meaning' for the operation.

A second instance comes from his arm gestures in relation to brackets (hugging the expression): this seems more a form of gestural-graphic onomatopoeia. Hewitt observes:

I often use images to help children recall something. In this case, there is the arbitrary notation of how brackets are written. Here, I try to evoke the image of the brackets hugging all that has been written up to this point.[5]

More important are Hewitt's attempts to have algebra emerge from arithmetic by a crucial shift of focus. I made mention (in the previous chapter) of Brian Rotman's work on the destabilising role of zero with regard to arithmetic and the question of whether all numbers are signs. In the same book he writes of two subjects, not arithmetic and algebra *per se*, but human 'subjects'. Nevertheless, his work can help to distinguish the school subjects of algebra and arithmetic.

96

Perceived internally, variables [the letter signs] present their familiar appearance as manipulable algebraic objects, as signs among signs within formulas.... and generally being treated as if they *were* number signs according to a common syntax. [Perceived externally] on the contrary, they are signs which meta-linguistically indicate the possible, but not actual, presence of number signs....

Thus, the algebraic subject [the algebraic equivalent of the one-who-counts] has the capacity to signify the absence of the counting subject, the displacement of the one-who-counts from an actual to a virtual presence. Now at certain points, when variables are instantiated by numbers, this displacement ceases to operate – the two subjects coalesce.... But this sort of arithmetic localisation [for instance, checking the result of replacing $x$ by 10 in an identity] is extraneous to the difference between the two subjects: when variables are manipulated as *algebraic* objects within formal calculations any such fusion between the counting and algebraic subject is precluded.

(Rotman, 1987, pp. 31–2)

I shall try to illuminate some of his complex account by means of the Hewitt lessons, while at the same time conversely indicating why I have singled out these particular features of these lessons for comment. Rotman's references to an internal perception is alluding to the role of letters as counterparts and the 'levelling' with regard to arithmetic symbols (in the same way that 0 is taken as a digit just as 1–9 are.) The external perception is with respect to their signification, and echoes Hewitt's characterisation of algebra with regard to the possible rather than the actual: 'how you might get [to an answer]'.

At times, teaching can be described in terms of acting as a 'vicarious consciousness', that is as a separate entity working alongside the pupil taking on certain cognitive functions that may be too much for the pupil at the time, thereby extending a pupil's potential attention by encouraging its focus on other things. A good instance of this is when Hewitt tells his pupils not to worry about what the $x$ is, he'll let them know later.

The 'I' who is doing the thinking of a number holds the 'reference' for $x$. Whenever the spoken phrases 'I'm thinking of a number' or 'Whatever number I am thinking of' are used, $x$ is written. Hewitt wants his pupils' attention to be on the operations, not on what $x$ is. He achieves this in part by having them instruct him on what he is going to write next. Their language is generative. Because *he* is taking care of $x$, their attention is free to focus elsewhere. In the lessons I observed, he only once evaluated the actual value for $x$. In Rotman's terms, this would be to confound the algebraic and arithmetic subject, and it is the very possibility of producing the former that Hewitt is working to develop.

In the one instance where Hewitt decides to push through the calculation to derive an actual number (using calculators), and not end with a complex arithmetic expression which *would* give the answer, the number proved to be a messy decimal. Almost as a throwaway comment, he says, "Oh, was that the number I was thinking of? I guess it must have been." This is one way of weakening the storyline meaning of 'I am thinking of a number'. There are always important decisions to be made in algebra lessons about when to stay with the form of the computations and when to press on to find the actual numbers in each case, connected to the shift from algebraic to arithmetic subject. His role as a teacher of algebra is to personify the algebraic subject as well as always looking for ways to indicate algebraic possibilities.

Hewitt embodies this role himself first, and then encourages pupils to see this possibility in themselves, thereby allowing them to work algebraically. He specifically contrasts the descent to the level of numbers in search for a referent for *x* with developing and maintaining awareness of the algebraic subject in the collective class focus. When he writes alpha or gamma ("that's what I heard, wasn't it?"), he is personifying the algebraic subject, while at the same time supporting them, "I'll let you know what that is later." (At the very end of the second rulers lesson a pupil is heard to remark, "What was the number yesterday? You didn't tell us." Hewitt dissimulates by way of reply, "Didn't I? I'm like that. I'm just like that." As ever in these classes, pupils are deliberately left with lots to think about.)

By means of think-of-a-number tasks, work is conducted directly on 'manipulating' equations; enough of a storyline is provided to ease concerns about what *x* is, and to permit algebraic working on symbolic expressions. Similarly, with 'rulers', the 'meaning' of expressions is pretty much left to individuals, the task provides enough to enable them to work at and experience direct equivalence of expressions. The tasks, and more crucially the teacher's placing and shifting of the group's collective attention, serve to sew the experience together.

When algebra is taught exclusively as 'generalised arithmetic', the algebraic subject may not emerge from the arithmetic one, resulting in an often unhelpful preoccupation with what *x is*. As exemplified by Hewitt's lessons, there are ways of working directly at symbolic-notational issues, which need not carry the pejorative label of 'rote' working, yet where nonetheless attention on the forms and transformations is uppermost. He also does this, in part, by encouraging them to work communally, corporately, tribally. And finally, recalling the comments I made in Chapter 1, I want to add, he works in some important sense *ritually*, that is with respect for external ritual forms.

## TECHNO-ALGEBRA

In the previous section, I have offered a detailed analysis of some non-traditional school algebra lessons, in part in order to highlight some of the complexities involved in invoking algebra. But I also did so as such direct teaching about working on algebraic symbolism (echoing Tahta's desire for 'specific techniques' that I cited in Chapter 1) is becoming rarer. Algebra teaching in UK schools (and elsewhere) is itself undergoing substantial transformation. I see two particular forces: one present, the other looming.

The first is a retreat from specific algebra teaching as a core part of secondary school syllabuses: in some sense, a giving up on the very teachability of algebra to most adolescents. The second, less generally present at the moment (though not for long), is the development of computer algebra systems. Lying supine behind these forces is a concern with the perennial questions: what is algebra and what is it good for? Will algebra always be a school subject?

Earlier this century, working 'rotely' at 'blind' manipulation resulted in a bad name for algebra; now, in the UK, investigative approaches to mathematics encourage numerical pattern-spotting and some expression of generalities, but little manipulation of them ensues. This trend emphasises the signification function over the counterpart one of algebraic expressions.[6] Such algebra that is invoked is near the surface and tied to the specific situation: without reason to manipulate, there is little force to work at perceiving equivalence or acquiring fluency at transformation. Hewitt's lessons are relatively unusual in their more direct algebraic focus.

There is an important balance to be struck among production, transformation and interpretation of algebraic symbols. Though this markedly changed emphasis in schools is an important curriculum process, I shall say no more about this here. (See Noss, 1994, for a discussion about the massive demise of proof from much of the English school curriculum in terms of competing ideologies about the nature of mathematics and mathematical meaning. In the US especially, there is a growing provocative perspective of avoiding algebra in pursuit of democratic goals of 'mathematics for all': see Kaput, 1994.)

The second shaping force is the rapid development of symbolic manipulation packages (which I shall generically label 'computer algebra systems') on reasonably priced computers and even a few up-market calculators. This technological development provides the main focus of this section. More than with the teaching of arithmetic in elementary schools, when confronted with cheap numerical calculators, there is growing confusion about what will be left of the upper-school algebra syllabus, now these devices can carry out many of the manipulations that seemed to constitute the very subject. What in algebra is to be preserved for students, what will machines do? Perhaps we need to find a different form of algebra, one that is still worthy of our pupils' attention.

The previous section illustrated the importance of action in relation to algebra, as well as various interpretations, static and dynamic, that are possible of algebraic expressions. Spencer Brown (1977) writes of how much mathematics involves the giving of instructions and the issuing of injunctions. He even distinguishes between the notions of *demonstration* and *proof* in terms of the former being a sequence of instructions, that is, imperatives, and that our role is one of seeing that they are followed correctly. He draws an analogy with written music as a sequence of precise instructions, claiming:

> When we attempt to realize a piece of music composed by another person, we do so by *illustrating*, to ourselves, with a musical instrument of some kind, the composer's commands. Similarly, if we are to realize a piece of mathematics, we must find a way of illustrating, to ourselves, the commands of the mathematician. The normal way to do this is with some kind of scorer and a flat scorable surface, for example a finger and a tide-flattened stretch of sand, or a pencil and a piece of paper.
>
> (1977, p. 78)

Written in the early 1970s, the above passage when read now neatly draws attention to one of the dramatic changes of the past twenty years, due to the development of computers seen as symbol-manipulating devices. One powerful affordance of the computer is the immediate *implementability* of certain mathematical language, producing feedback, frequently visual, generated by the arithmetic/algebraic code. Computers enable students to work with what has been called 'executable symbolism': it can be executed, but need not be.

In what follows, I look very briefly at Logo as a site for algebraic implementation on a computer,[7] before moving on to discuss the recent development of computer algebra systems. Logo has been available on microcomputers in schools for just over a decade. It is a fully implemented computer language, but has particular characteristics that make it appropriate for use in an educational setting. It is thus a hybrid 'manipulative', though its pedagogic use has resulted in a general perception of it being 'only' an educational language. The ability to name a sequence of commands as a single entity (one which behaves akin to a mathematical function) results in the ability to produce exactly repeatable sequences of actions. Even though these named procedures can be used as any actual primitive in the language, unlike the 'real' primitives, the code of a user-written procedure is open to inspection through the editor. Noss (1991), in his piece on mathematical density and depth, draws attention to the pedagogic value of Logo in offering a mathematically dense but relatively shallow environment to pupils.

Almost all implementations of this language mark the difference between the name of a variable and the current numerical value of that location, between "variable and :variable. This marking provides a nice reflection of Rotman's distinction between the algebraic and arithmetic subject; the notation :variable inviting the superimposition of both algebraic and arithmetic subject.

In the context of turtle graphics, Logo's quasi-algebraic formalism serves as a means to an end, rather than an end in itself. The pupil's focus is customarily on the turtle task, working *through* the language, in order to control the turtle on the screen, rather than directly on the uninterpreted form of the language itself, as is so often the case in more traditional algebra lessons. Previously, emphasis has been almost entirely on, in John Mason's words, 'doing someone else's algebra rather than their own'.

Working in the editor involves a mix of algebra and arithmetic; the effect on the screen is geometric. As I mentioned in Chapter 3, the only way to produce effects on the screen is by means of the code. There are different mathematical spheres of influence, but it is clear which is privileged.[8]

Consequently, the link between expectations and effect can be explored and revised. Machines can *implement* algebraic language – they are not worried about manipulating non-compact expressions, and so they provide a context where the trade-off between transparency and compactness is not so strict. On the other hand, pupils do frequently believe the machine to 'understand' the meaning of the variables, that is both the actual referent and their intentions behind the naming chosen. The formalism helps keep track of operations (what we *did*, rather than what we *got*) precisely because they cannot be immediately evaluated: they also stay written, available for inspection. But the machine can also do computations – it can be both algebraic and arithmetic subject.

Noss (1986) showed how pupils' Logo experiences could provide a conceptual framework for building algebraic intuitions: pupils can and do construct linkages between variables in a Logo context and in a more traditional school setting. He writes: "Logo thus provides a model of the ideas of function and variable which is reasonably consistent with mathematical usage" (*ibid.*, p. 337). The language offers a means for introducing algebraic notation in the classroom (pupils programming at their own level) as well as inviting the interpretation of an existing symbolism (offering Logo programs for them to work out what the code does and why). It also requires the perception and articulation of relationships, both specific and general: that is, how to see through particular programs in order to formulate relationships in general.[9]

Logo offers a forum where pupils, as well as using their own symbolism expressively, can work at possible interpretations of others' symbolism. Both of these aspects are central to pupils acquiring a fluency and ease with algebraic notation and ideas.

## Symbolic manipulators

Symbolic manipulators are a form of software. They customarily contain a number of facilities, such as graph plotting, algebraic manipulation (factoring, simplifying and equation solving), differentiation and integration of functions, and data-handling facilities. Powerful contemporary examples include *Derive*, *Maple* and *Mathematica*, though there are a number of far less sophisticated packages on the market as well. The symbolic output of such manipulators currently requires a very strong degree of interpretation on the part of the user. They are sophisticated devices to assist the knowledgeable, just as calculators are, rather than expressly pedagogic devices.[10]

Even more crucially, computer algebra systems allow the dynamic linking of these facilities. For instance, connections can be simply established between the algebraic expressions and graphical representation, to produce 'live' symbolic representations in different screen windows. Change in one evokes change in another.

One assumption that lies behind offering multiple, linked representations is that they are representations of the same thing. What I have started to argue in this book is that the mathematical concept is often derived secondarily to the erstwhile 'representation' and is somewhat dependent upon it. Cabri-geometry is a non-Euclidean geometry in a very particular sense, because the drag-equivalence classes of screen diagrams do not generate quite the same 'theoretical' referent as do static, pencil-and-paper ones. Second-order equations in two unknowns are not quite the same as sections of a cone. 'The' notion of function is actually subtly different, depending on whether it is accessed through algebraic forms, graphs or numerical tables.[11] Because the generative direction *from* representation *to* 'object' is seen as the reverse, the central role of representations in conditioning mathematics is insufficiently appreciated.

This change of representation also highlights some differences across these mathematical functionalities. For instance, the successive transformations of algebraic expressions have a direction in time (linear order on the page, marking before and after), whereas the superimposition of graphs on the screen reveals no such temporal ordering; some changes in algebraic form (e.g. multiplying an equation by a constant) have no visible effect on the corresponding screen graph. It is still very early with regard to classroom exploration of these devices. I shall restrict myself here to some speculations about the background presumptions as well as their possible effect on perceptions of the nature of algebra itself.

I can state my belief quite succinctly at the outset. I suspect that the linking of representations is never neutral: one will predominate and will, in consequence of this privileged position, lose much of its own representational status. My candidate is the graph. The machine may be providing too much to attend to at one time: human attention is usually caught by movement. The graphical window is likely to be the winner among different displays. I predict the algebraic forms will come to be seen as merely descriptive, suggesting that, as can happen with turtle graphics, the 'meaning' is the screen graphical representation, rather than maintaining two different, independent-but-linked representations. In other words the graph will become a counterpart, drawing attention primarily to itself, yet will be perceived as a referent.

The linking of representations can suggest causation and generation, in that changes in one (wherever my attention and subsequent action is) 'produce' changes in the others. Jim Kaput writes: "it [computer algebra systems] also links *actions* on F-1 [functional expressions $y = f(x)$] to their consequences in G-2 [coordinate plane graphs]" (1989, p. 179). I repeat: the most absorbing representation will be seen as the 'meaning'.

Kaput offers the hypothesis that work in such environments "can provide novel and potent means for remediating many of the classic manipulation errors that have been studied in recent years" (*ibid.*, p. 179). This reflects only a slightly variant belief from the 'understanding (through reference) before doing' camp. It takes attention away from the forms themselves and to graphical images as what algebra is 'really' about.

He writes:

the "meaning of A" (say, a polynomial expression) may be provided by a graphical referent B, in which case we would say "A refers to B", that is, "$16x^2$ refers to the parabola". We can also say that A represents B.

(ibid., p. 169)

Yet B here is also a representation and not an object. I can see $y = 16x^2$ as naming (calling-into-being) a parabola far more easily than I can see a parabola as referring to $y = 16x^2$. It was in this sense that Mandelbrot exclaimed so loudly about the term 'visualization' (see note 16, Ch. 2) The algebraic expressions often label the graphs, inviting them to be seen as the names for the graphs, and hence that the graphs are the referent, not merely another symbolic representation.

The perceived connections, which are metonymic, between visual properties of the graphs and formal properties of the symbolic expressions, become seen as semantic ones. "Transformations that preserve semantic equivalence are those for which the target and starting expressions have the same graph" (*ibid.*, p. 179). So, for instance, does $(x + 1)^2 = x^2 + 1$? The graphs are different, therefore it is an 'illicit' transformation.

If you are very attached to the graphical interpretation of algebraic equivalence solely in terms of no difference in the 'pictures', you may not even look at the forms to try to attend to differences or possible routes to get from one to the other. So the induced shift once again is from 'touch' (manipulation) to sight (graphs). If the machine can generate a route from X to Y, you can learn from the printout. If you ask only whether $X - Y = 0$, the machine only confirms yes or no. This criterion provides no reason for their equivalence, though, as Kaput points out, analysis of the residual difference X – Y can suggest what alteration is to be made. However, such an analysis requires considerable mathematical sophistication, unless the machine can be asked for an algebraic formulation of this resultant graph.

The invitation is for the graphs to be attended to, and to look for difference. With superimposition of graphs as my criterion of equivalence of algebraic expressions, I have to rely on my visual perception (over the range I am shown in the screen window, at least) – and the resolution of the screen. I come back to this point in the next chapter. The graph may show convincingly that these expressions are the same, but offers no insight into *why* they are the same. I believe it is the direct transforms of the forms produces the how and hence the why.

This perspective makes algebra about functions, and thus algebraic objects are not the forms themselves seen as counterparts, but now 'really' signify functions. There is also a changed perspective from manipulation to solution. With a solution, we may not need to see the route, if we aren't to learn how to solve ourselves. It even affords a recasting of an equation in terms of the superimposition of two graphs (and thus a solution as a point of intersection which is the invariant under 'legal' transformations).

Chazan argues:

> In other words an equation is a particular kind of comparison of two functions. $3x - 4 = x + 17$ is really a question. It asks, for what values of the shared domain (the default in this case is the real numbers) do the functions whose rules are $f(x) = 3x-4$ and $g(x) = x + 17$ produce the same outputs?
>
> (1993, p. 22)

Ironically, technology is being used to insist on screen (graphical) interpretation of algebraic forms. There is a strong presumption that symbolic forms are to be interpreted graphically, rather than dealt with directly.[12]

Thus, primarily in the US, there is currently a rapid process of redefinition of algebra, triggered I feel more by the potentialities of these new systems and the drawbacks of an over-fragmented mathematics curriculum than by any novel epistemological insight. The view of algebraic objects that is being strongly promoted in relation to symbolic manipulators is of algebraic expressions as functions.

For instance, Chazan (*ibid.*, p. 22) writes: "One oft-mentioned suggestion for revamping algebra is to have functions replace equations as the fundamental objects of algebra". (Five references follow.) The proceedings of an NCTM conference, *Algebra for the Twenty-First Century* (NCTM, 1993) has two strong, separate, declarations. Judah Schwartz writes:

> A proposal is made to restructure the post-arithmetic mathematics curriculum around the notion of function (and the entailed concept variable) as the central, and indeed the only necessary mathematical

and pedagogical object of the subjects now called algebra, trigonometry, pre-calculus and calculus. . . . These software environments
[that already exist] allow symbolic representations of functions to be
manipulated symbolically and graphical representations of functions to be manipulated graphically.

(*ibid.*, p. 26)

Jim Kaput offers four 'fundamental assumptions', including (*ibid.*, p. 26):
*'The algebra curriculum should be organized around the concept of function'* and
claims:

Historically, algebra has been identified with a formal propositional
language which served a small elite. The new media allow visual,
graphic representations of relationships that are likely to be more
easily learned and used by the greatly enlarged segment of the
population who must now learn and use them.

(*ibid.*, p. 32)

On the next page, the report of one of the working groups claims: "Algebra
is a study of functions" (*ibid.*, p. 33). Combined with this access aim is an
argument in terms of 'real-world' applications driving the algebra curriculum, where input–output models abound.

Welcome to year zero.[13] This proposal is at the opposite extreme from
those who claim that history should guide curriculum developments
(usually along the lines of some version of the Polya-promoted observation of the nineteenth-century biologist Haeckel: 'ontogeny recapitulates
phylogeny'). Many forms of algebraic thought and activity predated the
emergence of functions with Euler in the mid-eighteenth century. It is thus
a complete reversal of 'the lessons of history'.

Such redefinitions are not without historical precedent or mathematical
import (such as conic sections being second-order equations in two
variables, or Klein's reformulation of geometry as the study of a group of
transformations). However, what they do is to switch from description to
prescription: from the fact that it is possible to describe one thing in terms
of another, to the fact that it must be so seen. And in consequence of this
redefinition, the possibility is removed of discussing what gets excluded.
Definitions always include and exclude, stress and ignore. However, I am
not aware of substantial argument for the *mathematical* advantage of this
anti-historical perception – other than that it can make use of affordances
of computer algebra systems.

Such a reformulation of algebra may be mathematically tenable, but is
that sufficient reason to offer it to pupils? Function is becoming an
increasingly imperialistic mathematical notion, but as Wheeler (1989)
observes, it was one that was relatively late to emerge historically. Has
nothing been learnt from the dramatic effects of the combined over-

enthusiasm and myopia of mathematicians in the 1960s with regard to the universal applicability of the notion of set? The influence of machines is being felt in a new way in terms of their demands and affordances. Will they be instrumental in producing a new 'modern' mathematics?

### Is algebra necessary or is it merely nice?

The sub-section title mirrors a discussion in the area of metaphor (see Ortony, 1975) where the corresponding question is whether metaphor is essential (offering something that cannot be obtained otherwise) or reducible to direct language statements. The corresponding reduction in the case of algebra is to whether everything can be done graphically. The original question about metaphors boils down to a question of substitution rather than essentiality. If there is nothing attainable with algebra that we could not get without it, now we have machines to aid our geometric visualisation, while carrying out algebraic manipulations for us offstage, can we actually do away with it? Would I do any algebra personally if I did not need to?

On the one hand, the machine can manipulate algebraic forms alone: it has no need for or desire of 'meaning'. On the other, the multivalency of the device can trace such connections (initially by means of juxtaposed graphical imagery mirroring certain algebraic manipulations), assuming that the designer has intended this as an 'educational' computer algebra system rather than solely as an expert device. Is algebra 'necessary', or merely 'nice' – do all the manipulations have a corresponding 'meaning' (here, graphical interpretation)? I wonder whether use of such devices will *require* this to be the case, thereby helping to make it so.

> Stand firm in your refusal to remain conscious during algebra. In real life, I assure you, there is no such thing as algebra.
>
> (Lebowitz, 1982, p. 27)

In her advice to adolescents above, comedian Fran Lebowitz raises the possibility of the existence of unconscious processes at work when doing algebra. Doing algebra may make more explicit our human situation with regard to language in general, where meanings and connections are effective in the unconscious that we may only partly be aware of. A hundred years ago Paul Souriau (1881) queried the feasibility (and I, now, the desirability) of remaining fully in touch with the 'meaning' of algebraic expressions and manipulations.

> Does the algebrist know what becomes of his ideas when he introduces them, in the form of signs, into his formulae? Does he follow them throughout every stage of the operations he performs? Undoubtedly not; he immediately loses sight of them.

Interestingly, the algebraic forms are now what are receding for us, rather than the images. And in a way these forms may not be in our individual unconscious, but lie instead in a collective unconscious, stored in the programs of these machines. How are we to teach algebra, or will this aim wither away too (along with that of teaching certain numerical, pencil-and-paper methods), as merely another temporary aid from a pre-machine age?

There is a strong historical irony here in the development of algebraic manipulation, in that a machine that can liberate us from much of the computational tedium of algebra is also returning us to a partly-rejected strongly referential paradigm. In hand algebra, the paper may push back. With computer algebra, the pencil is taken from my hand, and graphic representations are offered as substitutes to take my attention.

The parallel sense of geometric reality being fundamental, and the algebraic description being secondary, became reversed in the eighteenth century (due particularly to Euler), resulting in properties of the algebraic equations (as objects in their own right) being taken as primary, such as the discriminant as determining the characteristics of curves. What we now have with the machine is a return to this perception, not to the Greek 'reality' of curves, but to the eighteenth-century view of Cartesian curves and more centrally functions. The fact is that a function doesn't 'look' like anything until a coordinate scheme is selected; the same as numbers not having digits until a particular, place-value numeration system is selected. Yet graphs are frequently perceived as pictures, offering direct seeings. I return to this situation in the next chapter.

This most contemporary approach is to return to geometric (or at least Cartesian) images. Thus, when solving a pair of simultaneous linear equations, the corresponding geometric transformations are offered to show what is 'really' going on. And nowhere is this clearer than with some computer algebra systems, where the power of the machine can be used for this end.

Is our mathematical understanding enhanced by this retention of the geometry on the surface? Once again computer software seems to be allowing us to reconnect with an earlier mathematical tradition, one which differentially privileges the visual, the geometric. Will algebra revert to being solely a descriptive language, rather than at times serving as a generative one?

But is my perception of the geometry whatever is 'really' going on, behind the algebra? Is this the unconscious meaning, operating below the level of my awareness, beneath the chains of signifiers? If so, where is my attention supposed to be? Experience with pupils working on turtle graphics suggests that the dynamic, graphic screen is the main focus of attention and it can be difficult to deflect attention onto the symbolic code which is generating the screen effects.

Currently, when working on algebraic forms, I am encouraged to suppress 'meaning' in order to automate and become an efficient symbol manipulator. In other words, I am encouraged to ignore the signification function and to see the symbols as counterparts until the very end of a computation. I learn to associate aspects of the forms with aspects of the situation (for instance, the numerical value of the discriminant in order to discriminate among various types of conic section), and work with them instead. This displacement of attention is a mathematical commonplace, and can also lead to very powerful theorems.

As someone schooled and fluent in pre-machine traditions and conventions of 'hand-algebra', I sometimes worry about loss, usually of control: a control that has arisen from expertise acquired at whatever cost (see Hatch and Hewitt, 1991). Traditions speak of investments – most strongly in those of us who, like Paul Simon, 'lean on old, familiar ways'. By the time I have been enculturated into a tradition, it will most likely have considerably affected my outlook. One paradox may be that the only way to understand a tradition is to partake of it fully – and that may then render it impossible to stand outside of in order to evaluate.

Our attention is modified by the old and the new acting together. At no time is that more true than currently with computational devices. There is a heady mix of devices and desires, of human intentions and wishes, in mathematics as elsewhere. We are in the midst of seeing the development of machines ostensibly to carry them out. What is lost?

Moreover, with computer algebra systems, the perceived locus of mathematics can shift outside of myself when confronted with such sophisticated devices, ones that no longer 'assist', but take over completely an area of functioning. Is the mathematics *in* the apparatus, is it *in* the machine? If I no longer see myself as the calculator, then does arithmetic necessarily reside in the machine? If the machine manipulates geometric screen images for me, do I need to see myself as someone who can manipulate my own? If the computer algebra system does my symbolic manipulations for me, then do I have no opportunity or need to see myself as an algebraist?

## ON SYMBOLS

In a Symbol there is concealment and yet revelation.

(Carlyle, 1836; 1987, p. 166)

In every chapter so far, I have found myself constantly using the word 'symbol', alluding to the power and efficacy of action on external symbolic forms. Mathematical symbols have more than one function: signification and counterpart are two central ones. To name frequently enables us to invoke, summon, conjure, make present: names allow us to distinguish things (though care needs to be taken here). Counterparts offer visible or tangible substitutes for 'manipulation'. Counterparts seem secular, of this sensible world; signs are often taken as spiritual, that is, other-worldly.

What is the origin of the word 'symbol' itself? Literary critic Northrop Frye (1987) writes of the Greek verb *symballein* meaning "to put or throw together", but also draws attention to the noun *symbolon*, which he glosses as: "a token or counter, something that could be broken in two and recognized by the identity of the break" (p. 3).[14]

Frye informs us that there is another etymologically close noun, *symbolos*, meaning "an omen" or "an augury", and in the final chapter I will make mention of mathematical origins and inaugurations. Symbols and the gap, the separation, between symbol and object are fundamental to the very possibility of mathematics.

> A *symbolon* is something that is not complete in itself, but needs something else, or another half of itself, to make it complete. A *symbolos*, in contrast, links us to something too complex or mysterious to grasp all at once.
>
> (*ibid.*, p. 4)

We symbolise when we want something that is absent or missing in some way – and then we work on or with the symbol as a substitute, and on occasion as a consolation. Through working with the symbol, we also gain experience of the thing substituted for. In the process, we can often lose sight of the fact that what we have *is* a symbol, and not the thing we originally desired. But Huxley (1956, p. 29) is at pains to remind us: "However expressive, symbols can never be the things they stand for".

The throwing[15] sense of 'symbol' from *symballein* follows into French, with the term *jeton* being the word for token (e.g. for the telephone – the verb *jeter* means "to throw", but also "to calculate" in the sense of "to cast up accounts"). There is also an anglicised version, 'jetton', a term used for some mediaeval coinage. Thus, symbols preserve the idea of the thrown (exceeding my reach in this manner, jettisoned out of my sight, possibly subterraneously), but also retain the link with money.[16] In both cases, they etymologically involve the hand and therefore invite manipulation. One central reason, then, for symbolising is that symbols allow us to *manipulate*, by proxy, things that are not easily handled, or which are even impossible to handle, by our physical selves.

What does this look at the past senses of words offer us? Goldenberg and Feurzeig (1987, p. 189) write directly of this discursive move, commenting that they are personally "always somewhat moved by the rhetorical device of evoking an etymology". They later add:

> But we should not use etymologies restrictively. An all too popular notion treats an etymology as the official key to the word's current

English meaning, ossifying the meaning rather than illuminating its source. Instead, knowing what a word used to mean, either earlier in the history of our language or in the language from which we borrowed it, can enrich our use of language, building bridges to other words.

This is the sentiment with which I offer such etymological discussions as appear in this book. Words accrete condensing layers of meaning. In the case of the word 'symbol', I think the senses of both these early root words can offer us an important perspective on symbol use in mathematics, as I start to explore below.

### Symbols as counterparts

How do actions on symbols connect to actions on the actual objects? How do arguments involving symbols relate to arguments about their counterparts? Seeing the symbol as part of the whole produces a reason for the link. Do we ever argue about the whole from the part in mathematics? Despite much turning up of intellectual noses at such an apparent mathematical solecism, there are a number of occasions when such generic arguments are used. Here are three:

- In Euclid's proof of the unlimited nature of primes, where he shows that if there were three primes, then he knows how to construct another one – and doesn't even make the remark that the proof goes likewise for any other number of primes.
- When working on particular elements of equivalence classes, in order to show what happens to the classes as a whole (usually with a general theorem in the background that the operations are well behaved with regard to class boundaries).
- When deciding where a derivative is positive or negative over an interval by finding the zeros and then testing an individual point (similarly for points in the plane satisfying inequalities).

The key feature here in all of these instances is that the argument presented is a particular argument that apparently does for all. (See Balacheff, 1988, for a discussion of similar modes of thinking in adolescent provers.)

With algebra, the symbol used is *not* an actual instance of what is being talked about, a letter is not a number in the main (*pace e* and *i*, and perhaps $\pi$). So there is more of a question about the relationship – and relating principle – between the symbol and the referent, as well as how an argument conducted on the symbols bears any relation (be it one of mimicry or something else) to what is the case for the actual members of the set. The Greek mathematician Diophantos' symbol for an unknown was a Greek letter s-like mark that is plausibly a relic of the last letter of the word *arithmos* ("number"), and a common choice of variable name is to use the first letter of the corresponding word name (*r* for radius, *t* for time). So here it is a part of the word symbol, rather than part of the actual object, that is used.

With arithmetic, early number symbols were either pictographic (using three strokes or objects for three) or used a residue principle based on the natural language word. (Attic Greek numerals, for instance, had $\pi$ for five, the first letter of the Greek word *pente*.) It is possible to see numbers both as bearing the same relation to referent experiences as with algebra (e.g. Martin Hughes's (1986) interviews with young pupils who baulk at intransitive, non-adjectival use of number words as things to be added), but also as individual numbers in their own right. (Try to make sensible use of '6' as an algebraic symbol; for instance, 'Let 6 be a group'.)

Generic examples of computations with simple surds such as $\sqrt{2}$ can sometimes be more illustrative than with an algebraic variable, in that they partake of particular number status without being easily reducible in computations, so it is possible also to gain from the structural, placeholder function that algebraic variables serve in highlighting every occurrence of the particular number in focus.

What about geometry? The same duality of symbol relation occurs. A geometric figure is symbolic of the general often, but is perceivable also as a particular element. I earlier wondered whether the ease of transformation of *Cabri-géomètre* or *Geometer's Sketchpad* drawings encouraged viewing a diagram only as an actual particular rather than as a general symbolic? And what of the singular perspective that it is not a single figure being transformed, but a continuous highlighting into attended awareness of distinct figures all equally present in potentiality. The continuity of deformation by the mouse again can act against this perception.

With any general argument in mathematics, there is an additional need for symbolisation. The relationship between the symbols and the things symbolised needs to be established (whether by synecdoche or some other means). Does one of the differences between geometry and algebra lie in the difference in relation between symbol and referent, and hence, in the different symbolic nature of arguments that are used to justify general claims?

## BONES AND STONES

> Nations and graves. Graves and nations. Land is sacred because it is where your ancestors lie.
>
> (Ignatieff, 1993, p. 93)

Dick Tahta has spun a tale surrounding the ancient megalithic site at Avebury in England.

The discovery of many isolated human bones, but no complete skeletons, in the ditch and the surrounding mound is striking. It suggested to him that it might have been that most of anyone's remains were buried in the family group barrows (funeral mounds, of which there are many in the surrounding area), but that one or two bones were thrown into the large ditch surrounding this possibly sacred site. One reason might be in order that Aunt Ann or Uncle Jack might partake of the communal continuity linking past and present.

I was particularly struck in his speculative account by the fact that the bone was actually part of Uncle Jack. So the action of choosing and placing the bone therefore employs a physical synecdoche (substituting a part for the whole, but suggesting and invoking the whole by the presence of the part), as well as producing a specific physical symbol.[17] The parallel with comparable issues about symbols in mathematics and their relation to the broken-off counterparts I found striking.

112

This photo from the 1908 excavation of the site shows the depth beneath the current ditch level at which the bones were found

The Vietnam Veterans Memorial in Washington, DC (also known as The Wall) offers an extraordinary embodiment of some of these issues. Made of smooth black marble, it starkly and sparely lists the names, in chronological order of their death between 1959 and 1975, of all 58,000 American military personnel killed or missing in action during the Vietnam war. The names are arranged so that the last is next to the first.

The Wall is complete: part of its force lies in the fact that in one sense there is no representation of the general, everyone is there. On another level, it demonstrates the strikingly powerful invisibility of the metonymic substitution 'name for the person named'. As with zero, a name's presence here marks another absence.

It is a memorial, not a tombstone: the bodies are not buried underneath.

113

The scale is dwarfing. People interact with it quite specifically, touching it, even taking rubbings of names (to create a counterpart that they might take with them). It provides a focus (as with a particular marker in a cemetery) for private, individual mourning: a colleague commented "I know someone listed. I always find his name whenever I go."

Unlike many war memorials, there is no image attempting to evoke a response through a depiction of the particular: my experience is that these root such sculptures in the particular (age, race, size, relation, . . .). The Wall's relation to and depiction of the general is quite different.

The above is a second monument erected almost on the same site in response to some veterans' unease that The Wall was too negative. For me, however, it has none of the impact. The particular can be powerful and moving. The nearby, newly opened Holocaust memorial offers individual stories to visitors as a different means of creating relation. But I am left with the forceful and overpowering impression that this complete list of names, presented in this way, made on me.

There is a remarkable film, directed by Bertrand Tavernier, entitled *La vie et rien d'autre*, which explores similarly evocative themes. It is set in October 1920 and details the efforts of French society at all levels to come to grips with the missing and the dead (both accounted for and unaccounted for) of the First World War. The main character, the head of the government research bureau, is obsessed by accurate numerical documentation, and numbers resound through the film. (At the very end he writes to the woman he loves: "These are my final dreadful statistics. Forgive me this crushing accuracy".)

He is accused, "Only your statistics count". He comments, *"Les chiffres, on ne joue pas avec"*, not for their inherent seriousness, but because of what they are counting: the dead, the missing, the unaccounted for, the cost. I see his haunting need for numerical precision, for exactness, as a necessary and not inappropriate defence to keep the horror at bay without denying it: a defence which enables him to continue with his work. He infuriates his superiors: "I bother them. Because I keep accounts that never come out right".

He sees his task thus: "I put names to faces, or vice versa", reflecting his belief in the fate and whereabouts of 350,000 soldiers still to be resolved, "349,771 to be exact". He has names and no referents, he has bodies (objectified and named as *les sans-noms*) with no identities. He works with all that remains: relics, the things (such as watches, rings, mugs) found near or with human remains. Countless families are engaged in trying to identify their relatives from them. He too is trying to match them, to reduce the uncertainty, the ambiguity in which so many families are living – he wants no unknowns.

But the other theme of the film, a powerful counterpoint to this search to uncover, to identify, to know, is a top-level secret mission to choose 'an unknown soldier', whose remains are to be buried under the *Arc de Triomphe*. It has to be certain to be a French corpse (no Germans or Americans), but that is all that is to be known. The research chief objects violently, they are identifying people all the time ("51,000 in the last two months"); this one may be identified next week. He issues a veiled threat, "It won't be me, but if it [the actual identity] leaks to the newspapers, then your unknown soldier's mystery evaporates and loses its symbolism". (The actual French is more resonant still for my purposes: *et votre soldat inconnu ne representera plus l'ensemble*.) It is to be both a particular body and yet any body.

In the penultimate sequence, we see the final choice made from eight candidate 'unknowns' issuing from nine geographic regions (even at the end, the numbers won't come out right). The chooser is one young soldier who survived the Somme (making him so unrepresentative) to select finally which one it will be. He chooses number 6 and is asked afterwards why he chose that one. "I'm of the 132nd. I added up the digits. And my regiment's the 6th corps." Even at this moment, he exhibits a faith in numbers to help choose, to enable him to decide, and in metonymic links to confer apparent connection and significance in the face of randomness and death.

At the end of Tavernier's film, the research chief sorrowfully decries the symbolism of the 'unknown' soldier. "It distresses me. But it reassures them. They had 1,500,000 killed. But now they'll only think of this one."

# 6

# MAKING REPRESENTATIONS AND INTERPRETATIONS

> There aren't two things like abstraction and representation, each must contain the other.
>
> (David Hockney, 1993)

Mathematics abounds with representations. In earlier chapters, I have described certain features of geometric, arithmetic and algebraic symbolism. This chapter concerns itself with both the processes of representing and the nature of representations themselves. In particular, it explores graphing and graphs as mediated by computers seen as dynamic imaging devices.

The table below purports to set out a range of representational processes claimed to be of relevance to mathematics. Each process comes with a context for the acquisition of skills and 'know-hows', as well as opportunities for application in particular contexts.

| From \ To | Situations, verbal description | Tables | Graphs | Formulae |
|---|---|---|---|---|
| Situations, verbal description | | Measuring | Sketching | Modelling |
| Tables | Reading | | Plotting | Fitting |
| Graphs | Interpretation | Reading off | | Curve fitting |
| Formulae | Parameter recognition | Computing | Sketching | |

(from Janvier, 1984, p. 29)

118

Janvier also offers the notion of 'translation process' from one form to another.

The metaphor of translation is not neutral, however. The presumption behind translation is one of preservation of meaning – yet there seem to be many non-preservations in the varied list, with 'modelling' providing the clearest instance. A naive view of modelling, and indeed of representation, seems to suggest it is a one-to-one mapping (for example, from a situation described in an arithmetic 'word problem' to a 'corresponding' algebraic equation). Dienes' multiple embodiments seem to suggest a many-to-one mapping, whereas my comments on *Cabri-géomètre* may suggest a many-to-many mapping. Dufour-Janvier *et al.* (1984, pp. 110–11) write: "certain representations are so closely associated to a concept that it is hard to see how the concept can be conceived without them". I wish to go one step further and argue that most (all?) mathematical concepts are only accessible through particular representations.

Anyone who has attempted to translate a text will be aware of needing to work simultaneously on what the linguist Michael Halliday has identified as the three major components of language: the forms, the functions and the meanings. The forms are the words and expressions that make up a language and in mathematics include diagrams, pictures, tables, graphs and charts, while functions include persuading, informing, challenging, stimulating, obscuring and concealing. Similarly, changing representation requires attention to all three of these aspects.

Of the three components, it is the notion of function that is most problematic. In general, who are you representing for (yourself, a teacher, some designated or generalised other), and why? What are you trying to achieve? In talking about representation as an abstract process, it is possible to lose sight of the one-who-represents and their purposes. One function of representation can be to allow access to some event, although any choice of representation carries with it certain stressings and ignorings. Another function is to render visible, so that the discriminating eye can come into play; a third, that of tangibility, so that manipulation by the thinking hand can occur.

Representation involves re-presentation. The prefix 're-' suggests it has been done before, and 'presentation' *tout court* would perhaps be a better term, in the sense of a way of making something be present. English syntax requires a representation to be a representation *of* something, placing it in a subordinate position to the original.[1] It is hard to imagine a photograph that is not a photograph *of* something, and in the second section I discuss in what sense any mathematical images, including computer screen ones, are akin to photographs.

Allied to the notion of representation is the word 'representative', which echoes the discussion of symbols at the end of the last chapter. I may be willing to deal with the representative for a number of reasons, while bearing in mind the varied ways in which a representative can relate to a constituency.

But these etymological observations still reflect a view of representation as derivative or secondary, as subordinate in some way, coming *after* the thing represented. An important notion until now has been the difference between counterpart and signification functions of symbols. With counterparts, there is always the issue of the basis for the resemblance: for example, geometric diagrams resembling something else, the *dessin* resembling the *figure*. And what about graphs of functions? Are all graphs, graphs *of* something? Is the relation there one of resemblance, and if so to what? Or are mathematical 'objects' called into being in order to preserve the more simplistic notion of representation?

A preferable term might be the less directional 'correspondence', which allows a more comfortable exchange of subject and predicate in a way that 'representation' does not. A graph can be made to correspond to an algebraic expression. An underlying theme throughout this book has been the acknowledgement of a more complex interrelation between symbols and objects, in particular with regard to the presumed secondary, ancillary nature of symbols.

## GRAPHING

> Graphs have traditionally served as display representations because the only readily available media were static. *But the static medium restriction is no longer in force!* With the advent of relatively inexpensive bit-mapped graphics displays, we are now free to move and manipulate graphical objects just as we have always been free to manipulate alphanumeric objects.
>
> (Kaput, 1989, p. 185)

The words 'graph' and 'graphic' contain a portmanteau of senses. One core meaning of 'graph' is "written or drawn" (thereby implicitly made with the hand): 'autograph' (self-writing, in one's own hand), 'graphemes' (minimal elements of writing), but also 'photograph' (light drawing) or 'lithograph' (stone drawing). 'Graphic' also carries the connotation of "vividly descriptive or very clear". Yet graphs, although drawn or made with the hand, are intended for the eye, and interpretations are certainly made by eye.

This is equally true whether the graphs are corresponding to algebraic relations or are displaying statistical data. Graphs can provide representations of functions, but can also be used as mathematical models to fit numerical data. Many schoolchildren appear to gain the idea that graphs are simply a pictorial representation of a situation, akin to a literal drawing: for instance, positive gradients on distance-time graphs are seen

120

as showing uphill walks (see Kerslake, 1982). Clement (1989, p. 82) too writes of students making a "figurative correspondence between the shape of the graph and some visual characteristics of the problem scene". In other words, graphs can be seen as providing directly iconic images. Since all graphs have some symbolic features, their meanings are not transparent but need to be 'read'. Graphs are the drawn result of an action, a process. But, once drawn, they come to have the status of things; static and symbolic artifacts like algebraic expressions or geometric diagrams.

One specific affordance of computer algebra systems and some graphic calculators can be graphs appearing at the touch of the button – often without any semblance of their being drawn, instead being conjured whole, ready-made.[2] Images appear, rather than being drawn; the drawer is out of sight, inaccessible. The machine helps me to create images now, and again conditions the images I may draw. Continuous graphs come to be seen as a single object, rather than as enormous composites of points. This is similar to how, in *Cabri-géomètre*, the software requires selection of a point on an object before certain constructions are possible: prior to that moment they are seamless, unitary items.

Janet Ainley and Dave Pratt have been carrying out an extended project exploring some of the effects of allowing young children (eight to ten years old) extended, ready access to laptop computers, including spreadsheet facilities. Among other things, they have been exploring children's ability with using and interpreting line graph representations of numerical information, data with which the children had a close connection. Computers can also introduce many graphical images into the classroom environment, at the pupils' own behest, which are then available as focuses for both discussion and use.

They were both surprised by the facility with which these pupils could interpolate readings and interpret trends in the absence of any explicit teaching about graphs, as well as subsequently produce and work with their own hand-drawn graphs. Indeed, Ainley and Pratt attribute much of this facility to the explicit *lack* of any teaching focusing pupil attention on matters such as scales, point plotting and interpolation.

Their claim about the importance of the computer-generated presentation of *complete* graphs as entities to be thought about in a context that was familiar and understood seems akin to Hewitt's introduction of algebraic symbolism, discussed in the previous chapter, at the precise point when the pupils' main attention was elsewhere. Ainley (1994, p. 8) argues: "If attention is focused on these [individual graphical construction skills], it is difficult for children to keep in mind the context and purpose for which the graph is being drawn". The computer-generated graphs can be seen as accompaniments, by-products of some other activity rather than direct pictures of it.

One power of this software is to suppress all sorts of detail, allowing pupils only to work with the shapes of graphs, whereas previously attention would have been more on individual values, even with a calculator to hand. The facility of producing graphic images (such as line graphs and pie charts) with these machines allowed many 'nonsense' graphs to be drawn (e.g. ones with data measured in different units recorded on the same scale), and Pratt (1994) explores the question of various valuings possible for such images (including illustrative pictorial-aesthetic ones), as well as of how to introduce children to interpretative criteria for specifically mathematical valuations.

These 'psuedo-mathematical' graphs have the correct 'form', and as such have resonance with variant 'countings' (such as 1, 2, 5, . . .) of much younger children; that is, distinguishing the category of number words from other words, but having yet to become attuned to the specific number order. Understanding before doing seems out of place in the counting context, and the work of Ainley and Pratt, although at an early stage, suggests it to be so in deciding on what pupils can and cannot do with graphs at certain stages.

Graphs used to be hand-made, but, as Kaput indicated, were customarily intended for display purposes only, rather than to be manipulated directly. In algebra, we can use symbols to express a perceived relationship and then manipulate the result to obtain new information and insights. Indeed, these transformations embody the essential power of algebra because, due to their concise and non-physical nature, symbols are much more easily manipulable than the things they represent. Graphs can now play the role of counterparts of functions far more easily.

### Picture windows and scale

> The only way we can get the colour of a spot is by matching it, which in practice means isolating it, but when we do that we change the apparent colour, for our perception of the apparent colour is affected not only by the colours of the adjacent areas, but by their sizes and illumination. It is this, for example, that makes it impossible to get a true colour reproduction of even an abstract diagram in colour, let alone of a picture, unless we make our reproduction of the same size as the original and give it the same texture. There is literally no way to make a true colour reproduction on a changed scale.
>
> (Ivins, 1969, p. 153)

Computers offer particular-sized and particular-shaped screen spaces ('windows') at or through which to 'look'. A normal window looks out onto a landscape and generates a view, but there is less sense of it being 'the view'. Similarly, we usually only see part of the graph, and from a particular perspective. One of the things that standard images produce is a sense that it is 'the' way to look. Quite an interesting task might be to show various graphs and ask whether any or all of them could possibly be 'views' of a particular function or equation.

An important aspect of recognition of anything has to do with scale and familiar orientation. Much fun can be had offering pictures of familiar objects from unfamiliar points of view, in particular using unfamiliar scales, to produce appearances far from those that fit the customary perceptual scale.

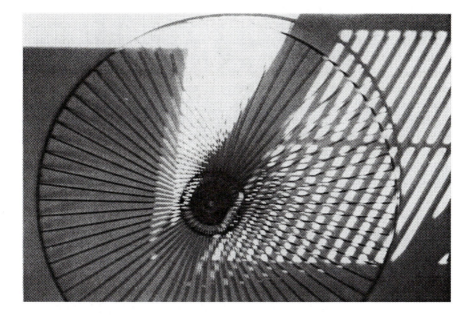

The same can be said of graphic presentations. It is common to talk about a graph as a picture of a function, or even more directly inviting students to *picture* the function $y = 2x + 5$. But I want to explore in what sense is it a picture of the function. And what is the 'best' distance from which to view it? The introduction mentioned the metaphor encapsulated in the perception 'a graph is a picture'. With computers, there is the problem of how to 'see' what appears on the computer screen. How are we to look through our own sight? Take the case of a graph of a function. Whatever you see, you think you see all of 'it', a single thing complete. What does a function 'really' look like?

With computer graphics, scale has to be included (either determined by the user or the machine's default settings). You always get a picture. It resolutely draws to scale (and so retains certain dimensions). As long as there exists the option of leaving automatic scaling off, the work of doing the mathematics does not become invisible.

If I change the scale, do I change the graph? Graphs become counterparts of functions and they themselves are being manipulated by scaling. If I change the scale I can turn a circle into an ellipse, but I can only turn a parabola into another parabola and not into a hyperbola or an ellipse. Thus, a circle is an ellipse (one for which $a = b$), in the same sense that a square is a rectangle. If I scale a cubic, I get another cubic of the same 'type'. In this sense, there are three different types of cubic. Work with computer facility at changing scale has highlighted how much image shape is not fixed, but highly dependent on scale.

Thinking of the computer screen as a window gives rise to all sorts of terminology: in particular, zooming in and out. The fact that the computer creates a new screen image from scratch (a 'magnification'), rather than bringing you 'closer' to what you were already looking at, is conveniently forgotten; the illusion is created that the detail was already 'there' in the previous image.

We are in an era of transition in screen 'fidelity': soon the semblance will be transformed, confusion of pixel with point, computer plotting errors (such as continuity across asymptotes) or visual misrepresentations such as diagonal lines as 'step' functions will all become things of the past, as screen resolution sinks below the visible threshold of distinction.

Paul Goldenberg (1987, 1988) has explored visual miscuing of pupils by linear and quadratic graphs on computer screens and denies that graphs of functions are inherently easier to comprehend than algebraic symbolism. He focuses on the visually barren nature of the screen scene, and the sparse interpretative support it offers to pupils endeavouring to make sense of what they are seeing. "Perceptual strategies that are sufficient for interpreting scale and relative position in real-world scenes are inappropriate when dealing with the infinite and relatively featureless objects in coordinate graphs of simple polynomial functions" (1987, p. 197).

In particular, he discusses pupils trying to derive the quadratic equation of a graph presented on a screen, and talks about the difference between their interpretation of their attempts and his in terms of illusions. Goldenberg provides examples of two pupils' work on finding an algebraic expression which will generate a target graph seen on the screen. The feedback they took from the screen was widely different from Goldenberg's.

To my eyes, what they are doing is bringing knowledge to bear of how to make two objects superimpose, without taking into account the privileging that functions have of vertical adjustments over horizontal ones. Their reasoning seems fundamentally sound in terms of curves (i.e. if the screen objects are primary), but not as graphs of functions. It is feasible for them to match the two graphs on the next page by a change of variable.

The point I made in Chapter 3 about mathematical seeing being projective in nature is particularly relevant here. When looking at such screens, my mathematical knowledge tells me in substantial part *how* to

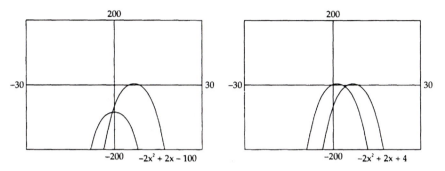

see what I am looking at. Without that knowledge, *must* I see these screens mathematically? This sounds similar to the discussion of Dienes blocks in Chapter 2.

Part of the difficulty has arisen through attempting to use the graph to gain access to the function, rather than have the graph being generated from an analysis of the function. Instead of graphs being associated with functions, but arduous to construct, they now 'come for free' on graphing calculators and computers, and are increasingly being offered as *the* route into functions.

I prefer to use the word 'image' rather than 'picture' in order to highlight the non-representational nature of what appears on the screen. With any photograph it is possible to ask 'What is this a picture of?'; the photograph has secondary place. The image on the screen is not a picture of anything: it is what is generated by a device.

A screen image is a particular kind of dynamic symbol and not the thing itself. Yet it invites such strong projections onto itself as to externalise the objects of the imagination in particular ways, as well as to feed back into the imagination what seems like direct experience of mathematical objects, apparently residing within the machine and under my and its joint control. The computer screen is not a window with us looking in. Functions are not to be found 'inside' computers. Computers generate screen images which are dynamic, interactive symbols – a very powerful new class of symbols.

## Seeming is believing?

> I am concerned not with the theory of objects, but with the appearance of things.
>
> (Bridget Riley, 1993)

David Lodge (1984, p. 295), in *Small World*, reports some delightfully creative translations of Shakespearean titles into Japanese: the best, when

125

retranslated, being 'The Flower in the Mirror and the Moon on the Water' for *The Comedy of Errors*. In the novel, a Japanese interpreter explains: "It is a set phrase . . . It means, that which can be seen but cannot be grasped."

'That which can be seen but cannot be grasped' is a perfect description of computer screen 'image-objects' fabricated from electricity and light. To the extent that the images stimulate and inspire us, they can act as sources of imagery for human mathematical activity of immense power. To the extent that they take over the imaging and seem to provide the actual objects, rather than merely transitional counterpart objects, they can detract from our working mathematically with them.

We are often reminded of the difficulty of distinguishing between how things seem to us and how things are. It was with this in mind that I offered the Gattegno quotation in the first chapter which identified us as 'liv[ing] in our images'. Currently, the gap between micro-computer screen portrayals of geometric and other graphical forms and our own images is sufficient for us to be reminded that we are not perceiving actuality, we are not looking through 'windows'.

When working with students on computer-generated graphs of functions, the question arises as to whether that particular feature comes from the mathematics (is it a property of the function) or is a computer-generated 'glitch'. The map at the moment is visibly not the country. But not for much longer, I suspect. The art of computer visual mimicry is developing apace, and soon, as with photography in the last century, computer screens will draw attention to themselves far less.

Wallace Stevens writes evocatively of seeming being 'description without place' (in a poem of the same name) and also notes that seeming differs slightly from reality, a result of 'the difference that we make in what we see'. He goes on to add (1967, p. 344):

Description is revelation. It is not
The thing described, nor false facsimile.
It is an artificial thing that exists,
In its own seeming, plainly visible,

Description without place is like image without referent object. My concern with computers is that some of the messages and metaphors that come with them suggest we are not being offered description, we are being provided with (false) facsimile. We are apparently viewing the object itself – geometric reality. And it resides within the machine, not ourselves.

Seeming, so close to seeing, is of crucial relevance when looking at images on computer screens. There is a temptation to see these screens as windows, and us as looking in, observing. We read we are to think of computers as microscopes, the metaphor of 'zooming in and out' is widely used (the metaphors lurking behind the naming of various computer functions would make a rewarding study), and of computers providing us with views of other worlds. In all of these images there is a suggestion of our being offered direct perception of mathematical objects.

But it is we, as always, who have to do the seeing. What is being generated are dynamic iconic symbols which are for us to interpret. When David Tall defines a differentiable function as one that when zoomed in on sufficiently eventually *is* straight (and not just *looks* or *seems* straight), he is merely continuing a long tradition in mathematics whereby first features of the form are used to signal features of the meaning – and then later come to substitute for them.

(An even number is one that ends in a 0, 2, 4, 6, or 8, provided numbers are rendered graspable in our familiar decimal numeration system. It allows us a very quick recognition of even numbers. But does it provide a rich description for developing a meaning of evenness? Once again we have come upon a tension between efficiency and understanding.)

'The computer screen is a window' is a metaphor, not a description of fact. I have written elsewhere (Pimm, 1987, Chapter 4) about certain aspects of metaphor in mathematics. Where the metaphor is offered as an initial means of gaining experience of a new phenomenon, it is important that it be taken literally early on if it is to have its full effect. However, it is equally important later on that its metaphoric status should also come to light – in this case, so that a separation between mathematics and machine can take place.

The most pressing problem I see is that of novices being able to see beyond the screen. Similar problems arose in working with Logo where the teacher wanted attention to the code that was generating the screen effects, whereas the pupil's attention was frequently taken up with the screen itself, and the status of the generative language was reduced to mere epiphenomenon. Simone Weil (1952, p. 128) writes of the transference of consciousness into an object other than the body itself as being characteristic of increasing skill and apprenticeship. Here, the invitation is apparently the reverse.

I am looking for ways to view the computer and two ways of looking at the screen are as a mirror or as a window. A mirror allows our own mental functioning to be perceived. When seen as a window, there are fantasy notions of breaking the glass and letting the human in, something that Lewis Carroll wrote about in *Through the Looking Glass*. The virtual world is on 'the other side' of the mirror, even though walking to 'the other side' of the mirror does not get you there.[3] Yet with either of these images, the source object is missing. I do not generate the images in the computer-seen-as-mirror, even if I do interpret how they seem to me.

## EXACTLY REPEATABLE PICTORIAL IMAGES

Exact repeatability and permanence are so closely alike that the exactly repeatable things become thought of as permanent or real things, and all the rest are apt to be thought of as transient and thus mere reflections of the seemingly permanent things.

(Ivins, 1969, p. 162)

Although I have been concentrating here on computer-generated graphic images, I am generally concerned with the nature of images and the role they play in mathematics. Children often view diagrams in mathematics books as merely decorative rather than making integral statements as part of the text. A separate belief is that a picture offers a 'true likeness' of what it is a picture of – pictures too are apparently always pictures *of*, never primary things in themselves. A similar debate about the nature of representation in art led Magritte to offer his paintings of artists' paintings substituting vividly for the 'reality' they depicted.

William Ivins (1969) has written a remarkable book on the history of the making of prints in Europe since 1500. Underlying this theme is an exploration of important differences between words and images for permitting symbolic communication about things. Words written or spoken in different handwriting or accent are seen as equivalent: "hand-made pictures, to the contrary, we are aware of as unique things; we see all the differences between them and know the impossibility of repeating any of them exactly by mere muscular action" (*ibid.*, p. 159). His recurrent theme is the emergence of the capability for the exact repetition of pictorial statements about things, and the remarkable effect this had on many spheres of knowledge.

Ivins records numerous developments in the production of graphic (hand-made) pictures, as well as contrasting the situation of exact reproduction of verbal statements. Since the invention of writing, the latter has been possible with spoken statements, though hand copying of books was the only method of replication. Automated printing allows the production of an unlimited number of copies, although, as Ivins points out, one way of viewing the effect of this development is merely reducing the amount of proof reading required.

A degree of 'verisimilitude' is required of any image: is it the same for a sketch, a diagram and a picture? There is a particular importance for accuracy of the representation when it is taken as a mathematical counterpart and work is done directly on the representative as if it were the object itself (such as measuring geometric drawings).

One debate concerns the question of the original, and the relation of the 'copy' to it. I spoke earlier of the relation of resemblance between counterpart and object. Michel Foucault draws a distinction between 'resemblance' and 'similitude', in terms of the former having a 'model' or original element, one "that orders and hierarchizes the increasing less faithful copies that can be struck from it. Resemblance presupposes a primary reference that prescribes and classes", while with similitude the common ancestor is missing: they are alike one with the other, with neither having a prior claim.

The situation with similitude exists with prints. A plate is made, but this is not the original. A limited edition may be run and the plate destroyed: while they are run in order, there is no original, only a first, a second, .... The same is true with photography: the negative is not the original, many positives can be made. There is no original. Originals leave room for the imagination, they are only what they are. If what we have is a copy, then it is constrained by having to be a copy *of*. In a society filled with reproductions, we have a preoccupation with originality. Inherent in the processes of print-making and photography is exact reproducibility.

> Resemblance serves representation, which rules over it; similitude serves repetition which ranges across it, similitude circulates the simulacrum as the indefinite and reversible relation of the similar to the similar.
>
> (Foucault, 1983, p. 44)

Computers offer a new technology for exact reproducibility of images. The above would suggest that it may be difficult to see such images as resembling. What is the source of authenticity for any mathematical image? Must it be one of resemblance to its erstwhile object? Do we not, in fact, create these mathematical 'objects' in order to have an original from which our 'representations' may then derive?

Ivins offers a historical commentary on the problems of science and art history arising from a past inability to make such exact copies of visual images. He writes:

> As we have seen, the Greek botanists were fully aware of the limitation upon the use of hand-made pictures as a means of communicating exact ideas of shapes and colours .... They could only make copies of pictures, and when hand-made copies are made from hand-made copies it takes only a small number of copies for the final copy to bear no practically useful resemblance.
>
> (1969, p. 161)

Consequently, even for a geometric diagram to be repeated accurately, a copyist would need to understand what role it played in order to stress and ignore correctly, tracing not being feasible. And the copier is always working from the substitute rather than the original.

I am interested in the ability of computer languages both to capture and to execute an exactly repeatable sequence of operations (which provides in some ways the definition of an algorithm). The implementability of computer languages provides a strong link between the exact repeatability of text statements (e.g. programs printed in a computer magazine) and exactly repeatable pictorial statements. The now-commonplace quality of this event has resulted in its becoming invisible. Are computer-generated mathematical images originals? Or are they copies, and if so of what? How are we to know? The relation between things seen and imagined in mathematics is particularly complex.

Ivins writes of photographs as a key stage in the making of exactly repeatable pictorial statements, indicating how it was only with the photograph that a distinction was perceivable between a maker and a reporter of a work of art. But he also points to the influence of the photograph in substantially determining how we came to see.

> As the community became engulfed in printed pictures, it looked to them for most of its visual information. . . . As people became habituated to absorbing their visual information from photographic pictures printed in printers' ink, it was not long before this kind of impersonal visual record had a most marked effect on what the community thought it saw with its own eyes. It began to see photographically, it stopped talking about photographic distortion, and finally adopted the photographic image as the norm of truthfulness in representation.
>
> (*ibid.*, p. 94)

> Thus by conditioning its audience, the photograph became the norm for the appearance of everything. It was not long before men began to think photographically, and thus to see for themselves things that previously it had taken the photograph to reveal to their astonished and protesting eyes. Just as nature had once imitated art, so now it began to imitate the picture made by the camera.
>
> (*ibid.*, p. 138)

The 'impersonal' photographic record meant that it was not hand-made, even though it was eye-made. With a photograph, the objects delineate themselves, rather than humans doing it with their hands. But the traces of the way of seeing rather than the way of drawing may be far less evident. At the moment with the current state of screen image technology, screen distortion ('straight' lines not being straight, for instance), puts us at the corresponding stage of still talking about 'computergraphic distortion'. How long will it be before we adopt the computer-generated image as the norm of truthfulness in representation? Behind all this is a resilient belief in the possibility of unmediated seeing which relates to the fantasy of perfectly transparent understanding.

Roland Barthes (1984) has written a meditative essay on photographs and photography. He points out that with a photograph the signified 'adheres' to the signifier and claims the essence of a photograph to be the assertion: 'that-has-been'. With a photograph the object needs to have been present. "A specific photograph . . . is not *immediately* or *generally* distinguished from its referent (as is the case for every other image . . .) by the way in which it is simulated" (*ibid.*, p. 5), adding that because "a photograph always carries its referent with it", it is far harder to perceive the photographic signifier: "a photograph is always invisible: it is not it that we see" (*ibid.*, p. 6).

> Photography's Referent is not the same as the referent of other systems of representation. I call "photographic referent" not the *optionally* real thing to which an image or a sign refers but the *necessarily* real thing which has been placed before the lens, without which there would be no photograph. Painting can feign reality without having seen it. Discourse combines signs which have referents, of course, but these referents can be and are most often "chimeras". Contrary to these imitations, in Photography I can never deny *the thing has been there.*
>
> (*ibid.*, p. 76)

With computer screen images, what are they images of? They are undrawn by human hand, yet are projected as photographs are coming to be. The relation between the image and what it may once have been an image of is becoming more complex with the possibility of storing, editing and displaying of photographs in computers. The fact that digitised images can be edited on a computer and then printed out again, means that any sense of a photograph necessarily being a representation of something else is fading. Photographs are taking on a new life as entities in themselves, belying Barthes' observations of a mere ten or so years earlier.

Computers generate images and not pictures, even if photographs are subsequently made of them (such as beautiful ones available of fractals). How are we to decide whether the image is dependable, to authenticate it now a screen image is becoming the norm, rather than a paper one? For Barthes (*ibid.*, p. 85): "The photograph's essence is to ratify what it represents".

The static, time-frozen rather than compressed nature of photographs also points to their singular nature. Can photographs aim for a generality, or are they for ever particular? Are what *Cabri-géomètre* offers us 'stills' because of the possibility of motion to generate generality through continuous juxtaposition of particulars, turning a photograph into cinema? This is one reason for valuing drawings rather than screen 'photographs' for their generality rather than particularity.

One of the claims Ivins makes in the transfer from hand-made to light-made images is the freedom from the tyranny of the grid (the 'net of rationality' as he terms it), the coordinate framework that determined the seeing, in order to enable the representation to be rendered. In response to an increased demand for information, more lines needed to be used in the wood-cut, finer and closer together.

The generalised abstract mesh of lines sounds so much like the Eulerian coordinate plane (Descartes chose his axes relative to the particular geometric figure he was studying and not conversely). The symbolic saving in grid-related descriptions over Greek verbal *symptoms* provides a good example of the staggeringly compact efficacy that certain symbolisms can make – as well as the immense amount of structure that is contained in the 'infliction' (to use Dieudonné's term) of innocuous-looking coordinates on the plane.

I believe there is an averaging effect of cameras which re-enacts the averaging effects of making particular etchings or of using coordinate axes. However, the effects of these representational choices get forgotten and things become necessary and 'the way they are' rather than highly contingent. The rise of functions (and the consequent privileging of $x$ over $y$) has obliterated the study of curves, many of which are not graphs of functions.

The pixel grid of a computer screen is still there, in the same way that the dot resolution on a film is there, still consistently influencing our seeing without being discriminable by eye. But 'zooming in' on a computer-drawn graph does not reveal the 'grain' of the screen (which is nonetheless there) as it would a blown-up picture; the graininess that serves to remind us ultimately that what we have is a picture and not the real thing. No, what we are shown is a different screen image, just as in algebra we are presented with a transformed equation; instead of a sequence of equations, we have a sequence of screen images, apparently bringing us closer to the 'true nature' of the mathematical object.

### Camera obscura

Concern and confusion about the nature and consequences of developing technology is not limited to mathematical devices. I wish to continue discussion of photography, while shifting focus from the nature of the photographic image to recent developments in the devices for taking them: cameras. I hope through this apparent digression to bring out some features of the educational use of new technology in mathematics. Over the next couple of pages, I discuss the situation in photography with new automated, 'point-and-shoot' models replacing, among others, single-lens reflex cameras. While the parallel between cameras and calculators and computers is far from exact, I feel there is enough similarity to make the comparison interesting.

In photography, there are now inexpensive automated cameras for which aperture function (measured in f-stops, usually in seven increments numbered 1.2 to 16) and shutter function (measured in fractions of a second), as well as focus and even the speed of the film (measured in ASA numbers)[4] are calculated or read off by a microchip integrated into the device itself. Consequently, the only thing the photographer does (the only function that is actually still available to her) is to compose a picture and release the mechanism that initiates everything else. This does not encourage precise composition nor a studied approach – the former primary values of photography being control over the image and a great degree of optical flexibility.

Such cameras, because of their design, determine to a great extent what can and cannot be done. The user cannot manipulate depth of field, nor choose how to readjust the lighting, nor decide to blur the image purposefully to create an effect. The result is an averaging which produces the 'best available' picture given the pre-determined balance (and the aesthetic that lies behind this) among these functions that is hard-wired into the camera.

Such functions are locked together – they cannot be selected, paired or controlled independently in order to *create* an image. Indeed, some cameras won't allow you to take a picture (by locking the shutter function) if it adjudges there to be insufficient light. Light meters in particular are averaging devices and can badly mislead if there is high contrast, reinforcing the fact that the average is not a data point.[5] The automated camera cannot stress and ignore, emphasise or isolate in the way the human eye can: these human abilities result in a seeing that a photographer can vainly strive to capture.

All of the discussion so far has been from the point of view of taking decisions away from a photographer who is used to being able to control these functions manually. What is the effect on a novice learning photography when the only camera available is such an automated 'point-and-shoot' one? Photography clearly becomes a different experience.

What happens is that novices might see something yet lack the ability to incorporate the desired subtlety of their seeing into the picture – because it is set against the averaging effect of the device. It may be that the mechanism automates the function so successfully that it effectively disappears: the user may be unaware that other possibilities exist. Such devices also carry the subtle implication that there is a 'right' or 'best' picture to be taken.

On the other hand, one advantage of such an automated device is that the novice does not have to worry about mechanical or technical aspects at the outset. Almost all technical detail is suppressed and need not interfere with the intent or desire. If photography is conceived as composing, seeing and choosing a decisive moment, beginners are freed to work directly at this *ab initio*. It also may be that they do not wish to become photographers, but would nonetheless like to take pictures – and they can get more than satisfactory results from these cameras.

However, such a view implies that technical and compositional aspects of imaging through a camera are independent of one another, whereas one way of learning about producing a desired effect is through experimentation with precisely these technical aspects. The possibility of gaining technical fluency at the same time as photographic awareness is no longer there. The technology, while providing easier, less sophisticated access, is also partially determining what pictures *can* be brought into being. The camera is a recording device: but it can also serve as a seeing and an editing device, despite the human eye being much more sophisticated than the camera.

Whichever technology is in use serves as an extension, amplification or diminution of some human functioning and its design capabilities are always limited. Such inventions also may alter or even serve to determine the genre – similar to the way in which photography took over from portrait painting in the nineteenth century. Early photographs attempted to mimic the look and conventions of oil painting, such as using soft focus (achieved by putting a gauze as a filter over the lens). Barthes (1984, p. 30) observes: "The first man who saw the first photograph must have thought it was a painting: same framing, same perspective".

Seeing photography initially in terms of oil painting is an example of a metaphorically structured perception. Metaphors are inherently conservative and backward-looking. They are about seeing the new in terms of the old. This also offers a reason why for contemporary experts schooled and fluent in the traditions and conventions of the technology of the recent past, such technological change seems always to be solely a loss, usually of control: control that has arisen from their expertise acquired at whatever cost. Yet another technology can offer new, as-yet-unperceived possibilities.

The position with arithmetic calculators, geometry software, graphic calculators and computer algebra systems in the light of the foregoing discussion is quite interesting. If you cannot vary something, it is hard to get a sense of the possibilities. Does machine-automated functioning preclude exploring questions such as:

• What is it actually doing?
• How does it do that?
• Do all machines do the same thing?
• Could I aspire to doing that without the machine?
• How was it done before machines?

Calculators and computers have both means and methods hard-wired or deep-programmed into them on grounds of speed and efficiency. But these are not generally accessible to the user. As with taking pictures, such devices are very efficient: they can save time and energy, they are portable and provide simple access to computations of many kinds. They are very useful devices for operating in the material world. But for some of us at least who are involved in mathematics education, our greater concern is with students encountering and engaging with mathematics than solely with their successful functioning in the outside world.

# 7

# SYMBOLS AND MEASURES

To measure the inaccessible consists in mimicking it within the realm of the accessible.

(Serres, 1982, p. 85)

This chapter starts to explore how parts of mathematics (and its symbols) are related and 'applied' to events in the material world, by means of the process of measurement. The range of what and how humans have chosen to measure has both widened and deepened over the ages, as have the techniques and devices for doing so. The expression 'to get the measure of something' (as well as 'to have someone's number') implies it is then satisfactorily known.

There is a deep connection between symbols and measures. Measures have come to be taken for the thing measured, and this process echoes the way in which symbols come to stand for the thing symbolised. The measure becomes the name for the thing measured, and because numbers can serve as counterparts too, these things are manipulated by means of the measures. I also take a look at 'measuring' mathematical entities themselves.

For instance, a secondary teacher said to his class of twelve-year-olds, "I'll put these angles on the board and I'd like you to say whether they are acute, obtuse or reflex." He then wrote: '30°, 75°, 145°, 200°, 350°, 5 right angles, 6 right angles' (thus using two different units of measure: the degree and the right angle). He used the measure of the angle metonymically as the name for the angle, in some sense substituting the measure of the angle for the angle itself (with the tacit assumption that all 200° angles, for instance, are the same). This is a commonplace mathematical practice.

In the 1960s, there was an attempt to pull apart useful, functioning confluences (such as numeral-number) in the name of clarity, correctness and precision. Yet the intent of the above task was to allow a property of the measure (namely numerically less than 90°, bigger than 90° and less than 180°, or bigger than 180° and less than 360°) to determine whether an angle is adjudged to belong to the categories of acute, obtuse or reflex angles respectively. The measure of the angle is identified with the angle, and then properties of the measures are used to 'manipulate' the angles themselves. In some ways, the angles are being named through their measures and brought into existence by using the number name.

For instance, is it the doing, the turn, that is the right angle, or is it the static end result? Which is to be stressed? There are many situations where seeing angle as dynamic, rather than static, is beneficial to understanding. For numerical measures to be useful, they should be constant, which suggests that the thing measured is static. Earlier I described the metonymic move from '1, 2, 3, 4, 5' to '5', from counting to count, as well as from drawing to drawn. Mathematics in general, and measurement in particular, repeatedly turns processes into objects. Measurement involves the placing of numbers onto the world, rather than the extraction of numbers from it.

Numbers are a human invention, and the world is not inherently numerical. The numbers are in some way acting as counterpart symbols for the actuality. They are then worked with (compared, ordered, averaged, . . .) and then the results transferred back and interpreted in the original situation. It is quite possible to specify how to measure something without being clear on what the thing itself is. The familiarity and apparent solidity of the numbers help to assuage any lingering doubts.

Coding information into numerical form has a tendency to lend it spurious objectivity. Once the world has been quantified into the form of numerical data, it is increasingly likely that they will be fed into a computer. The capacity of computers to store data on a massive scale has seduced us into attempting to measure ever more facets of our world, as well as providing the prospect of manipulating them, something that would have previously been unimaginable.

Some of the implications of this are discussed in Joseph Weizenbaum's book *Computer Power and Human Reason*, whose telling subtitle identifies the tendency to move 'from judgement to calculation'. One of its central themes is a lament for the systematic replacement by calculations of the use of human judgement in situations: computations being increasingly carried out by computers without the apparent involvement of humans at all. As science and technology develop, the gap between what is measured, and the actual object about which measurement claims are being made, increases. This conceptual distance can allow human distancing as well. A current charged example of this is that of pilots who bomb targets by aligning two points of light on a computer screen, which may allow them to believe that they are not therefore directly killing human beings. This is one way in which our society is becoming increasingly mathematised, and in ways which are increasingly invisible. I return to this theme in the next chapter.

The first section below details examples of measurement as well as the accompanying language and symbols invoked in the everyday world which surrounds me. The subsequent section looks briefly at certain features of human measurement of the social world and links directly to the next chapter on the contexts of mathematical problems. The third section explores briefly an instance of measurement of the physical world, including a discussion of the nature of measurement itself as well as its relation to the senses of both touch and sight. In the final section, I turn to the question of exactness and the measurement of certain 'supernatural' objects of mathematics such as the circle or square.

## MEASUREMENT IN CONTEXT

NEDDIE SEAGOON: How far is it to the valley?
MAJOR BLOODNOCK: Roughly sixty miles.
NS: I know it's roughly sixty miles, but what is it exactly?
MB: Seventy miles.
NS: We'll go roughly, it's ten miles shorter.

(The Goon Show Scripts)

Any urban environment is symbol-dense: symbol-displaying devices made by human beings abound. Many arithmetic symbols are employed together with geometric elements in measurement displays, diagrams and charts, graphs and other ways of providing, storing and representing information. For example, a whole range of human uses of mathematical (mainly arithmetic) symbols is revealed when driving along an English road: one road sign has a 50 in a red circle, another bears the legend 7% with a sloping line, a third advises 'Weight limit 7.5 tonnes'. A motorway sign bears the symbols 'A508' and lower down on the left a '15' and on the right '½m'; on another 'M. Keynes 25' and on a third 'Petrol **** 51.3'. There are signs with \\\ or \\ or \ on them just before a motorway service station or exit, and signs saying 'Road works 400 yards'.

On the dial of a car radio, there are two number scales, one labelled MHz and the other kHz. A device on the dashboard of a car reads 8:51, a rotating pointer on a second indicates 75 (the dial is labelled mph), while a third offers whole numbers between 0 and 6, with many divisions in between, and is cryptically labelled 1/min × 1000. Signs on the backs of cars label them as 3.2s or 2000s, etc.

Any adult living in England is likely to be able to interpret most or all of these symbols, and, in some sense, to 'say what they mean', though often that will mean they can *use* the symbolic information in order to control the device. On a radio dial, for instance, the numbers can be used to locate stations without any sense of what an Hz might be or what it is being used to measure. You might know that the tachometer measures engine speed, in 'revolutions per minute', and the information can be used in order to guide when to change gear (while engine noise, although unquantified, is another possible indicator), without a clear sense of 'revolutions of what', how they are measured or what the indicator 1/min × 1000 refers to. Some of the numbers (such as 2.8) on cars may refer to the engine capacity in litres or cubic centimetres, while others may have no such measurement function.

Numbering is a general term for a range of processes by which numbers are attached to different objects or situations in our world. Besides using numbers as names (recall the delicatessen queue instance mentioned in Chapter 4), transitive counting and measuring (the focus of this chapter) comprise the two fundamental means of numbering.

There are two distinct uses of numbers in the above collection of arithmetic symbols in contexts. These are:

- *Numbers as labels* Some uses of number are primarily for the naming functions of identifying and distinguishing, such as house, telephone or social security numbers; the central principle is that no two distinct objects are to have the same number. The quantitative aspect is ignored or irrelevant – such as a road number or a car labelled 9000 Turbo; an even clearer example would be a Number 15 bus. (With the recent British privatisation of bus routes, different companies used the same familiar route numbers and so a court case arose in order to decide the 'meaning' of a bus route number.)

  The number is being used primarily as a convenient name. (In Boston, underground lines have colour names – Red line, Orange line; in

London, some have names relating to station names – like Victoria or Bakerloo;[1] in Montreal, they have numbers.) Certain namings do relate to some measured feature of the situation, however, as with a C60 audio-cassette or an E180 videotape (where the number refers to playing time in minutes). Some, like road exit numbers, allow certain properties of numbers to be taken advantage of. (In England, motorway exits are numbered, hence ordered; in Germany, where there are many more, they are named only by the next town.)

• *Numbers which actually measure something* There is an implicit or explicit unit (the speed limit is in miles per hour, the odometer reading is in miles, the clock reading is in hours and minutes). As with many of the above examples, the context is frequently required to supply the units. The tendency is to use the numbers alone, with the units suppressed.

However, much of the application of number to the physical and social worlds comes about through measurement of certain attributes of objects or situations. Measurement introduces numbers directly into the world.

The central use of measuring is that of comparison. Is this *bigger* than that, *longer* than that, *older* than that? We don't always need numbers if we wish to compare things. In order to achieve a direct comparison, the two objects (situations) need to be brought 'next to' each other in some sense, so they touch: two children can stand back to back to decide who is the taller, two small objects can be put in opposite pans of a balance and directly visually compared with respect to weight, and so on.

But often objects being compared cannot be brought next to each other in this way: they may be too small, or too far away from each other, or be immovable for some reason.[2] For example, you may want to check whether a heavy piece of downstairs furniture will fit into an alcove in an upstairs bedroom. A third object can be used as a measure – one that can be moved from one to the other, laid against one and then laid against the other: a portable common comparison.

Measuring can be used to short-circuit the problems of comparing directly. By measuring numerically, we assign a number to each object and then the numbers can *always* be 'brought together' (mentally) to be compared with one another. Once you have worked out which is the larger *number*, that becomes the basis for deciding which *object* is the larger/older/heavier/.... The numbers become the counterpart of the material-world object, process or situation. And an important justification for using numbers as measures is that any two numbers can be ordered; that is, in principle we can always decide which one is the bigger, and which the smaller.

With actual measurement, there is always the question of the units involved. Often, they are somewhat vague and seldom specified in the actual context. With measurement of continuous quantities (like lengths, weights or capacities), there is also the recurring question of approximation – the numerical answers can never be exact – they are actually signalling an interval of numbers. But they *become* the length, and so become exact.[3] The numbers come to stand for or symbolise the quantity measured. (I have postponed until the last section of this chapter the question of the exact 'measurement' of geometric objects, such as the length of the diagonal of a square of side one unit or the area of a unit circle.)

## The language of measurement

The English language offers structures for comparison and part of learning to speak mathematically involves acquiring these spoken forms: 'bigger than', 'lighter than', 'the tallest or heaviest', 'as long as', 'twice as wide', 'a third as long', 'in every', 'for each', 'per unit of'. All of these constructions offer qualitative or quantitative ways of measuring or ordering events, objects, experiences.

There is also a language of approximation: there are *about* five minutes left, there are *roughly* forty pages to go, we have *between* two and three hundred members, there is *approximately* half a pint still in the bottle. These words are used with quantities, but also indicate that the numerical values are not to be taken literally. Such approximations are quite interesting statements: for instance, there are about 190,000 inhabitants in Milton Keynes. When would this claim be false? (For much more on the linguistics of approximation as one part of vague language use, see Channell, 1994.)

Some statements also illustrate the category of 'round' numbers which tend to be employed with approximations: a sign says 'Office space for rent: 50,000 sq. ft'. In part, what a 'round' number is will depend on the context and the object being measured, but there is something clearly anomalous about statements like, 'There are approximately four houses of this type in the street' (from a surveyor's report). More acceptable is the match box which reads 'average [or approximate] contents 48 matches', or bottles of wine having 75 cl e on the label (where the e means 'estimated').

There is also the comparative, ratio language of 'per': miles *per* gallon, revolutions *per* minute, people *per* square mile, feet *per* second *per* second. All prices are explicitly or implicitly 'per', meaning 'for every'. At petrol pumps, the prices are in pence per litre; on fruit and vegetables, pence per kilo; on clothes, pounds per item. Changing units is about numerical equivalences, and need not refer to anything about the actual objects at all. Dollars into pounds, inches into centimetres, pounds into kilograms, °C into °F, degrees into radians, pence per litre into pounds per gallon. All involve the notion of a rate, a substitution of this for that, so many of these per so many (often 1) of that, though a direct comparison is often offered by means of a conversion graph or chart.

## Units of measure

The metric (SI) system of weights and measures has a structure just as the imperial one does. The parallel with different numeration systems is quite close. Knowledge of this structure[4] can help make sense of or even allow you to work out what certain measures must be, purely on linguistic evidence alone. Kilogram and kilometre[5] bear the same relation to gram and metre respectively: and so a kilojoule must also be 1000 joules, even if you do not know what a joule is a measure of, or the particular size of one joule. There is also, thus, a certain irony in that 'a kilo' has become a common abbreviation of 'a kilogram' in the particular context of weight.

The same is true for radio dials marked in kiloHertz (kHz) and mega-Hertz (MHz). Whatever a Hertz is, a kHz is thousand of them and a MHz (a megaHertz) is a thousand kHz, or a million Hertz. There are then three distinct types of knowledge required for successful handling of measuring units in context. These are: structural knowledge of the SI metric system coded into the naming system, experience of what is being measured, and having a sense of the actual size of the unit.

The notation for units mirrors algebraic symbolism, even to the point where, in secondary physics, discussions of the dimensions of units feel very like algebraic cancellation. Square centimetres are often written as cm × cm or even $cm^2$; the sense of 'per' is rendered by the division line, metres per second comes out m/s. The units given on the tachometer, 1/min × 1000, reflect a process where whoever reads the dial is invited to perceive the numbers directly rather than to scale the number on the dial by multiplying by 1000 and then to interpret that number as revolutions in one minute.

It is perhaps not surprising that pupils in school tend to ignore the units of measurement. Indeed, in the midst of a computation, it is common mathematical practice to drop the units and work with the numbers alone. The counterpart function has temporarily superseded the naming-signification one. (For an insightful look in general about elementary school practices involving measurement, see Janet Ainley's (1991) challenging piece 'Is there any mathematics in measurement?') However, when solving actual measurement problems elsewhere, other forces come into play. Jean Lave reports a 'Weight-watchers' class, whose participants were preparing their meals:

> In this case they were to fix a serving of cottage cheese, supposing the amount allotted for the meal was three-quarters of the two-thirds cup the program allowed. . . . He filled a measuring cup two-thirds full of cottage cheese, dumped it out on a cutting board, patted it into a circle, marked a cross on it, scooped away one quadrant, and served the rest. . . . At no time did the Weight Watcher check his procedure

against a pencil and paper algorithm, which would have produced
¾ cup × ⅔ cup = ½ cup.

(1988, p. 165)

From my perspective, there are at least three points worthy of note here. The first is that the problem was solved by operating directly on the cheese, rather than mathematically to obtain the right amount which was then to be measured out. The solver (who had studied calculus) found a way to take three-quarters of a particular quantity of cheese (namely two-thirds of a cup).

The second is that Lave's account of what would be the written solution seems slightly awry. She writes: "which would have produced ¾ cup × ⅔ cup = ½ cup". But the problem was to find ¾ of '⅔ cup', while the arithmetic solution finds '¾ × ⅔' cup. The first number is acting as a numerical operator on the quantity, while the second is a measure of the quantity. Arithmetically, we can see that the same amount would be obtained by finding ⅔ of '¾ cup', but that is to interchange the (very different) roles of the two numbers in the actual problem, analogous to the percentage example which is to be offered shortly.

The third point is one about classroom contexts for such erstwhile measurement problems. If it were posed as a verbal problem, would a pupil ask: has he got a measuring cup and a cutting board handy? Such problems often ask pupils to engage with quite implausible situations (in order to make them mathematically tractable), such as baths filling with plugs out. I look at this issue in more detail in the next chapter.

Cups and tablespoons as cooking quantity measures seem to speak of familiar, household objects. You and I probably have them in our kitchens. Yet when employed as a semi-formal measure of capacity, they have a particular function. The context of use allows for some variation (my 'cup' as a sufficient substitute for the recipe's 'cup', for instance), just as two eggs in a recipe are not usually of specific size.

But what about a more formal unit of capacity? What is a cubic centimetre? At one level, it is a physical entity, one which embodies the property of which it is a measure, and $cm^3$ (formerly, cc) is its symbol. So, in this instance, its dimensions are 1 cm along every edge. Its weight, however, is not relevant, nor is what it is made of (provided its edge lengths and shape are pretty stable). So the question 'How heavy is a cubic centimetre?' can have no consistent answer, although any given embodiment will have a particular weight, as it must be a physical object.

We talk about a cubic centimetre in the singular, yet is there one or are there many (more or less the same)? There is a sense in which a cubic centimetre is also an abstract 'thought object', one which stacks perfectly, of which every one is the same, allowing perfect repeatability. The desire for 'exactness' in measurement moves units more closely in the direction

142

of mathematical objects, and in terms of their being 'handled' through thought alone, closer to the 'manipulations' of geometry and algebra rather than that of hands directly. In some sense, a unit is an ideal and cc is one symbol for that ideal. Physical units may seem concrete, and very much of the physical world, but the closer we get to what they are and how they are used, the less concrete and the more abstract they become.

The same is true of an inch or a millimetre. At one level, it is a marked length on a ruler, yet its use also involves the presumption that every one is the same as any other. The ability of humans with the aid of machines to fashion objects very similar to one another, exactly repeatable physical statements, results, among other things, in a widespread availability of measuring instruments. The metre used to have a physical referent (a singular, unique metal bar kept in Paris under certain physical conditions, such as a particular constant temperature). But rather like paper money which no longer has a physical referent in terms of a certain weight of gold, the metre is now specified in terms of wavelengths of a certain type of light and so has lost much of its tangibility. And certainly nothing would have been allowed next to it for fear of contaminating its physical properties. Its reference status became purely symbolic.

Contrast this discussion with the notion of percentage with its accompanying symbol, %. What sort of symbol is it? It looks in some ways like a unit, of which you can have a certain number, as, for example, when hills are labelled 13% as a measure of their slope. The symbol itself is indicative, stylistically representing a fraction. We can press the % key on a calculator, which suggests it is an operator like + or ×, although the way it operates is different from them.

However, per cent (sometimes written 'percent', which reinforces the sense of unit) is an abstract compound unit of numbers: five per cent meaning five in every hundred. Interestingly, North American newscasters have started talking about 'percentage points', thereby making a percentage into a number of units rather than a rate, and hence 5% becomes just like 5 metres. (I have never heard asked the question: what is a percentage point?) Percentages are used to compare rates which are otherwise difficult to compare. In the case of a 5% pay award, 5 per cent more is implied and it also carries with it connotations of fairness – the same rate for all – despite the effect of a constant percentage increase being to widen absolute differences.

Percentages are often used in the context 'of' something: 50 per cent *of* some quantity and the use of 'of' signals multiplication. Which is more, 17% of £50 or 50% of £17? We are up against a similar split perception as that between arithmetic and algebra. You can know that $2(3 + 4) = 2 \times 3 + 2 \times 4$ either by working them both out and seeing that they give the same number (14), or you can directly know they *must* be equal (through an algebraic perception about properties of the operations). The two percentages given above can be seen to be the same by calculating them both and obtaining the same number of pounds. You can also see that they *must* be the same through an algebraic perception of equivalence because the word 'of' signals multiplication and multiplication is commutative.

Why does the context involving percentages and pounds serve to confuse this? Because there is no direct way of perceiving the sameness *in the context itself*. It is a counterpart property alone. As I mentioned earlier, in many computations, it is common to ignore the units, along with the fact that the numbers are measures, and work mathematically with the numbers alone, only at the end reinterpreting the numerical answer back into the context. One power of abstraction is that it is possible to recognise samenesses that were not readily perceivable in the context itself.

## MEASUREMENT OF THE SOCIAL WORLD

> Everything that exists, exists to some extent, which can therefore be measured.
>
> (Thorndike, 1973, p. 17)

The above claim draws attention to an increasing tendency to quantify the world. Certain quantities, such as length, weight or temperature, seem relatively easy both to conceptualise and to quantify (and the quantification comes after the conceptualisation). Quantification, however, is a growing feature of areas of life where the phenomena purportedly being measured are far more ambiguous or vague, and their definitions, therefore, more contentious. Such an example is given by Richard Noss, who writes:

> A recent example of the extent to which this myth [of mathematics as dehumanised and hard-edged, invoking meaningless problems] is culturally accepted involved a TV interview with a sociology professor who had just given birth to the notion of the QALY – a Quality Adjusted Life Year – which allowed him to judge the relative 'values' of two human lives so that scarce funds could be 'scientifically' allocated to the most deserving cases. The interviewer, seeking perhaps some rationale for the ideas, asked the professor whether this was a helpful way to think about the value of human life, or perhaps 'only a mathematical formula'.
>
> (1988, p. 265)

This century's massive increase in (mainly numerical) data about people can be difficult to grasp. A glance through any newspaper will provide a welter of examples: health statistics, estimates of risks (a 1 in so many chance) and economic reports, to name but three. The information collected and analysed for various ends from the national census provides a further instance. Mary Douglas (1991, p. 6) writes: "Now we are so used to thinking statistically that we hardly notice how much we are besieged by politically serviceable numbers, averages and chances".

A significant shift in what was measured occurred in the late nineteenth century, with the development of modern statistical techniques. Such measures included attempts to quantify people's potential and their educational achievement and brought with them particular problems. For instance, in the use of IQ tests, the act of measuring at first gives an indicator, then later becomes an entity in its own right, thereby *creating* that which it is supposed to be measuring. It thus seems to provide an 'objective' way of comparing or judging individuals.

The measurement of 'intelligence' by IQ apparently made it a trivial process to decide which of two individuals was 'the cleverer'. Yet ever since its introduction, there has been marked wrangling over precisely what is being measured and the purposes to which such measurements were being put (see, for instance, Stephen Gould's (1981) book *The Mismeasure of Man*). Additionally, questions have been raised and concerns expressed about how *stable* the measure is (that is, measuring the same thing should produce the same sort of answer), whether an objective, general measure of intelligence could be captured solely by one number, and how accurately it is possible to measure such a subtle human quality. The entire intellectual diversity of human beings has been collapsed into one number.

But, as the Noss quotation about QALYs implies, the fact that we have produced numbers suggests that they must be the measure of some well-specified thing. I want to suggest that the relation between a quantity and its measure is akin to that between an object and a symbol for it. The number does duty for the thing purportedly measured. And the existence of the symbol (here, the numerical measure) is taken as proof of the existence of the object.

A particularly good example of the complex relation between object and measure is provided by money.[6] The measure (money) has a physical existence of its own and seems much easier to understand in terms of its function than either its purported underlying quantity 'value' or its referent, despite the familiar adage about the importance of 'getting value for money'. What money represents is a complex phenomenon (involving the perilous history of the 'absolute value' of the gold standard) and shares some attributes of the number/numeral distinction that I discussed in Chapter 4. It is also an object itself that can be bought or sold and thus must itself command a price. There is no scope here to go into this fascinating topic, but an excellent account (linking the notions of zero, vanishing points in art, and paper money) can be found in Brian Rotman's (1987) book *Signifying Nothing*.

The context of money problems offered in schools provides the possibility of looking more closely at certain relations between school mathematics and the so-called real world. One example which has relevance for mathematics teaching is the practice of 'shopping', not least because it is a common presumed point of contact between the primary (and increasingly, the secondary) school and the everyday world of the pupils outside school. In school, it is frequently used by teachers as a means of working on number.

In a chapter entitled '2p doesn't buy much these days', Valerie Walkerdine contrasts the learning of children about money at home and at school, and looks in detail at a lesson where the teacher's aim is to practise forming complements in ten, using a 'shopping' game, where small denomination coins are exchanged for goods.

> The problems here do not resemble practical problems either in their content or their methods of solution. In this sense they are 'fake' practical problems and most of the children seem to recognise this. The practical context is a foil for the teaching of certain mathematical relations, so that everything about the task is different from shopping.
>
> (Walkerdine, 1988, pp. 146–7)

She later comments:

> The purpose here is not to practise shopping but to calculate a subtraction. In this sense, the practical format can be misleading and sometimes downright unhelpful. . . . Everything about this task, then, testifies to the disjunction for the children between this task in mathematics and the knowledge of money which they have obtained outside school. The two practices barely overlap. The pedagogy assumes that children learn about money only from the handling of small coins which leads to the real understanding of arithmetic processes, whereas the understanding of money on the part of the children is one in which large sums of money are involved, these sums have important value attached to them and are inserted into crucial domestic economic practices.
>
> (ibid., pp. 147–8)

This section has discussed some contexts in which measurement is embedded and hence what knowledge and patterns of thought are required. I continue to explore the theme of contexts for mathematical thinking in the next chapter by means of looking at the tradition of word problems. But more significant problems for the development of mathematics itself arise from attempts to use mathematics to measure the physical world which surrounds us.

## MEASUREMENT OF THE PHYSICAL WORLD

The height of a pyramid is related to the length of its shadow just as the height of any vertical, measurable object is related to the length of its shadow at the same time of day.

(Plutarch)

One of the historical associations with the development of mathematics has been varied and ingenious attempts to ascertain the scale and scope of the physical world. The very word 'geometry' connects it with measurement of the earth. Mathematics and measurement have also been involved in astronomy, for example, as far back as we have written records. Babylonian tablets record astronomical measurements to quite remarkable accuracy, and it is a residue of their base 60 numeration system that we have 60 minutes[7] in an hour, as well as 360 degrees in a full rotation.

One of the fundamental reasons for symbolising is when something is missing or inaccessible. Under these circumstances, a substitute is employed to stand in place of the missing object. In the seventeenth century, the development of optical instruments such as telescopes and microscopes brought many previously inaccessible phenomena within the range of the perceptual and hence, the measurable. Even before the development of greater optical precision, much physical measurement was indirect. Something else, which *was* directly accessible, was measured and then, by means of a mathematical argument about mathematical objects, an inference was made about what a correct measurement might/should/must be. These proxies or substitutes have a symbolic relation to what they are standing in stead of. But unlike in earlier chapters, the counterparts here are *mathematical* – numbers and geometric figures.

A famous example of indirect measurement is the attempt by Eratosthenes to measure the circumference of the earth. Carl Boyer (1968, pp. 178–9) writes:

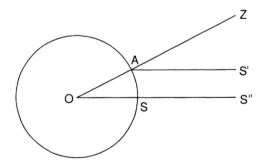

Eratosthenes observed that at noon on the day of the summer solstice the sun shone directly down a deep well at Syene. At the same time at Alexandria, taken to be on the same meridian and 5000 stades north of Syene, the sun was found to cast a shadow indicating that the sun's angular distance from the zenith was one fiftieth of a circle. From the equality of the corresponding angles S'AZ and S"OZ it is clear that the circumference of the Earth must be fifty times the distance between Syene and Alexandria. This results in a perimeter of 250,000 stades, or, since a stade was about a tenth of a mile, of 25,000 miles.

This account indicates how such indirect measurements can become theory laden, usually involving explanations from both mathematics and physics, in order to connect the numerical data the instrument provides to the intended observation or measurement. A more recent instance of this is provided by measuring the distance from the earth to the moon by leaving a circular reflective dish on the moon's surface during one of the moon landings and then bouncing a laser beam off it, timing how long it takes to return. Another pair of even more arcane instances might be direct measuring of ultrasound echo images of foetuses or bubble track pictures from particle accelerators.

## What does it mean to measure?

One of the oldest stories of Greek geometry is of Thales' determination of the height of the pyramids. The philosopher Michel Serres (1982) talks of Thales' 'ruse' in using shadows to compute heights. The measurement was an 'as if' one, made *as if* the shadow were the pyramid itself, and then allowance is made for the fact that the pyramid is not its shadow.[8]

The ruler is applied directly, but to the substitute, the counterpart. But the link between the desired and actual measurements is indirect. The light of the sun transports the inaccessible height to us and delivers it in the form of a shadow. Mathematics, in particular, geometry, provides the detailed nature of the link: in the case of Thales' theorem, the key notion is similarity. This process illustrates the fundamental sense of *applied* mathematics. Whenever that term is used, we should ask ourselves not only: what is being applied to what?, but also both how is it to be applied? and what is the means of application? Serres writes:

> Accessible, inaccessible, what does this mean? Near, distant; tangible, untouchable; possible or impossible transporting. . . . measurement is the essential element of application; but primarily in the sense of touch. Such and such a unit or such and such a ruler is applied to the object to be measured; it is placed on top of the object, it touches it. And this is done as often as is necessary. Immediate or direct measurement is possible or impossible as long as this placing is possible or is not. Hence, the inaccessible is that which I cannot touch,

that toward which I cannot carry the ruler, that of which the unit cannot be applied.

... in the final analysis the path in question [of mathematics, that these ruses take] consists in forsaking the sense of touch for that of sight, measurement by "placing" for measurement by sighting. Here, to theorize is to see, a fact which the Greek language makes clear.[9] Vision is tactile without contact. . . . The inaccessible is at times accessible to vision. . . .

As far as I know, even for accessible objects, vision alone is my guarantee that the ruler has been placed accurately on the thing. To measure is to align; the eye is the best witness of an accurate covering-over. Thales . . . brings the visible to the tangible.

(1982, pp. 85–6)

To summarise Serres' argument, he seems to be saying that even to measure the world accurately, it must after all be measured by eye.

I have quoted extensively from his chapter not just because of his profound observations about measurement, but also because it identifies so clearly the involvement of *sight* in measurement as a way of extending the power of adjacent touch for comparison, an extension that is fundamentally mathematical. This provides yet another instance of my developing theme about the links and contrasts between these two senses in contributing to mathematics.[10]

In conclusion, Serres (*ibid.*, p. 85) also offers the following quotation from Auguste de Comte:

In light of previous experience we must acknowledge the impossibility of determining, by direct measurement, most of the heights and distances we should like to know. It is this general fact which makes the science of mathematics necessary.

Thus, mathematics both embodies and employs indirection, sleight of hand.

## THE 'MEASUREMENT' OF MATHEMATICAL OBJECTS

The foregoing section invokes mathematics in order to enable conceptual measurement of inaccessible quantities. But similar questions can be asked of mathematical objects themselves, as such exact relations need to be called upon in successful measurement of the material world. Mathematical objects are inaccessible in a different sense: they are supernatural. Sight alone is insufficient to measure them: Euclidean figures cast no shadows.

Euclidean geometry also disavows movement: congruence theorems offer examples of criteria for equivalence and comparison, that apparently do not require figures to be moved, let alone be 'superimposed'. (This is just as well, as Einsteinian relativity theory tells us that if Euclidean lines were material, then movement would affect their length!) It is possible to see some Book I theorems from Euclid's *Elements* as effectively performing this function: one tells how to copy an angle somewhere else, whilst certain postulates and common notions assert general constructibility rights: for instance, 'to draw a circle with any centre and any radius'.

Mathematics has often been developed as 'thought measurement'. Archimedes' famous treatise *On the Measurement of the Circle* (which among other things derives $^{22}/_7$ as an approximation to $\pi$, but also offers $^{223}/_{71}$ as a better one) contains the word 'measurement' in the title, but its use is metaphoric – in the sense that there is no measurement of physical objects with instruments. But there is measurement in the sense that numbers have been systematically *applied* to geometrical entities. There is also comparison, of one geometric figure with another. From this perspective, much of mathematics can be seen as involving measurement.

This confusion, in particular of the involvement of measuring instruments in geometry, continues. Jeremy Gray (1988, p. 16) writes as follows about Descartes' use of the phrase that 'curves should admit of exact and precise measurement'.

> Descartes' instrument is really one that it is better to hold in the mind than in one's hands – but that, in a way, is Descartes' point. It is a thought-device for showing that curves more complicated than the circle can nevertheless be considered just as accurate, for the purposes of geometric construction, as ruler and compasses. This was not a prospectus for precision scientific instrumentation business, but a philosophical investigation into the foundations of geometric truth.

And John Aubrey, in his famous anecdotal collection *Brief Lives*, penned a thumbnail sketch of Descartes, an approximate contemporary of his.

> He was so eminently learned that all learned men made visits to him, and many of them would desire him to shew them his Instruments (in those dayes mathematicall learning lay much in the knowledge of Instruments, and as Sir Henry Savile sayd, in doeing of tricks) he would drawe out a little Drawer under his Table, and shew them a pair of Compasses with one of the Legges broken; and then, for his Ruler he used a sheet of paper folded double.
>
> (in Fauvel and Gray, 1987, p. 308)

We are back in the world of appearances and the symbolic nature of geometric diagrams. Although much of the language of mathematics (particularly geometry) suggests that it is a practical subject to do with measurement, there are some important differences. One of the difficulties in school mathematics education is offering a sense of the exactness of certain (usually geometric) relations among various figures or parts of a figure.

For instance, in the case of the angle sum of any triangle, there are two problems. The first is recognising the invariance: the fact that the angle sum of any two triangles is always the same. The second is arriving at the numerical value of the invariant: 180°, two right angles, half a circle, $\pi$ radians. Is angle summation direct geometric 'addition' of geometric objects, or measurement of the angles and then addition of the numbers?

It is not possible to come to the triangle sum theorem by direct measurement, that is using counterpart drawings. (See Balacheff, 1991, for an account of classroom research based on this mathematical result.) Much school work is done in terms of tearing paper triangles and 'rearranging' the angles. Yet the problems of 'exactness' and the fact that triangles are not made of paper remain. If protractors are used, how often in practice do the angles of a triangle add up to the required sum? At best, it may be possible to come to the plausiblity of the desired conjecture, though a more plausible one might be that the sums do differ, but not by much.

## Comparing world-views

One of the more interesting watersheds in Western history of mathematics has been moving from what might be called the geometric to the arithmetic-algebraic world-view. The latter involves assigning numbers to everything (thereby identifying the measure with the object),[11] and seeing letter-names as inherently numerical, rather than 'merely' as a name for the quantity itself. By contrast, much Euclidean geometry involves operating with lengths or areas as geometric objects in their own right.

For instance, Pythagoras' theorem tells us how to add two areas, non-numerically, and it plays a key role in a sequence of results in the finite content theory of plane polygonal regions. The difference between the phrases 'the square *on* the hypotenuse' and 'the square *of* the hypotenuse' reflects the above distinction, the former viewing the hypotenuse as a line segment and the latter as a number.

There is frequently a proposition lying concealed behind any definition, verifying that the definition does indeed do what is wanted (see Pimm, 1993b). Euclid Book IX, definition 9, for instance, asserts: "Equal solid figures are those contained by similar planes equal in magnitude and multitude". From its use, the required sense of *equal* is 'same volume'. For us, 'same volume' is a numerical equivalence not worthy of mention, in part because the numerical measure *is* the definition of volume. I have long been worried by the *purpose* of Euclid's *Elements* common notion 4: "All right angles are equal to one another". It makes no sense as a requirement when a right angle is one that is 90°. Once again, when starting with

151

the material world and an apparently straightforward procedure of measurement, we have ended up in deep mathematical and philosophical waters.

# 8

# LIVING IN THE MATERIAL WORLD: SYMBOLS IN CONTEXTS

It is of democratic importance, to the individual as well as to society at large, that any citizen is provided with instruments for understanding the role of mathematics [in society]. Anyone not in possession of such instruments become [a] 'victim' of social processes in which mathematics is a component. So, the purpose of mathematical education should be to enable students to realise, understand, judge, utilize and also to perform the application of mathematics in society, in particular in situations which are of significance to their private, social and professional life.

(Niss, 1983, p. 248)

This chapter predominantly looks critically at the nature of many problems offered as a central part of school mathematics, some of the simpler problems to which mathematics is apparently applicable *outside* of the sometimes hermetic world of pure mathematics itself. Mathematical problems invoking such human contexts have a number of interesting features and reflect long traditions as well as offering a focus for some recent changes in views about what a mathematics education is for.

A long tradition exists among textbook writers and the problems they offer for the study of mathematics. It is possible to trace the lineage of many problems back to the Middle Ages and even further. Elements include both apparently realistic and completely unrealistic settings, though the numbers seem chosen on many occasions with other ends in mind, whether to illustrate some feature of note in an algorithm, or to mask some complexity.

The notion of usefulness was cited in the opening chapter as one common core justification[1] both for teaching mathematics at all, as well as for the pre-eminent position it often holds within the school curriculum. Much, too, has been written in the past fifteen years on the increasing use of mathematics qualifications as a 'critical filter' for many jobs in our society, despite evidence that little of a content nature is actually required by many such positions.[2]

Common questions for mathematics education include: what relationship does mathematics have with the material world? More recently, one question has been given particular sharpness: how is mathematics used in our society and should discussion and exploration of this process itself be part of what is to be taught under the heading of school mathematics?

Traditionally, there has been little in the training of mathematics teachers to encourage them to be alive to the social uses of mathematics (especially statistics) within the traditional applied mathematics of the upper secondary school (physics or economics, for example, let alone in social arenas). Teachers of mathematics have not been expected to explore and contend with broad moral or philosophical questions as part of their job. A Danish mathematics educator, Ole Skovsmose, expresses this view quite succinctly:

> It is necessary to increase the interaction between ME [mathematical education] and CE [critical education], if ME is not to degenerate into one of the most important ways of socializing students (to be understood as students or pupils) into the technological society and at the same time destroying the possibilities of developing a critical attitude towards precisely this technological society.
>
> (Skovsmose, 1985, p. 338)

For instance, when grappling with a problem, there are many ways in which problem solvers can represent the information at their disposal for their own understanding. A vast amount of information is conveyed visually in our society. Graphical or other representations can be used to distort and thereby to manipulate other people (the most common sense of the word 'manipulate' – see Chapter 10), so any such interpretation must attempt to take account of possible intentions which underlie the making and offering of the graphs, diagrams or tables. When confronting other people's representations, therefore, we have to interpret them, including their purposes. Realising that the graph is not the reality (just as the map is not the country), for instance, can allow pupils to get between the representation and what it purports to represent.

Both these aspects of representation could be reflected in the school mathematics curriculum. Pupils require opportunities both to interpret complex representations and to work in rich contexts where they themselves can engage in purposeful representation. Learning to read, and read behind, other people's presentations can be enhanced by presenting their own data as well. Both elements are necessary in order for them to develop a mature sense of what various forms of representation can do for them and how various purposes relate to and help determine the form.

Some argue against a divisive distinction between two types of mathematics, of higher and lower status, as historically embodied perhaps in the association of Euclid with grammar schools and 'commercial arithmetic' with former secondary modern schools. Others, in different contexts, have feared for the exclusion of certain groups (ethnic minorities, girls) from the knowledge of the 'high culture' (be it Shakespeare or Euclid) which gives access to power. It was certainly common earlier this century for there to be two versions of 'Arithmetics', one for boys and one for girls, each with problems reflecting their presumed experience and interests.

I have indicated the possibility of failing to recognise assumptions behind decisions or claims based on numerical data. It is possible to go further and deliberately 'massage' statistics to promote a particular vested interest. Niss and Skovsmose both write of the importance of developing in their pupils a critical awareness of these sorts of issues. This can meet with some initial resistance, however. Lesley Lee writes of her attempts to interest her students in questioning data and surveys that had been carried out, thereby challenging some of the presuppositions about the 'objectivity' of statistics.

> There were times though when students resisted my methods. A particularly painful memory occurred at about mid-term in one of my college statistics courses when, after some discussion of the term's project [which was] group or individual criticism of a major statistical study of their choice, [and] answering questions such as 'Who paid for it?', 'In whose interests are the results?', 'What questions were left out?', two students indicated their rejection of the project. In a discussion with them after class, they said they had taken the course 'to learn statistics, not to criticise them'. They viewed any kind of criticism as a degenerate activity, malicious, and a sign of depression in the critic.
>
> (Lee, 1990, p. 55)

There remains a sharpening debate about working for a balance between examination of mathematical content and context and purpose of use. In considering some of the materials available, Lee also writes about Frankenstein's book *Radical Mathematics*:

> It became increasingly unclear as to whether her aim was to use mathematics to develop the ability for critical political analysis or to tap the political involvement of students in order to teach them some mathematics. Put another way, is the principal objective the teaching of mathematics or fostering political involvement?
>
> (*ibid.*, p. 55)

Ole Skovsmose has gone so far as to talk of society being 'formatted' (as with a computer disk) by mathematics, and to conclude that the primary role of mathematics education in a democracy should be to alert and educate pupils to its effects. However, while I agree with Niss's and

Skovsmose's contentions that being in a position to examine the role that mathematics plays in society is one important reason for teaching it, and while I support the development of more critical attitudes as *one* goal (of any school subject), surely the sole or even most important purpose of mathematics education for our society cannot be to criticise it. My prime purpose is providing thoughtful access to the ways of seeing which mathematics affords, while not being blind either to the costs involved or to presumptions about it offering the right or best such ways.

It is nonetheless true that there is increasingly widespread criticism and disagreement on the purposes and goals of mathematics education for school pupils, some focused under headings such as 'education for democracy' and 'anti-racist mathematics', but also under 'ethnomathematics'. Elsewhere, my colleague Eric Love and I have written concerning:

> a much more radical challenge to received thinking about mathematics that has been gathering strength over the last decade which comes from those who might be described as the 'ethnomathematicians' – although they would reject any such title. Their concern is that the mathematics implicit in everyday practices at work or leisure has been systematically denied while 'official' mathematics as taught in schools and in higher education is elevated as the only true form of mathematics. Moreover, a major effect of school mathematics is to disable people from operating in the informal and semi-formal world of ethnomathematics – both by legitimizing school mathematics as the only real mathematics and, as a result of the way in which it is taught, by undermining the confidence of a large part of the population in their ability to function mathematically. For this reason, those adopting this standpoint challenge the right of mathematicians to decide what counts as mathematics, and would like their view to be no longer especially privileged.
>
> One concern that underlies the arguments of the ethnomathematical critique, but which is shared more widely, is that not knowing mathematics leaves people at the mercy of those who do understand. Hence, one movement is to help empower people for the world they live in. Because our society describes itself as a democracy, the issues of democratic competence and what part mathematics and its teaching might play in that come to the fore. What at first sight might seem a preoccupation of a fringe group can very easily become matters for wide debate when there is an explicit national curriculum and anxiety about the use of technology. In other countries, for example Australia or Denmark, the official curricula are attempting to address such notions (Skovsmose, 1990); they are likely to become more prominent in this country.
>
> (Pimm and Love, 1991, p. vii)

Much of the direction of the work in ethnomathematics has been arguing to extend the bounds of recognition of classical mathematical topics and sources to include the skilled work which goes into traditional craft activities,[3] as well as wider, cultural embodiments of patterned thought. However, Chevallard (1990) offers a trenchant and penetrating analysis of some of the difficulties inherent in the notion of 'culture' in mathematics education, and in particular his distinction between 'ethnomathematics' and 'protomathematics', the latter offering fertile sources for mathematisation without itself *being* mathematics.

Sociologist Harold Garfinkel (1968) has provided an illuminating account of the reasons why he coined the term 'ethnomethodology'. His initial exploration in 1945 was of the function of being a juror, by means of the question 'what makes them jurors?' He tells how he was going through files in the Yale library looking for a term to describe the methodological concerns and preoccupations of these people with 'being jurors'. He found many tags like 'ethnobotany', 'ethnophysiology', and 'ethnophysics'.

> 'Ethno' seemed to refer, somehow or other, to the availability to a member of common-sense knowledge of his society as common-sense knowledge of the 'whatever'. If it were 'ethnobotany', then it had to do somehow or other with his knowledge of and his grasp of what were for members adequate methods for dealing with botanical matters.
>
> (*ibid.*, p. 7)

Garfinkel goes on to detail the ways in which ethnomethodology has become a shibboleth and comments: "I think the term [ethnomethodology] may, in fact, be a mistake".

My concern with some uses of the label 'ethnomathematics' is not the studies themselves of particular cultural practices, but the absence of any sense that the members of the particular culture believe they are doing mathematics or are concerned with mathematics when working on, for instance, sand drawings or making baskets. The knowledge they have may just as well be said to be about the activity itself (and hence is better seen as 'protomathematical'). It returns us to some of the questions about 'illustrative' manipulatives from Chapter 2.

There are serious difficulties in ascertaining when someone, who appears to be engaged in other activities, is 'actually' doing mathematics. Gerdes (1988, pp. 140–1) provocatively claims:

> The artisan, who imitates a known production technique, is, generally, not doing mathematics. But the artisan(s) who discovered the technique, *did* mathematics, was/were thinking mathematically. When pupils are stimulated to *reinvent* such a production technique, they are doing and learning mathematics.

This seems to me to be an over-extension of what is to count as doing mathematics, one which sees mathematics as consonant with traditional everyday activities rather than somewhat separate and distinct. In part, I think this arises due to the *over*valuation of mathematics as a cultural force and therefore reflects an increasing need to find broader and more inclusive sources. But it does highlight the problematic boundary between mathematical and other forms of thinking – something I return to at the end of this chapter.

## 'REAL-WORLD' PROBLEMS

Below are a couple of mathematical problems. What in the world might these problems be about?

> It takes three men six hours to dig a ditch. How long does it take two men to dig the same ditch?
>
> (Traditional)

> Suppose a scribe says to thee, Four overseers have drawn 100 great quadruple hekat of grain, their gangs consisting, respectively, of 12, 8, 6 and 4 men. How much does each overseer receive?
>
> (Problem 68, *Rhind Mathematical Papyrus*)

The syntax and style of writing make them stand out as arithmetic problem texts and are unlikely to be mistaken for anything else. Ancient texts are immediately recognisable today. Pupils' school experience teaches them that these problems are supposed to be self-contained, that all the information necessary for dealing with them is present. There is no need to go elsewhere to search for an answer. Where do they learn how to abstract the 'irrelevant aspects' of the problem, and how to read a sum *into* the text, rather than extract one *from* it?

One story which is told by mathematics educators is that embedding mathematics in familiar contexts makes it easier. Much work has recently been done on 'thinking in context' or 'situated cognition'. Rather than looking for a pupil's 'general ability to think', researchers have examined what children can do in certain situations and not in others, despite the fact that from a mathematical perspective, the tasks in these different situations may be structurally identical.

Jean Lave (1988) has studied learning about mathematics in school and compared it with ways of problem solving which occur as part of cultural activities and practices beyond the school gates. In particular, she has compared arithmetical problem solving in and near supermarkets with similar problem solving in school or other learning settings. Performance in context is frequently greater than out of context.

The widespread experience of teachers is that when children tackle textbook word problems, most of the time is spent in getting to grips with the intended mathematisation of the problem and discarding the 'container' of verbiage. This may be due, in part, to a difference in intention.

According to one view, children are offered a familiar, everyday context in which they can operate intuitively and hence engage with a particular manifestation of a mathematical idea. If the imagery provided by the context will help, then it can offer problem solvers a powerful way of thinking themselves into the relations required by the question – enabling them to draw on their own knowledge and experience.

In the second view, the essential mathematics is implicit and needs to be identified in order to solve the problem. Here, the task is one of developing modelling skills, in order to solve the actual problem which itself is the important focus. Self-styled 'real' problem solving provides one extreme instance (see Open University, 1989). Unfortunately, there is frequently a confusion between these two intentions, leaving obscure the rationale for why a particular problem has been offered.

When pupils do not recognise the context, they may simply say: 'I don't know about this', even though it could be possible to work out what the context is about and to follow cues. Christine Keitel provides a converse classroom anecdote where the solver's experience of the actual setting interfered with the intended solution to the 'mathematical' problem.

> The second case I met in an English comprehensive school, but it could have happened anywhere in Germany or France as well. It was a lesson under the heading of 'ratio and proportion' and the teacher told me that she wanted to approach the mathematical concepts in a practical way. So she offered the following question: 'Somebody is going to have his room painted. From the painter's samples he chooses an orange colour which is composed of two tins of red paint and one-and-a-half tins of yellow paint per square meter. The walls of his room measure 48 square meters altogether. How many tins of red and yellow are needed to give the room the same orange as on the sample?' The problem seemed quite clear and pupils started to calculate using proportional relationships. But there was one boy who said: 'My father is a painter and so I know that, if we just do it by calculating, the colour of the room will not look like the sample. We cannot calculate as we did, it is a wrong method!' In my imagination I foresaw a fascinating discussion starting about the use of simplified mathematical models in social practice and their limited value in more complex problems (here the intensifying effect of the reflection of light), but the teacher answered: 'Sorry, my dear, we are doing ratio and proportion'.
>
> (Keitel, 1989, p. 7)

There seems to be more to this anecdote than a missed opportunity. It concerns the fact that the teacher's perspective on the problem and that of her pupil are quite different. The teacher is attending to the mathematics, ratio and proportion, and this determines what she 'sees' in the setting. Indeed, the setting has been chosen precisely because she feels it embodies what she would like her pupils to work on. From this particular pupil's perspective, he sees the problem to be about tins of paint and making walls the same colour as the sample. His experience is brought into play in order to solve the problem as stated. He 'sees' something quite different in the problem.

The possibility of being diverted from the mathematical structure of the problem and engaging with the narrative content of these arithmetical situations has been beautifully captured by novelist Philip Roth in this description of the problems a father used to pose his child.

> His idea of amusing me was to teach me to solve the sort of arithmetical puzzles at which he himself was a whiz. '"Marking Down,"' he would say, not unlike a recitation student announcing the title of a poem. 'A clothing dealer, trying to dispose of an overcoat cut in last year's style, marked it down from its original price of thirty dollars to twenty-four. Failing to make a sale, he reduced the price still further to nineteen dollars and twenty cents. Again he found no takers, so he tried another price reduction and this time sold it.' Here he would pause; if I wished I might ask him to repeat any or all of the details. If not, he proceeded. 'All right, Nathan; what was the selling price, if the last markdown was consistent with the others?' Or: '"Making a chain." A lumberjack has six sections of chain, each consisting of four links. If the cost of cutting open a link-' and so on. The next day, while my mother whistled Gershwin and laundered my father's shirts, I would daydream in my bed about the clothing dealer and the lumberjack. To whom had the haberdasher finally sold the overcoat? Did the man who bought it realize it was cut in last year's style? If he wore it to a restaurant, would people laugh? And what did 'last year's style' look like anyway? 'Again he found no takers,' I would say aloud, finding much to feel melancholy about in that idea. I still remember how charged for me was that word 'takers'. Could it have been the lumberjack with the six sections of chain who, in his rustic innocence, had bought the overcoat cut in last year's style? And why suddenly did he need an overcoat? Invited to a fancy ball? By whom? . . . my father . . . was disheartened to find me intrigued by fantastic and irrelevant details of geography and personality and intention instead of the simple beauty of the arithmetical solution. He did not think that was intelligent of me, and he was right.
>
> (Roth, 1985, pp. 36–7)

This ability to throw away the 'outer' container of 'irrelevant' information in what the teacher perceives as an essentially arithmetic task is a skill which teachers attempt to teach in schools. Yet the contexts in which these problems are embedded do also carry considerable social implications for the perceived uses and usefulness of mathematics. Parables are important and, at their best, certain mathematical problems can act as parables, providing contextual wisdom and understanding of important mathematical ideas and processes. But there is a danger with convincing parables – the problem setter may perceive the essence of a problem as proportional thinking, while the solver sees a problem about digging ditches.

There is also at issue the social contract established in mathematics classrooms. Being good at mathematics is frequently perceived in terms of being fast at answering questions, the more done the better. One consequence of this is the less time spent thinking about or engaging with any particular question, the better, which can result in a devaluing of the questions and the embedded situations themselves.

## Old problems never die

I found a stone, (but) did not weigh it; (after) I subtracted one-seventh, added one-eleventh, (and) subtracted one-thir[teenth], I weighed (it): 1 *ma-na*. What was the origin(al weight) of the stone? [The original weight] of the stone was 1 *ma-na*, 9½ *gin* (and) 2½ *se*.

This text comes from a Babylonian stone tablet *circa* 1700 BC, along with other such problems and answers, none indicating how the answers were reached, and all involving a stone of 1 *ma-na* when weighed. (*Ma-na, gin* and *se* make up a system of weights and measures, and we can deduce their relative values from the arithmetic of such problems.)

It is clearly *not* a practical problem about the weight of an unidentified stone – if it could be weighed half-way through the problem, it would have been better to weigh it at the outset. And anyway, the tablet gives the weight at the end. For at least four thousand years, many problems have been posed *as if* they were about something practical and justified as providing practice in working on the difficult question of how mathematics relates to the everyday material and social worlds. However, a more likely intention seems often to be to help students to recognise certain standard problem types and apply standard algorithms.

One of the common characteristics of collections of mathematical problems dating from as far back as 2000 BC has been the use of 'familiar', 'everyday', and 'real-world' settings, situations and contexts in their exposition. This common feature allows the confusion to continue, namely whether the reason for learning mathematics is presented in terms of being able to solve these particular problems (or problems *such as* these) or whether such problems are 'merely' a way of dressing up, disguising the mathematics itself in order to appeal more to the learner's presumed interest. The former allows for the pupil to reject mathematics on grounds of lack of interest in such problems, while the latter invites the complaint about teachers not coming clean about what the task actually is.

In his book somewhat misleadingly entitled *Capitalism and Arithmetic*, Frank Swetz (1987) provides us with access to a translation and commentary of the first printed arithmetic book (known as the *Treviso Arithmetic*) which includes such unlikely questions as: "If 1000 pounds and 1/5 of cinnamon are worth 130 ducats and 1/4, what are 14616 pounds, 9 ounces, 5 sazi and 1/3 worth?" The author of the *Treviso* holds out the lure of 'gratifying usefulness' for attentive students (how attempts at 'motivation' remain constant over time).

Do these 'practical' (i.e. commercial) problems offer potential source material for a form of social archaeology? Can we find out about historical conditions or get a feel for life at the time through the problems in arithmetic texts, getting the goods on the cost of renting a mediaeval house in Sienna, or the usurious level of interest rates then prevalent, or even learning that one single merchant imported all these spices for the rich of Europe? What image of the concerns and preoccupations of our society would present-day textbook problems give?

One tension still with us is between 'nice numbers' and 'realistic prices': in other words, between numbers chosen for mathematical reasons and numbers that happen to be current, and therefore subject to both the complexities and the simplicities of actual commerce. With the availability of calculators today, there is a move towards the use of 'real' data, as if there were any inherent mathematical value in topical actuality. This would only be the case if the particular situation offered were where attention was to be placed – which is not common. (On occasion, this enthusiasm can be reminiscent of the worst Soviet demands for realist 'fiction' which led to wonderful, fantastic novels opening with ironic claims that 'nonetheless this really happened'.)

What are credible purposes in offering such questions? Some possibilities include the following.

- Perceiving underlying models (there are standard questions about common situations of this type – this is a 'leaky bath' type of question, or I can think about it in terms of balls in urns). This requires pupils to see through a particular context, and possibly therefore strip some of it away.
- Practising algorithmic skills in interesting settings.
- Being able to apply mathematical skills in a wide range of contexts.
- Developing growing awareness for the wide applicability of mathematical ideas.
- Exploring mathematically aspects of humanly important contexts.

How plausible and relatively important are these? A key point is that most of these do not just come about by having pupils do lots of problems. The most *mathematically* important of these intents may be in terms of providing generic arguments and situations to think about that when seen in a particular way embody a mathematical principle or process. (The label 'telegraph poles and spaces' serves me as a reminder that I need to count one on some occasions and the other on others – and that the answers differ!) Whether more detailed and focused study of a few such embodiments will serve this purpose better than doing many questions, routinely and relatively unthinkingly, is a different matter.

Despite these observations, I argue in the next section that it nevertheless does matter what contexts are offered, even in traditional-style questions, not for technical mathematical reasons, but for the social education of children as well as for the attitudes formed about the uses and abuses of mathematics in our society. The central question to be looked at further is that of the purpose(s) – for both teaching and learning – for such contextualised questions.

### Social concerns

So perception is stricken by algebra, for algebra sees only what is right under its eyes; memory is confounded, since when the second sign is found algebra pays no further attention to the first; imagination goes blind because algebra has no need of images; understanding is destroyed because algebra professes to divine. The result is that young men who have devoted much time to algebra find themselves later, to their great dismay and regret, less apt in the affairs of civil life.

(Vico, given in Fisch and Bergin, 1944, p. 125)

Do problem settings merely reflect the passing interests of the textbook author? Below are some problems from nineteenth-century, North American arithmetic texts which offer varying 'realities'. Despite the apparently realistic settings, no one could actually want or need to know the answers. It appears more to be about arithmetic computation through ostensibly 'familiar' settings, providing a veneer of realism: yet recall my discussion of the film *Life and Nothing But* in Chapter 5.

An army loses 12,000 men in battle, 1/6 of the remainder in a forced march and then has 60,000 men left. Of how many men did it first consist?

(*Treatise on Arithmetic*, 1880)

There were 7 farmers, 3 of whom drank rum and whisky, and became miserable; the rest drank water and were healthy and happy. How many drank water?

(Emerson's *The North American Arithmetic*, first part, 1838)

163

A human body, if baked until all the moisture is evaporated, is reduced in weight as 1 to 10; a body that weighs 100 pounds living, will weigh how much when dry?

(Franklin *Arithmetic*, 1832, cited in Freeman, 1960, p. 52)

A gentleman left his sons 3600 dollars, his daughters 1375 dollars, his grand-children 570 dollars, the American Bible Society 4600 dollars, the Orphan Asylum 500 dollars: what was the amount of his estate?

(William Slocomb's *The American Calculator*, 1831,
cited in Bidwell and Clason, 1970, p. 12)

If one Confederate soldier kills 90 Yankees, how many can 10 Confederate soldiers kill?

(Cited in Elson, 1964, p. 329)

Strong features of society come to mind from the fact that questions such as these were offered to pupils to learn about the 'application' of mathematics to the material world. What messages do they offer about connections between mathematical ideas and human values, and judgements about what is worth knowing? Jenny Maxwell, in an article called 'Hidden messages', juxtaposes examples of such material-world 'containers' for arithmetic problems from different countries and cultures, in an attempt to draw attention to some of the political and social values implicit in them.

A Freedom Fighter fires a bullet to an enemy group consisting of twelve soldiers and three civilians all equally exposed to the bullet. Assuming one person is hit by the bullet, find the probability that the person is (a) a soldier, and (b) a civilian. (Tanzania)

Once upon a time a ship was caught in a storm. In order to save it and its crew the captain decided that half the passengers would have to be thrown overboard. There were fifteen Christians and fifteen Turks aboard the ship and the Captain was a Christian. He announced that he would count the passengers and that every ninth one would be thrown overboard. How could the passengers be placed in a circle so that all the Turks would be thrown overboard and all the Christians saved? (USA)

(Maxwell, 1985, p. 18)

It is hard to see what is going on in offering these settings to pupils, other than a simple, ugly reinforcement of some locally convenient valuations extraneous to the subject matter at hand. One reason for my having chosen examples of problems distant in time or space is that such peculiarities, emphases and choices can be far more visible. In this way, we can hope to 'make strange' the familiar collections of problems that inhabit our textbooks at whatever level, and hence see their comparable characteristics.[4]

However, it is worth remarking on the similarity between classical word problems about digging ditches, paying wages, inheritances, filling baths, and so on, and nursery rhymes and fairy tales. In both, there is the problem of the apparent unreality of the situation; in both, there is an adult sense that these are not tales to be taken at face value. For both, they are analysed in terms of their 'structure', although more is enshrined in them than just their structure. Nonetheless, in mathematical word problems, the structure is customarily more important *pedagogically* than the context. It is worth remembering that *all* word problems, whether from Egyptian papyri or mediaeval Italian manuscripts, are devised to be teaching instruments. And that such teaching is seldom directly about the material world we inhabit. The questions reflect other intents.

This may be one reason for resisting attempts to make 'word problems' more realistic (both in terms of settings and answers) – provided that the unreality is noticed and remarked upon from time to time – perhaps by being joked about and the opportunity for spoof questions invented which exaggerate these features even more as a way of drawing attention to them.

### Psychic concerns: thinking about the unthinkable

There is one universal functioning without which nothing is noticed. This is the *stressing* and *ignoring* process.

Without stressing and ignoring, we can not see anything. We could not operate at all. And what is stressing and ignoring if not abstraction? We come with this power and use it all the time. I know that the pitch of my brother and the pitch of my father differ but I ignore the difference so as to comprehend that the words of one are comparable to the words of the other. I ignore that it is only the eye of my mother that I can see when she comes close to my cheek and kisses me. If I did not, the eye quite likely would frighten me. But I ignore this, and I stress the smell of the person. From this I know it is my mother. That is, I can shift my attention to another attribute that also belongs to her. If I did not do that I would not know that it was my mother that kissed me. To stress and ignore *is* the power of abstraction that we as children use all the time, spontaneously and not on demand ... And teachers insist that we *teach* abstraction to children through mathematics at the age of twelve!

(Gattegno, 1970, pp. 11–12)

It is all very well to encourage the skill of ignoring the overt content of many problems, but there will be times for all of us when we are asked to think about situations which excite or disturb us. An instance of an educational invitation where the context seemed too insistent to repress comfortably concerned a videotape for the teaching of mechanics, one

165

section of which dealt with the topic of impacts. The first sequence of images showed billiard balls moving toward and colliding with one another. The second was a high-speed car crash in slow motion that was repeated over and over again. Where was the invitation for the viewers to place their attention?

A second example is provided by Richard Noss, who described visiting a school where the class referred to the problem below as 'The Falklands Question' (though world events have transpired to render this an out-of-date naming). It comes from an English national examination in mathematics for academic pupils.

> A pilot flying an aeroplane in a straight line at a constant speed of 196m/s and at a constant height of 2000m, drops a bomb on a stationary ship in the vertical plane through the line of flight of the aeroplane. Assuming that the bomb falls freely under gravity, calculate (a) the time which elapses after release before the bomb hits the ship, (b) the horizontal distance between the aeroplane and the ship at the time of release of the bomb, and (c) the speed of the bomb just before it hits the ship. (15 marks)
>
> (Noss, 1985, p. 38)

This is surely not a 'practical' problem either. Even in the event of any pupil being about to bomb a ship, it is doubtful whether having worked on this question would assist them. The filters necessary to render the problem mathematically tractable remove the most salient features of the actual situation (the excitement and fear from the fact of trying to destroy human beings and conversely, a non-stationary boat with a non-constant speed trying to avoid destruction, and so on).

What are my options as a pupil, if I have been educated to use my personal imagery to engage with the contextual elements of a problem I have been faced with? If I refuse, out of a sense of preservation of mental self, to think about that situation mathematically, I lose fifteen marks in an important examination. However, does that imply that teachers and examiners should only offer anodyne, non-controversial applications and contexts which will not disturb the sensibilities of any members of the class?[5] What, for instance, of gambling, playing cards and throwing dice which can be an anathema to some members of particular cultural groups?

Part of the teacher's authority resides in the power to direct attention, to decide and rule on what is 'relevant' to the matter in hand. Yet, there can be some unfortunate (and possibly unintended) results of this. Recall the quotation from Keitel given above: "Sorry, my dear, we are doing ratio and proportion". This can be read quite clearly as a demonstration of power.

One important aspect of working mathematically involves repressing meaning and stressing only the symbolic, and this ability may be one casualty of attempting to 'sidestep' algebra. From working successfully on word problems, you can learn how to de-emphasise particular, personal meaning, as well as take part in the public repression of particular meanings. It can result in symbolic knowings (e.g. how to add fractions) and 'just' ('only') working with the symbols, both of which are potentially powerful and enabling. But they also have their price.

In mathematics, it can be efficient for the pupil to understand just enough initially to know what to do. If I have faith in my teacher, I may be willing to submit to him or her, trusting to pattern, trusting to order (to account for why it is, for instance, that $-1 \times -1 = 1$). Yet precisely those skills of becoming a successful mathematician may well disempower me from being an insightful observer and critic of political aspects of situations. There is an important sense in which political and mathematical awarenesses can prove antithetical to one another, something which may prove damaging to the aims of those who wish to offer mathematics for political enlightenment.

In work in mathematics, meanings always get attached, but some also end up hidden or suppressed. There is always the question of cost.

## THINKING RATIONALLY AND MATHEMATICS

My final focus here is mathematicians' seemingly imperialist claims in the area of thinking in general. Recent writing, for example on problem solving, has reflected ill-defined boundaries between mathematical thinking processes and thinking processes in general. It is common for such writers to claim many general thinking processes for their own, a territorial grab that at times beggars the imagination. It is also common to see rationality referred to as objectified, with rules and procedures of its own – despite current discussions with regard to *whose* rationality, discourse, rules and procedures (e.g. Belenky *et al.*'s, *Women's Ways of Knowing* or Gilligan's *In a Different Voice*).

Richard Noss (1994, p. 5) has also written:

> It [the general superiority of mathematical proof over everyday justification] stems from the wider view that mathematical thinking is superior to practical thinking, a view deeply embedded in Western culture; it forms part of the ideology of what it means to think abstractly, perhaps even what it means to think.

Mathematical thinking is precisely that: ways of thinking developed to work on mathematical forms and entities. To see it as ubiquitous, infallible or necessarily better than other forms of reasoning for particular tasks is to fail to make important distinctions. To take an example: probability is not part of the material world. It is not observable. It is about the general, rather than any particular; about the possible rather than the actual. It is about group phenomena. Everything that happens in the material world happens with 100 per cent probability every time. And, as an individual, I am often not interested in *average* expected gain. I am interested in the actual outcome when I carry out a specific action – and probability has almost nothing to say to me about that singular occurrence that has never happened before nor can again.

Consider the following situation. I have to decide whether or not to inoculate my child against whooping cough. I am told that the statistics about the vaccine causing brain damage are 1 in so many. I am also told that the statistics on child deaths from whooping cough are 1 in some other many. What do I do? Defer judgement to calculation?

My decision cannot be just to compare the two rates, for that would be to compare unlike things. My vaccination decision is *now* – and at the end of it I will either have a brain-damaged child or I won't. The statistics on death from whooping cough only refer to a future *possibility* – once my child catches whooping cough. So I am trying to compare an about-to-be-actual present state with a possible future state.

But these apparent probabilistic 'facts' fail to make important distinctions – the rates are not uniform geographically, nor across social class, to name but two. I can continue to make distinctions, until I get down to the actual circumstances of our life, even the genetic make-up of my child. Because that is what I am interested in – not average rates and likelihoods.

I mentioned earlier that the human price for thinking mathematically about certain situations may be too high. I also mentioned Weizenbaum's concern about the disallowing of human judgement and the acceptance of the results of computer-implemented mathematical models. Mathematics may also feed unhelpful desires and expectations in ourselves, unless the distinctions among awarenesses are clearly maintained.

The vision of earth from space confirms the highly finite and interrelated aspect of our home. Certain ways of thinking that mathematics encourages, indeed at times requires, cut across this. One such 'fantasy' that our mathematical imaginations support is that we can go on for ever without getting tired, that an operation once carried out can be repeated (in the imagination) as many times as we wish. Valerie Walkerdine has written powerfully in this area, most notably in her book *The Mastery of Reason* (1988).

I believe mathematics actually plays a far smaller and less significant part in rational thinking about the material world around us than many mathematics educators and others would have us believe. The complex, troubled relation between the actual and the possible, between physical reality and human imagination, mirrors the uneasy links between the material world and mathematics.

In conclusion, in a piece on perception, Aldous Huxley quotes Blake – and I think in what follows that 'Angels' could easily be replaced at times by 'mathematicians':

"I have always found", Blake wrote rather bitterly, "that Angels have the vanity to speak of themselves as the only wise. This they do with a confident insolence sprouting from systematic reasoning."

Huxley then goes on to acknowledge that:

Systematic reasoning is something we could not, as a species or as individuals, possibly do without. But neither, if we are to remain sane, can we possibly do without direct perception, the more unsystematic the better, of the inner and outer worlds into which we have been born.

(Huxley, 1956, p. 77)

Mathematics can be at least partially characterised by its particular use of and emphasis on symbols. I mentioned in Chapter 3 that the possibility of direct, unmediated perception of mathematical forms and ideas comes to the fore most strongly with geometry. The incursion of computers as image-generating devices is also evident in providing both synthetic geometric images and graphical representations. The extent to which they allow us 'direct mathematical perception', however, is quite another matter. This book has in large part discussed the problematic nature of ever gaining direct experience in any part of school mathematics – that is, experience unmediated by symbols.

# 9

# ON FLUENCY AND
# UNDERSTANDING

the words a writer uses, even now, go back and back into a written
history. Words are not simple things: they take unto themselves, as
they have through time, power and meaning: they did so then, they
do so now.

(Weldon, 1991, p. 17)

In this chapter and the next, I start to uncover some of the 'cover stories'
I mentioned in Chapter 1 with regard to mathematics education. I do so
as one means of integrating several themes that run throughout the
previous eight chapters. The first has been an increasingly complex search
for reference, for mathematical objects, to underpin mathematical language and notation, necessary to preserve a naive, descriptive view of the
function of language. A second, related theme has been a questioning of
the automatic presumption of the primacy and anteriority of the object in
relation to the symbol.

The third has traced different manifestations of the counterpart (for
manipulation) and signification (for naming and pointing) functions of
mathematical symbols. And lastly, there remains the important question
of what the need is for fluency (in computation) in an era of electronic
devices that perform the same computations faster and more accurately
than most of us can ever hope to aspire to. Is fluency now no longer an
aim in mathematics teaching? If so, is greater understanding the only other
aim worth pursuing?

The most central, recurrent tension in mathematics teaching is between
the presumed conflicting goals of 'understanding' and teaching for understanding on the one hand, and fluency or automaticity of performance
(and teaching for that) on the other. There are also entrenched views about
which has to come first in a teaching context, or indeed whether they may
be developed relatively independently of one another. Geoffrey Howson
(1982, p. 21) summarises the views of sixteenth-century mathematics
teacher Robert Recorde: "Understanding is vital therefore, but mastery of
a technique may well precede understanding." What are 'rote' methods

(somehow always connected with 'memory') and why are they always to be shunned?

Can you be *too* fluent, can you have *too* much understanding? Can an excess of one actually detract from the other? Understanding in mathematics is automatically assumed to be a universal good, and the more the better. Yet it is recognised in other arenas that too much understanding can inhibit action, as the complexity perceived can inhibit decisions. And to be too understanding can prevent suitable boundaries from being maintained.

I start here to examine the force and role behind the words 'fluency', 'meaning' and 'understanding' as the dominant terms in many discussions of mathematics teaching and learning, reflecting a relative poverty of language for talking about 'doing' mathematics. Fluency is centrally about doing. Was fluency ever an end in itself? If not, what was it seen as a means to? Once fluency becomes an end in itself, it masks the fact that it may no longer serve any useful purpose.

There is an irony in the Nuffield-promoted motto of the 1960s, 'I do and I understand', as it actually can be seen as embodying an earlier story about 'doing (computations) first and understanding coming later' ('I do and [so/then] I understand') that Nuffield was attempting to supplant. A current, simplified version of this revised belief might be that understanding will help you do, particularly if stuck – 'I understand, so therefore I can do'. But, so this story goes, understanding may also help you to mechanise and hence to forget.

While there are concerns about the 'blind manipulation of number symbols', most of the expressed concern in mathematics education publications over the past century, unsurprisingly perhaps, has been in the area of algebra.

> Drill in mere manipulation is necessary at every stage in school algebra. That this should be thorough, so far as it goes, will be admitted by all teachers, but it should in the main be given *after* its necessity in applications has been perceived by the pupil and not *before*.
>
> (MA, 1934, p. 10)

The phrase 'mere manipulation' shows up a value system *inside* mathematics, implying that no insight was required, and perhaps that the result was 'only' a mechanical one.

Yet there was no doubt about the necessity of *both* 'understanding' or meaning' *and* technical skill, facility and fluency in manipulation. By 1979, in the HMI report *Aspects of Secondary Education*, we can read: "Success in repetitive exercises on (say) technical points involving the manipulation of fractions or decimals was, in itself, not taken as sufficient evidence of competence." We come up against another of these key words, 'technical' and the related term 'technique', as well as the desire of teachers to be justified in reading competence from performance.

Machines now allow the complete automation of certain mathematical functionings. It may nonetheless be important to offer the possibility of fluency, in order that students have something to reflect upon. For instance, this may require that in school contexts we need to redefine algebra in such a way that humans can continue to do it: one possibility might be a shift from the mechanisation of arithmetical operations to reflective awareness of what it is *we* (and not the machines) are doing. As a second instance, Gattegno's approach to arithmetic through language (rather than through the counting of objects) yields a facility that is then available for reflection, and neatly reverses the presumed order of 'understanding, then fluency'.

There are different dreams associated with the notions of fluency and understanding. The fluency dream goes back at least to Leibniz and his wish for a universal calculus (and a rational calculating device), so that problems of whatever sort may be reduced to symbols which are then manipulated to enable universally applicable answers to appear. One presumption underlying this dream is of a universal (mathematical) structure to the world and its processes that is independent of the particular content or setting.[1] The imperialist identifying and collapsing of thinking into mathematical thinking that I mentioned at the end of the last chapter is very evident.

The dream of understanding is harder to state. It includes seeing with a clarity so transparent that all that is needed is to look – without resort to codified or calculated methods. 'Behold' is the only word apparently accompanying a diagrammatic proof attributed to Bhaskara of Pythagoras' theorem. This understanding is integrated into me, so I no longer have to work at remembering, certainly no 'rote' learning is required, nor is accepting something on anyone else's authority. I am at one and as one with whatever I am trying to understand.

To end this opening discussion, here is part of a short article entitled 'A matter of relationships', written by Caleb Gattegno and published in a Canadian teachers' journal. With perhaps uncharacteristic humour, he teases out some inconsistencies in the way we talk about our goals in the domain of early arithmetic, focusing particularly on a tension between immediacy and understanding, as well as what 'knowing' means.

> All teachers will agree with me that their teaching of arithmetic is based essentially on the use of counting, which would appear to be the simplest of all ideas. Is there not a logical foundation for saying that $6 + 4 = 10$ is true because $6 + 1 = 7, 7 + 1 = 8, 8 + 1 = 9$ and $9 + 1 = 10$, hence the answer? Yes, but are we to be content with that? We do not stop at proving that $6 + 4 = 10$, we also want it to be remembered, and that is where logic no longer operates.

6 + 4 = 10 is only found to be true if I resort to counting; if you ask me what it is, I shall use my fingers, or counters, or whatever I have. But that is not what you want; you want me to say at once that six and four makes ten. Counting is not to be used because it wastes time. Why, then, did you 'teach' me to count if I am not allowed to use it?

"I taught you to count", you will say, "so that you would know your numbers and understand addition. Now I want you to drop counting and 'know' addition bonds."

"If I said I know addition bonds, would you believe that it is because you taught me to count?"

"Yes, how else could you know that 6 and 4 makes 10?"

"If I said I just know it because I can remember strings of words, then would you be satisfied?"

"No, because I want you to understand what you do."

"Then I must use counting to find 6 and 4 makes 10."

"No, since you should, by now, know it."

"But if I don't, may I count?"

"You may, but you should know that 6 + 4 = 10 soon, otherwise there must be something wrong with you."

"Similarly, you 'teach' me the multiplication tables, and I can recite them. But you want me to give the answer at once that 7 × 8 = 56; if I say 1 × 8 = 8, 2 × 8 = 16 . . . 6 × 8 = 48, 7 × 8 = 56, you get cross with me and say I should 'know' it. Is it not knowing if I am able to stop at 56 in the sequence of tables I so laboriously learnt? You wanted 7 × 8 and now I am telling you that it is 56."

"Yes, but you should *know* it by now, otherwise there is something the matter with you."

"Then why did you 'teach' me the tables if what you want is the products?"

"So that you would understand that we obtain the answers by always adding 8 to itself."

"But that is precisely what I did to find 7 × 8 = 56."

"Yes, but you must not use the tables any more, you should know the answer at once."

"But why, then, did you 'teach' me the tables in the first place?"

(Gattegno, 1963b, pp. 80–1)

## ON FLUENCY

What might fluency mean as a central goal for mathematics education in an age of machines which can perform arithmetic and (more recently) algebraic routines with far greater efficiency and accuracy than humans? Where does speed enter into this discussion as a desirable characteristic of mathematical performance (rather than merely as a gatekeeping technique of exclusion)? Teachers often went for speed, taken as an indicator of fluency and efficiency, and the former became a substitute for the latter.[2]

In general contexts, the word 'fluency' is primarily used of language speakers and writers, and has etymological root imagery of flowing. Common contexts of use include: reading aloud, speaking, writing in one's native tongue (usually of young children striving for mastery) or a foreign one (usually adults). Another is music performance ('I can read music or play this piece fluently'), arguably an extension of the human voice. A third, a fluent translator from one language to another, or from one embodiment of language to another (including working from written music). It is not common to talk of computer productions as fluent, though possibly I can be a fluent *user* of certain software or other media. In computation using calculators, you seldom see any intermediate effects – every computation is like $7 \times 8 = 56$!

For me, fluency is about ease of production and mastery of generation – it is used also in relation to a complex system. 'Fluent' may be related to efficient, or just no wasted effort. It is often about working with the *form*. Finally, it can be about not having to pay much conscious attention. Speed can be a by-product of fluency, but is not an important goal in itself. Nonetheless, speed is visible and can often be what attracts someone else.

Speed is an interesting element in its own right, as it can, sensitively used, provide a means to block attempts to understand consciously and deliberately and endeavour to engage more fundamental processes. It may require a deliberate letting go of conscious control over the process of generation of responses. One key element of working with Nicolet-Gattegno geometric films can come from control being elsewhere, and I can choose to subordinate myself to the film, in particular to the pace and rhythm of the images. In the Gattegno piece about arithmetic bonds, one key phrase is that the results be given 'at once', with apparently no thought, intervening steps or working out. The number 'bonds', whether additive or multiplicative, are demanded to appear fluently, without hesitation.[3]

Algorithmic, arithmetic, and algebraic fluency are all common expressions. Arithmetic fluency is not the same as algorithmic fluency. Algorithms are about ways of doing.

> Their confidence [seven- and eight-year-old pupils of Cuisenaire], and the swiftness and accuracy of their work are so impressive that many visitors to Thuin [where Georges Cuisenaire taught] find it difficult to believe they are as young as they are. Long vacations do not seem to affect the skills acquired, and we no longer assess them in terms of memory: it is true understanding that the children have found for themselves. . . . They can answer in a fraction of a minute

at the age of eight questions such as the following. . . . This rapidity is not achieved as a result of undue time or effort. On the contrary, the pupils quickly come to need only 15 minutes of arithmetic a day to remain proficient.

(Gattegno, 1963a, p. 13)

In this quotation we have some attributes of fluency, namely speed and accuracy, mention of the level of maintenance practice involved as well as the contrasting of 'true' understanding with memory. These are common elements in discussions of mathematics teaching still some thirty years later.

There is a problem of specifying fluency in relation to existing technology. When you get access to a new one, there is a need to separate fluency with the medium from fluency with the ideas. For instance, only very young children for the most part struggle for fluency with a pencil – at least with regard to writing (artistic drawing is quite another matter). The computer can help with early stages of writing because the letters are already formed on the screen (like notes from that other keyboard, the piano, as compared with the violin).

Symbolic manipulators are currently in hands of experts who already have considerable symbolic fluency with manipulation: they report a massive amount of interpretation is required. What awarenesses do they develop or block in novices? Do they free students from spending an inordinate time learning and practising particular techniques, affording instead the prospect of focusing on significance of techniques in whatever context they are working? What are costs of handing over the manipulations?

There is a key role for symbols in developing fluency, involving, in particular, the distinguished functions of signification and being a counterpart. At one level, fluency with symbols involves being at one with them, so they can be seen through: transparent signification is the dream here. Yet there is also a simplifying substituting value in opacity (which Schmidt aligns with the counterpart) in order not to be distracted by what may be going on 'underneath'.

## On technique

I am a teacher, and therefore I am interested in search and growth, schools and methods. Or does it work the other was round? In education as in handicraft, I am interested in questions of meaning and technique.

(Richards, 1989, p. 99)

Techniques are something to be valued, but can also be devalued. To say 'He is all technique' in music, or in painting, is to denigrate a person's skill, and to suggest that something is missing. In Gestalt psychotherapy, the comparable unease is with a set response, rather than being as flexible as possible to actual situations.

Recall the Tahta quotation I gave in the Introduction which complained about insufficient attention to actual techniques to help people gain symbolic facility in mathematics. Technique is a means of operating on and interacting with the task or problem. Arithmetic pattern spotting can be quite advanced yet offers no insight into the problem – but it does offer a technique. Techniques allow us to avoid a need for generating particular insight. It is hard to offer insight, much more simple to offer techniques. One consequence is that we tend to give instruction in the processes we have developed techniques for. Arithmetic and algebraic algorithms provide excellent examples of this didactic transposition – the re-emphasising that takes place merely as a result of having to *teach* mathematics in a classroom setting.

In Serres' discussion of the traditional legends of the origins of geometry among the Egyptian pyramids, he draws our attention to the tacit knowledge of technique and action.

> What is the status of the knowledge implied by a certain technique? A technique is always an application that envelops a theory. . . . If mathematics arose one day from certain techniques it was surely by making explicit this implicit knowledge. That there is a theme of secrecy in the artisans' tradition probably signifies that this secret is a secret for everybody, including the master. There is an instance of clear knowledge that is hidden in the workers' hands and in their relation to the block of stone. This knowledge is hidden there, it is locked in, and the key has been thrown away.
>
> (Serres, 1982, p. 89)

This is a very difficult area. I mentioned in Chapter 4 Noss's (1991) insightful work on the notions of mathematical depth and density in relation to computer software and hardware. I think it provides a way forward in regard to identifying the force of offering mathematical functionings and techniques installed in machines for the mathematical education of pupils.

Among many other things, Logo's turtle graphics capability can serve as a means of making explicit the mathematics inherent in drawing certain figures that the hand already knows. It also serves as a reminder of the link between technique and technology. Certain technology embodies and automates[4] mathematical techniques and carries them out for the user. So the technique no longer is available for our inspection or reflection, it is no longer *our* skill that is the focus of or source for reflection. It is locked up in the device even more tightly than the stonemason's knowledge is.

176

## On practice

Precepts are not given for the sake of being practised, but practice is prescribed in order that precepts may be understood.

(Weil, 1952, p. 112)

One of the challenging questions in mathematics teaching at the moment is that of how to, when to, how much to and why encourage practice. These are questions of central importance to all teachers and yet it is far from clear what is to be done by way of moving towards resolving them. One dictionary sense of the verb 'to practise' is to visit habitually or to haunt. 'A repeated performance or systematic exercise for the purpose of acquiring skill or proficiency.' Children are very good at practising certain things until they have mastered them – they are willing, it seems, to pay the necessary attention.

One thing is clear, however, and it relates to a point made earlier about the independence of questions in textbooks one from another: it crucially matters *how* pupils approach practice in terms of what they get from it. Traditionally, one of the central roles of textbooks was providing precisely such a resource of graded problems for pupils to work at.[5]

Do we practise 'mere' repetitions? If so, is this enough? One difficulty is in deciding what it is that is being done again. It is rare to offer pupils the same problem twice – usually they are invited to work at 'the same but different' – and stop when the different has become the same. There is a common tension here. Do I (as their teacher) want them to think of this problem as itself (a new situation, attend to particularities and exploit them as you wish in order to reach a particular solution) or do I want them to think of it as material for 'the same but different', as potential algorithm fodder.

One key point is that if I approach a series of exercises (be they mathematical or musical – there are similar practice issues here) with my eye out for the general, for what there is in common across these activities (which is, after all, likely to be the main teaching point, concept or algorithm), then I am better mathematically attuned to what is of importance. If I go through the exercises one after another, as something to get through (or just enough to get by or as many as I can in the time), then my attention is crucially missing from the central focus, from the point of view of teaching. Sets of exercises where there is no connection between one and the next destroy the possibility of such focused practice.

Some mathematics teachers now voice the concern that 'we never seem to practise at all, now', while others relish their sense of liberation from drudgery in exactly the same words. Practice need not be a repetitive drill to fix a particular action or process in automaticity. But you can gain fluency through practice. What are some arguments against rote practice? The most prevalent is that this erstwhile practice destroys meaning and inhibits understanding, perhaps even denying the possibility that anything mathematical can be understood. Yet, recall Hewitt in Chapter 5 commenting how he does not offer 'reasons' for conventions. Not everything in mathematics is to be understood, and certainly not in advance.

Is the fact that frequent repetition of a word seems inimical to retaining its meaning linked to concern at the role of repetition in creating automatisms?[6] Recall the comments on ritual I made in the first chapter. We have experience of repetitive devotional acts (for instance, Jewish *shuckling* at the Western Wall, or focusing *mantras* to be said over and over),[7] as well as obsessive repetition of actions, the myth of Sisyphus, or Freud's account of the hand-washer. One overt intent of the former rituals is to profit from the loss of conventional meaning (and of self) which such repetition brings in order to break through into a different realm of experience. Chanting (whether of multiplication tables or other things) rhythmically can on occasion offer a similar opportunity.

## ON MEANING AND UNDERSTANDING

The questions "What is length?", "What is meaning?", "What is the number one?" etc., produce in us a mental cramp. We feel that we can't point to anything in reply to them and yet ought to point to something. (We are up against one of the great sources of philosophical bewilderment: we try to find a substance for a substantive.)

(Wittgenstein, 1958, p. 1)

Method for understanding images, symbols, etc. Not to try to interpret them, but to look at them until the light suddenly dawns. Generally speaking, a method for the exercise of the intelligence, which consists of looking.

(Weil, 1952, p. 109)

I return here to a discussion I started in Chapter 1. The words 'meaning' and 'understanding' are often conflated or used interchangeably. I think meaning has a closer connection to reference. A referent offers something to *refer* to, a focus for attention but also an underpinning for language. In Chapter 2, material objects were offered as sometime referents. At other times, in mathematics, the symbols serve as referents as well.

One central function of any language is to enable the speaker to 'point'. The root verb *deuten* of the German verb *bedeuten* ("to mean") means "to point with a finger at something". As I progressed through this book, one central question that recurred was: what are these 'things' that mathematical language apparently points at? (Recall from Chapter 3 the link between the action of pointing and the mathematical notion of point.) And mathematicians do more than point: they 'manipulate', as the ubiquitous metaphor has it.

Michael Halliday has written a book about a two-year-old's acquisition of language, a book he entitled *Learning How to Mean* (1975). By using the normally transitive verb 'to mean' intransitively, he has drawn attention to the fact that young children need to learn *how* to use language to achieve their own ends, whatever these may be. Likewise, children need to learn how to mean *mathematically*, how to use mathematical language to create, control and express their own mathematical meanings, as well as to interpret the mathematical language of others. In part, this is so that they might experience and be able to attend to mathematical ideas and meanings that others have generated and valued.

The French verb 'to mean' is *vouloir dire*, a composite of two verbs and literally means "to want to say"; in other words, the feel of *intention* is uppermost. In consequence, it is even harder to have things 'wanting to say' on their own, than meaning something by themselves. 'To understand', in French, is *comprendre*, but it has a second meaning, "to include".[8] The motto 'Tout comprendre est tout pardonner' is striking perhaps because once understood something is inside and part of us, rather than outside and hence separated from us. The French double sense reminds us that understanding is a process of inclusion, of incorporation. One powerful way of educating the imagination is by taking the outside and turning it into inside.

The literature on understanding in mathematics education is legion.[9] I cannot nor wish to attempt either to summarise or survey it here. It would be very nice at the end to be able to say something simple. For instance, in mathematics, meaning comes about through the signification function of symbols, while fluency comes about through the counterpart function. There is certainly some truth to this observation, enough perhaps to bring those promoters of illuminatory manipulatives up short. Electronic devices hide the counterparts and seem to offer direct access to mathematical meanings through the dynamic signs, the geometric screen images of *Cabri-géomètre*, the arithmetic or algebraic symbols of computer algebra systems. If computers come to mediate much of school mathematics, where and how are we to learn about the counterpart, calculational function of mathematical symbols, which permits their manipulation to mathematical ends?

### A touching sight

Earlier in this book, I drew attention to the fact that the two most common metaphors for understanding derive from the language of touch and sight, and this is one reason I have attended to these two senses particularly. It is to this that I wish to return now, in order to summarise some observations about the role of computer technology.

William Ivins, once curator of prints at the Metropolitan Museum of Art in New York, has also written a book on art and geometry, and draws attention to the differing balance and predominance of the tactile-muscular and visual sources of space intuition present both in Greek art and mathematics, and subsequently. He characterised Greek perceptions as almost totally tactile-muscular, while the reverse he felt was true of Renaissance and post-Renaissance mathematics and art.

In the opening chapter, he reports on some sense experiments he carried out, endeavouring to isolate effects of sight and touch. Of particular interest to me was when he wrote:

> Now, as against all this fading in and out, this shifting, varying, unbroken continuity of quite different visual effects, what do we discover when we examine the tactile-muscular sense returns given by the exploring hand? . . . To begin with, as we all know from our experience in finding our way about in completely dark rooms, tactile awareness for practical purposes is not accomplished by a gradual fading in and out of consciousness, but by catastrophic contacts and breaking of contacts. My hand either touches something or it does not.
>
> (Ivins, 1946, p. 3)

I was struck by the similarity between his description and the 'all-or-nothing' sense of understanding, of grasping something, that seems to leave no room for my overwhelming experience of understandings coming in and out of focus, subtle shifts in my understanding, blurring and gentle fading as well as occasional sharp, bright 'seeings', moments of insight. Instead of asking 'Do you or don't you understand', perhaps asking a pupil to 'show me your understanding' would leave more scope for an informative response.

What John Mason has termed 'mouse mathematics' seemingly returns us to the pre-language interaction of very young children where they are able to act directly on the physical world with their hands. This interface diminishes the difference between screen and material-world objects markedly. Mouse mathematics also offers the illusion of direct interaction and control over screen objects, as if they were the mathematical objects themselves, rather than suggestive machine-generated symbolisms.

This apparent ability to move screen objects by hand offers a sense of manipulability similar to the manipulation of physical apparatus discussed in Chapter 2. In my earlier book, *Speaking Mathematically* (Pimm, 1987), I discussed some of the ways in which screen objects can serve as intermediaries between public and private as well as between the physical and the purely mental. The illusion of grasp and of manipulation supported by means of the mouse offers a powerful extension of the sense of touch into this hybrid realm.

The illusion of continuity afforded by the mouse privileges the perception of a static geometric diagram as particular, given the ease of transformation (whether seen as moving from one configuration to another, or deforming one into another). This is at the expense of seeing a static geometric diagram as being a symbolic representation of the general, analogous to an algebraic formula or expression.

I wish to comment on the rebalancing of the senses involved in doing mathematics as a result of the affordances of the computer. My first remark is somewhat at variance with Ivins' central dichotomy. The experience of using the mouse, although firmly tactile-muscular, is one of continuity, not disjointedness. The sense of drag and continuous response of the figure, however, although not accompanied by any sense of resistance, provides the confirmation that touch can offer that there 'really' is something there: in Ivins words, that there is a 'reachable and touchable form'. But it is the eye that observes and confirms the effect.

> In any continuous pattern the hand needs simple and static forms and it likes repeated ones. It knows objects separately, one after another, and unlike the eye it has no way of getting a practically simultaneous view or acquaintance with a group of objects as a single awareness. Unlike the eye, the unaided hand is unable to discover whether three or more objects are on a line.
>
> (Ivins, 1946, p. 4)

There is an importance in balancing the senses, but also in being able to rebalance them, so that patterns are not set so hard that it is difficult to break out of them to perceive otherwise. Technology tends to amplify one sense in particular, and although expanding the imaginative possibilities available, an over-reliance on one form of technology can result in a swamping of the other senses by the augmented one.

## ON TRADITION

> Tradition is a genetic code. Its persistence in a culture certifies its function, however tacit that function is.... tradition combines innovation and rules from the past to invent new forms.
>
> (Davenport, 1987, pp. 24–5)

A colleague, Christine Shiu, was in China talking with a group of mathematics teachers about problem solving and investigative work in mathematics. One commented, "Yes, but you must learn from the Ancestors first". One reason for attending schools is to be among knowers of the old ways, in a 'community of memory', in order to be an inheritor of traditions. There is perhaps no more fundamental split between a perception of the primary function of schooling as inculcation into the traditions and one of preparation for the future; sometimes this is unhelpfully polarised between the backward-looking and the forward-looking.

It is important not to put tradition and individual creativity in opposition. It is precisely the interrelation between these elements, over and over, that is the material for the teacher in a classroom. While many other school subjects experienced a move away from communicating the traditions as the primary or sole focus (the extreme case might be in English, moving away from predominant attention to written linguistic forms to unfettered individual expression in the late 1960s), in mathematics it was not until the problem-solving movement of the mid-to-late 1970s that a similar, marked swing occurred in mathematics teaching in England. This had not been the focus of the new mathematics reform movements, which primarily altered content alone. As ever, questions of authority and the nature of teacher guidance (derogatively termed 'imposition') were central.

> It is, of course, this element of *direction* that is the ideological crunch. For a variety of reasons, not always consistent, there is a developing disinclination by teachers, or by the influential teacher-training establishment, to be seen to be too heavily 'directive'. Pupils are to be encouraged to work at 'their own mathematics', at mathematics which is variously seen as being culturally dependent, gender independent, and struggling to be free from the shackles of tradition. Wallis' investigative method has somehow in recent times acquired the accompanying restriction that it has to be virginal – innocent of other than self-created knowledge. Although it is – rightly – sometimes considered a virtue to share with fellow learners, pupils are not always so obviously encouraged to share with tradition, with textbook, or with teachers.
>
> (Tahta, 1988, p. 311)

With the new machines we are placed in a challenging position of dramatic tension with regard to our mathematical heritage and traditions. Traditions speak of investments. Investments result in resistance to change – not necessarily a bad thing as stability can be one result. To argue that human beings have always used mechanical aids for mathematical computation is to stress historical continuity without necessarily having knowledge of what particular assistance was rendered at different times. It is also to ignore the fundamentally new. These devices are not just 'more of the same, only a bit better, faster, more reliable'. I find it unquestionable that calculators and computers are extremely useful items in the everyday world. What I am struggling with is their particular usefulness, and at what cost, in the learning and teaching of mathematics.

Davenport (1987, p. 72) writes: "Art is the great abbreviator of experience into vivid symbols" and later adds:

The arts are a way of internalizing experience, allowing us to look with wonder at a past that is not ours, but enough of ours so that all stories are, as Joyce says, always "the same anew". It is not therefore surprising that the best books are old books rewritten. The tribe has its tales.

*(ibid.*, p. 83)

I feel the same is true of mathematics. The degree of vividness of the symbols comes mainly from the condensation of experience that has gone into them, but they can also serve as a prompter of experience. Attention does change over time, though there is still a strong *commonality* across time and culture of certain experiences (which Chevallard (1990) terms 'protomathematical') that give themselves over to becoming mathematics, over and above what such experiences have to offer in themselves. They stake a claim to our collective attention.

There is a powerful Australian aboriginal belief that everywhere you walk, you walk where others have walked before you, but also that as you walk, you are leaving your footprints for others to walk in. This resonant image speaks of continuity and community, of chains linking past to future through ourselves. It accompanies a belief in the importance of the naming of the dead, and trusting the power of language both to carry the culture and to allow us to recreate it continually while investing the storied events and forms with new meanings and significance.

Such beliefs also bear an interesting relationship to the way in which the particular and individual comes to take part in the creating and maintaining of a culture which is more enduring (as well as endearing). The symbolic forms survive, and yet can still offer both access and insight into the very individual and idiosyncratic ways of seeing and thinking that gave rise to these forms. This is despite the efforts of centuries of certain mathematical traditions to cover over and smooth out these idiosyncratic human hand-traces[10] from the artifacts – the human individuality necessarily imprinted and impressed on the forms.

# 10

# ON MANIPULATION

[Geometry is] a science quite the reverse of what is implied by the terms its practitioners use . . . . The terms are quite absurd but they are hard put to find others. They talk about 'squaring' and 'applying' and 'adding' and so on, as if they were *doing* something and their reasoning had a practical end, and the subject were not, in fact, pursued for the sake of knowledge.

(Plato, *Republic*; given in Fauvel and Gray, 1987, p. 70)

This book has offered an exploration of the metaphor of 'manipulation', asking what (and at times, who) is being manipulated, if anything at all. Throughout this book, I have found myself using the term 'manipulation' over and over as the key metaphor for 'doing' mathematics. I am interested in the language we have for talking about engaging in, performing or carrying out mathematical activity – and what sort of activity the ways we talk about it suggest it to be. For instance, how are we to entertain algebraic things – does manipulation require us to have mathematical *things* to be manipulated?

The metaphor of 'manipulation' requires a thing to be manipulated, which in mathematics is, of necessity, a counterpart. Plato complained about the language of geometry, suggesting that it made it seem to be about physical things. In the absence of the object (forever the case in mathematics), what is often manipulated by proxy is the symbol. So much of school mathematics is about transformation of symbols in various guises and to various ends. With symbolic systems, the action is restricted to 'mental manipulation'.

Michel Foucault, writing in *Les Mots et les Choses*, speaks of "that less apparent syntax that causes words and things (next to but also opposite one another) to 'hang together'" (quoted in Foucault, 1983, p. 4). He adds (p. 7): "The relationship of languages to the world is one of analogy rather than signification; or rather, their value as signs and their duplicating function are superimposed". The issue of fluency and understanding is right here in this superimposition: working with the counterpart duplicates permits increased fluency; working with the indicative function of signs encourages greater understanding. Mathematical notation acts as symbol for something else as well as providing an object to be manipulated in its own right. Rather than being unfortunate, the ability to confuse symbol with object in mathematics is essential to much mathematical activity, and certainly to any sort of fluency in calculation.

Is mathematics about things or about appearances? Rotman seems in no doubt that the latter is true and argues extensively in his book *Signifying Nothing* for the illusory nature of the seeming anteriority of things to signs, not just in mathematics, but certainly there. I find his writing complex, fascinating and persuasive. In my exploration of the nature of the term 'manipulation', I want to suggest that this pushes the tactile 'things' point of view, by requiring that we turn mathematical 'words' into things.

An attempt to present pupils solely with objects as the focus of mathematics, even to the extent of rebus mathematics (recording with things) in order to see meaning as even primarily referential, is to miscue fundamentally and in consequence contribute to the common failure to function mathematically with fluency. Mathematicians use and produce symbols, endlessly. Rather than recording as occurring after the event, such a view shifts attention and recognition of the primary act from object to sign, from presence to presentation. The language of 'manipulation' is a completely dominant metaphor and, as such, is to a great extent invisible. Symbols become objects, the things of mathematics themselves. Ironically, manipulation is about touch, whereas symbols are predominantly about sight, resulting in mathematics being in the grip of a powerful mixed metaphor.

## ON METAPHOR IN MATHEMATICS

Metaphors are actually about ways of seeing (seeing 'as if'), rather than being fundamentally linguistic entities. To be offered to others, they must be codified in language – and, once codified, they enter the cultural resources of that language.

- *Metaphors are conservative and backward looking* They are about seeing the new in terms of the old. Marshall McLuhan talked about "driving with your eyes on the rear-view mirror" and offered the example of 'the train is an iron horse'. One risk of metaphor is that you may miss what is fundamentally new. How appropriate is the metaphor of manipulation to describing computer-mediated mathematics?
- *Metaphors express particular stressings and ignorings* Using metaphors unawarely (including 'dead' metaphors) can result in them stressing and ignoring for you. Why do we need *two* core metaphors for understanding, touch and sight? Conversely, by solely using the language of

manipulation (connected to grasp), are we losing sight of other ways of thinking/seeing?

- *Metaphors can generate a creative tension* They can bring new perceptions into being (thereby reversing my earlier point – the language coding the seeing can actually *generate* a new way of seeing for the hearer). Their interpretation is far less tightly prescribed by the semantics of the language. I have to work much harder to produce a meaning – where do I *look*? And how?

Many people feel there is no place for metaphor in mathematics itself – that metaphors are inexact and flowery, and therefore inherently unsuitable for mathematical work. I would like to try to indicate a deeper reason for this feeling of inappropriateness, without endorsing the view itself which I do not share.

In order to do so, I provide quite a lengthy quotation (given in Fauvel and Gray, 1987, p. 52) from a prose poem, *The Way of Truth*, written by Parmenides, an ancient Greek philosopher (early fifth century BC), one of whose students was Zeno. It is not the clearest of texts.

And the goddess greeted me kindly, and took my right hand in hers, and addressed me with these words:

> Young man, you who come to my house in the company of immortal charioteers with the mares which bear you, greetings. No ill fate has sent you to travel this road – far indeed does it lie from the steps of men – but right and justice. It is proper that you should learn all things, both the unshaken heart of well-rounded truth, and the opinions of mortals, in which there is no true reliance.
>
> Come now, and I will tell you (and you must carry my account away with you when you have heard it) the only ways of enquiry that are to be thought of. The one, that [it] is and that it is impossible for [it] not to be, is the path of Persuasion (for she attends upon Truth); the other, that [it] is not and that it is needful that [it] not be, that I declare to you is an altogether indiscernible track: for you could not know what is not – that cannot be done – nor indicate it.
>
> For never shall this be forcibly maintained, that things that are not are, but you must hold back your thought from this way of enquiry, nor let habit, born of much experience, force you down this way, by making you use an aimless eye or an ear and a tongue full of meaningless sound: judge by reason the strife-encompassed refutation spoken by me.
>
> I shall not allow you to say nor to think from not being: for it is not to be said nor thought that it is not: and what need would have

driven it later rather than earlier, beginning from the nothing, to grow? Thus it must either be completely or not at all. Nor will the force of conviction allow anything besides it to come to be ever from not being. Therefore Justice has never loosed her fetters to allow it to come to be or to perish, but holds it fast. And the decision about these things lies in this: it is or it is not.

What powerful phrasing: "the unshaken heart of well-rounded truth", as well as the exhortation to "judge by reason the strife-encompassed refutation spoken by me"! But most resonant for me is the final maxim: 'it is or it is not'. We have Socrates claiming: "Clearly he always either is or is not a man" as well as subsequently Shakespeare posing the question: "To be or not to be". John Fauvel (1988, p. 6) has drawn our attention to how precisely this form mirrors and echoes mathematical statements that appear around Parmenides' time. Plato argues: "To double the square, either you double the sides, or you do not". Aristotle writes: "Either the diagonal and the side [of the square] are commensurable, or they are incommensurable". In Euclid, we find: "Either G is a prime other than A, B or C, or it is not".

The way of thinking embodied in the simple phrase 'it is or it is not' is profoundly mathematical. (In passing, there are interesting resonances in Parmenides of proof by contradiction – arguing apparently from what is not. There is also a hint of the shock our century has had to contend with when accepting arguments for the existence of *undecidable* propositions – ones for which we will never be able to say whether 'it is or it is not'.)

I think it is for this reason that metaphor can be found to be so profoundly disquieting in mathematics. For the very essence of metaphor, if it is to function as it should, is its assertive ambivalence: to be able to claim at one and the same time that 'it is *and* it is not'! I assert 'a function is a machine' (and yet I also know it is not one) – the strength of the metaphoric assertion comes through the use of the verb 'to be' – yet it carries with it implicitly its own negation. To lose one or other force – the assertion and its negation made simultaneously – destroys the creative potential that metaphors can achieve.

## THE METAPHOR OF MANIPULATION

The phrase 'symbol manipulation' seems so set, such a familiar pairing, that it can be hard to imagine that it was ever otherwise. Yet according to the *Oxford English Dictionary*, until the early nineteenth century, the word 'manipulation' had only a technical meaning in mining, referring there to a method of extracting silver ore[1] – the Latin root of the word means "handful". During the course of the nineteenth century, the word became more widely used, first to refer to the handling of physical objects, and then (in the 1850s and 1860s) to mean operating on things with the mind. The verb 'to manipulate' was coined only then.[2]

The *OED* is organised along historical lines, with the oldest recorded meanings first. A recent attempt by Collins to produce a dictionary where order within an entry reflected frequency of current usage depended on the compilation of an extensive computer database. I explored the evidence in the Bank of English, the corpus built by COBUILD[3] at the University of Birmingham, and found that by far the most common occurrence of 'manipulate' and 'manipulation' was of people (the next word – connected to the direct object – in order of frequency, was 'it', 'their', 'his', 'her', 'them', 'people', 'him', 'others', 'me') and then economic and political contexts – 'prices', 'opinions', 'media' being what was manipulated. One of the most common preceding adjectives was 'skilful'. Bones are *manipulated* when in traction or at an osteopath. A relatively new occurrence is with the metaphoric collocation 'genetic manipulation', to refer to a range of gene splicing and other recombinant DNA techniques.[4] There were virtually no references to mathematical manipulation in the 200 million word database.

I find it interesting that the most common use of manipulation is in its negative sense of manipulating people, yet there is apparently no trace of this in the mathematical connotations. Manipulation is about imposing my will, directly or indirectly. To be thought 'manipulative' is to be seen to be endeavouring to control and impose my will on others, though on occasion this 'handling' may be done with skill: being manipulative of other people reflects a view of treating people as if they were objects.

'Manipulative' and 'calculating' are both quite pejorative labels. To be a 'calculating' person, in the words of one dictionary, is to be 'selfishly scheming', to be explicitly conscious of what you intend to do – yet calculators render actual computations tacit and implicit, inaccessible to either inspection or control. My will is acting indirectly on and through the electronic calculator, rather than directly – an important shift in locus of control as I mentioned elsewhere.

In *doing* mathematics, there is an overwhelming emphasis on the hand, of which *manipulation* is one central component. According to another dictionary, to manipulate means 'to handle a person or things with *dexterity*'. Does the fact that we have the common collocation 'fluent' with 'manipulation' rather than 'dextrous' indicate that we realise that it isn't, at bottom, done with the hands?

'Manipulate' is a very odd word for working with symbols, treating them as if they were objects to be rearranged physically ('take the $x$ over to the other side and change the sign'). And if they are the 'objects', then the 'meaning' of the symbols may not easily be present as well. Counterpart and signification functions can prove uneasy companions.

With the computer, the development of the mouse as a control interface embodies this sense of manipulation, and invites the language of 'picking up' and 'dropping'. But it is actually gaze that is controlling, and future developments in computers may act directly in response to gaze direction, to an act of attention. This merely serves to reinforce my sense that sight and touch (tangibility and visibility) are key themes in relation to mathematics.

## IN CONCLUSION

The word connects the visible trace with the invisible thing, the absent thing, the thing that is desired or feared, like a frail emergency bridge flung over an abyss.

(Calvino, 1988, p. 77)

I began this book with an anecdote. I end it likewise.

While walking through an underpass on the edge of Green Park in London, I heard a young girl experimenting with echoes. What struck me was that the word she insisted on using repeatedly to generate the effect was 'ec-ho' itself – no other word would apparently serve.

Some words seem magic in conjuring effects in ourselves – and even, on occasion, in the outside world. They seem particularly resonant, giving us back an echo. Some words seem closer to the events themselves, succeeding in making them vividly present. Words and other symbols are portable; they can help to keep contact with traditions, to maintain rituals and values which emerged in places far off both in space and time. Symbols offer visibility, providing substitutes for manipulation and transformation.

This book has been about the place and importance of words (among other symbols) in relation to objects, images and meanings in mathematics – in particular, about the echo relation of call and answer between symbol and object. What do we emit and what information do we receive back? But it has also been indirectly about the crucial third term – the person for whom the signifier signifies.

I have explored some of the varied and complex relations which hold among word, image and thing, between symbol and the thing symbolised, which are particularly to the fore when teaching mathematics at any level. The symbolic aspect of doing (whether manipulating apparatus, exploring geometric images, working on naming numbers, carrying out arithmetic or algebraic calculations, interpreting graphs, solving 'real-world' problems) must be a focal point for attention, both by teacher and pupil.

In the Introduction, I posed one general dilemma which to me seems to be at the heart of many practical and theoretical debates about the teaching of mathematics in schools at all levels, namely the presumed precedence of understanding (and the consequent emphasis on the presence of 'concrete' referents, such as Dienes apparatus for place value) over fluency in symbol manipulation. I here extend the quotation from Dick Tahta that I gave in the Introduction (p. 9).

> In some contexts, what is required – eventually – is a fluency with mathematical symbols that is independent of any awareness of concurrent 'external' meaning. In linguistic jargon, 'signifiers' can sometimes gain more meaning from their connection with other signifiers than from what is being signified.
>
> Linguists have called the movement 'along the chain of signifiers' *metonymic* whereas 'the descent to the signified' is *metaphoric*. . . . The important point is that there are two sharply distinguished aspects (metonymic relations along the chain of signifiers and metaphoric ones which descend into meaning) which may be stressed at different times and for different purposes.
>
> (Tahta, 1985, p. 49)

The key point I want to make is that it is not an either/or, that 'understanding' *must* precede 'doing' or conversely. We do not have to choose to teach solely 'metaphorically' or 'metonymically' or even the one way before the other.[5] We can offer both Cuisenaire rods *and* finger complements and other numeral games. Rods seem to offer a model – i.e. a metaphor, namely numbers are in some respects like lengths. Complementing feels like metonymy. What are the fingers in this case? We can offer material-world situations *and* mental imaginings *and* direct work on symbolic forms. All are potentially mathematical. All contribute to the development of mathematical meaning. All therefore deserve time and place in classrooms.

Understanding and appreciation, while taking work and attention, may not involve someone 'getting caught up in the action'. The pursuit of greater fluency, within whichever part of mathematics is currently under study and in whatever form it takes there, remains for me a central goal of a mathematical education, despite the incursion of machines – just as in photography or music, disciplines which I have used in various places for comparative examples.

It was Simone Weil who offered the challenge of individualising machinery – a challenge which has particular resonance at this point in human mathematical development. If the core school mathematical experience is to become machines manipulating symbols for us, the pupil may end up "twice removed from the centre of things" (in the words of George Moore in Tom Stoppard's play *Jumpers*). How, for instance, are we to come to an algebra that is still worthwhile for our pupils to engage in?

Even though at the end of this book, I am still concerned with origins: the end, after all, 'is where we start from'. Michel Serres has inspiringly written:

The tale of inauguration [of mathematics] is that interminable discourse that we have untiringly repeated since our own dawn. What is, in fact, an interminable discourse? That which speaks of an absent object, of an object that absents itself, inaccessibly.

(1982, p. 97)

Serres' word 'inaccessibly' echoes the earlier discussion about measurement and how mimicry is a key way to make the inaccessible accessible. Absent objects, like absent parents, engender fierce longings. We crave the actual object; we are offered substitutes, 'cover stories', counterpart symbols – and necessarily so. It cannot be otherwise. Some of us learn to be good mimics, but at what cost?

Meaning seeps away when attentions change. Our shifts of attention wreak changes in the mathematical entities themselves. Stevens writes:

Our sense of things changes and they change,
Not as in metaphor, but in our sense
Of them. So sense exceeds all metaphor.

(1967, p. 431)

Meaning comprises a continual dance invoking denotation and connotation, metaphor and metonymy. And if our collective attention falters, then these 'objects' that the language and symbolism of mathematics have conjured and called into being also flicker and start to fade. If the counterpart is eliminated, then its paired part also starts to disappear.

What is mathematics about? It seems to me it is fundamentally about we human beings ourselves: our languaging and attentions, our wills and desires, and the astonishment that these can conjure. It becomes a place we invest with our dreams of precision, exactness and permanence. It is about the structures of our attention in relation to our inner and outer experience, our inner and outer meanings, our inner and outer worlds.

For the future, I am increasingly intrigued by the roots of mathematical meaning and its relation to the unconscious. Gaining automaticity is partly about moving certain functionings to the unconscious. What they connect to there, as well as the price we pay for having them there, we may never fully know.

# NOTES

## 1 INTRODUCTION

1 The fascinating article by Higbee and Kunihira (1985) discusses the specific design and use in Japan of mnemonics for learning mathematics, and provoked a lengthy discussion around the theme of 'doing mathematics without understanding it' in the same issue of the journal.

2 For further speculations on such powerful human connections, see Pimm, (1993a, 1994).

3 For more on the mathematical import of these terms, see Tahta (1991).

4 In this book, I use the terms 'pupils', 'students' and 'children' almost interchangeably. I like Gattegno's (1963a, p. 7) simple characterisation: "Pupils are children of various ages who acquire that name by going to school". Primary schools in England roughly match elementary schools in North America in involving the first seven years of education.

5 And James Joyce adds: "rite words in rote order". Right words in wrote order refers to the efficacy of the invention of writing to allow exactly repeatable verbal statements, formulations of procedures to be followed, evoking Ivins' (1969) identification of the historical and intellectual importance of being able to make exactly repeatable *pictorial* statements. See Chapter 6.

6 A similar view can be found in Carlyle (1836; 1987, p. 166): "By Symbols, accordingly, is man guided and commanded, made happy, made wretched. He every where finds himself encompassed with Symbols, recognised as such or not recognised: the Universe is but one vast symbol of God".

## 2 MANIPULATIVES AS SYMBOLS

1 I think that viewing the calculator and computer as manipulatives is worthy of consideration. But they are both purely *symbolic* objects, however material they may seem. Through the ages, different devices employing contemporary technology have been developed to assist and facilitate mathematical computation. Ancient Babylonian scribes apparently used tables of reciprocals and squares; abacuses of various sorts have been and continue to be used all over the world; Napier's bones and slide-rules, as well as more mechanical calculating devices, have been relied on, prior to our familiar electronic devices of the last twenty or thirty years. One progressive development this sequence of inventions has followed is the increasing inaccessibility of the means of functioning to the surface observer – as well, I would argue, as the increasing irrelevance of any understanding of this for successful use.

2 Dienes' use of the term 'embodiment' produces in me the right sense – something has been rendered physical in order that it may be directly manipulated by my body.

3 The mistaken sense of mathematics being seen as *in* the manipulatives recurs with calculators and computers. Is the screen object usefully thought of as a manipulative in this sense? Or is it distance education, where you may not have to get *too* involved: a hands-off experience? Where is the interpretative space for such experiences? See Chapters 4 and 6.

4 There is an important distinction to be made between the mathematical *task* offered and the pupil *activity* generated in response to it. See Love and Mason (1992), Chapter 3.

5 John Mason (1980) has proposed a 'manipulating – getting a sense of – articulating' helix with regard to mathematical action.

6 Papert offers the turtle as another object to think with, and it plays a role of transitional object (a term the psychoanalyst Donald Winnicott employed). However, if screen objects come to be taken as mathematical objects themselves, then the computer will perforce come to be seen as the *locus vivendi* of mathematical objects.

7 Another useful separation (here of language and action, and controlling the former by the latter) can occur with having one pupil be the 'head' and a second 'the hands', and only the head can talk and give instructions, and only the hands can cut, draw or stick, according to what they have understood. The constraints of the activity are 'artificial', but provided they are taken on by the children, then the constrained situation can offer a powerfully focused context for learning.

I saw a most striking instance of this separation in a saxophone master class, where the teacher had the pupil provide the breath only, and the teacher put his own arms round the pupil from behind and moved the keys, in order to make a point about the independence of the breath from production of the particular notes. This provided for me a clear illustration of Bruner's notion of 'scaffolding' by the teacher in order to focus pupil attention quite narrowly.

8 Actually, volume, but as the blocks are made with uniform thickness, either area or length becomes the salient variable.

9 Walkerdine (1988, p. 169) writes of Dienes' apparatus: "In all these examples of the children beginning place-value, the teacher, in a sense, *tells* the children what they are supposed to be experiencing and discovering. . . . she is providing the children with cues which reveal the properties of place-value which the objects they are manipulating are supposed to supply".

10 This list comes from one in Jaworski and Pimm (1986).

11 These verbs refer to the *role* the pupil's tactile activity is playing in relation to the mathematics to be brought into being.

12 Art does not reproduce the visible but makes visible. The very nature of graphic art lures us to abstraction, readily and with reason. . . . The purer the graphic work, that is the more emphasis it puts on the basic formal elements, the less well suited it will be to the realistic representation of visible things. . . .

Something has been made visible which could not have been perceived without the effort to make it visible. . . . we must be very clear about the aim of 'making-visible'. Are we merely noting things seen in order to try to remember them or are we also trying to reveal what is not visible?

(Klee, 1964, pp. 76, 454)

I shall say more about making-visible in Chapter 6 on mathematical representation. The issue here might be better described as the value of making-intangible.

13 The child putting things into her mouth is about 'incorporating' things into herself – literally making them part of herself, taking the outside and turning it into inside. (At a certain stage it seems as if *everything* is in a baby's food chain.) To *grasp* is the necessary preliminary step to incorporation.

## 3 GEOMETRIC IMAGES AND SYMBOLS

1 A similar making static can be seen in talking not about 'moving' but 'a motion', a process into a thing, a verb into a noun.

2 These fascinating speculations are continued in Tahta (1990a). We also find in Plato's dialogue *Republic*: "And what is more, it must, I think, be admitted that the objects of [geometrical] knowledge are eternal and not liable to change or decay". Geometry has been one regular recipient of a human desire for and investment in the eternal.

3 'Freud says of the maternal body "there is no other place of which one can say with so much certainty that one has already been there".' (Barthes, 1984, p. 40.)

4 This activity is due to Peter Gates.

5 A similar issue lies behind the 'arithmetisation of analysis' due to mathematicians Bolzano and Weierstraβ during the last century. The notion of variable involved motion, something (a variable) moving somehow through a static sea of points. An alternative individual conception involves checking (through generality) intervals one by one (this particular delta interval works for that particular epsilon) for the given function.

6 For an excellent general discussion of issues related to the use of film or video, see Tahta (1981b).

7 In what follows, I shall predominantly talk about *Cabri-géomètre*, with which I am more familiar. There are many similarities and some differences between these two programs. One of potential importance is the fact that with *Geometer's Sketchpad* you must select the objects first to which you intend to apply any construction (which requires you to know what they require ahead of time), whereas with *Cabri-géomètre* you must select the construction first and then stipulate the objects to which it is to be applied.

8 The one thing that is absent from this set-up currently is any direct (inertial) feedback to the hand from the mouse. Such Newtonian 'pushing back' is one thing that 'virtual reality' devices can offer.

9 Rotman writes:

> To move from abacus to paper is to shift from a *gestural* medium (in which physical movements are given ostensively and transiently in relation to an external apparatus) to a *graphic* medium (in which permanent signs, having their origin in these movements, are subject to a syntax given independently of any physical interpretation).
>
> (1987, p. 13)

10 See Douady (1985), for more on this important distinction. This is a similar shift of perspective to that to be discussed in Chapter 5 of seeing an algebraic expression at one and the same time as both a single, unified object and as a means of calculation. Being able to contend with such multiple perspectives is one important criterion for mathematical success.

11 *Geometer's Sketchpad* has a primitive called 'Mirror' which achieves this reflection directly. It is very difficult to enquire into system primitives, yet as

with Logo, their choice is central to the possibilities for creative exploration. The use of primitives also echoes the restriction of much Greek geometry to unmarked-ruler and collapsing-compass constructions.

12  In Archimedes, the curve is introduced by its symptom ('abscissae are as the square of the ordinates') rather than a definition by genesis (saying what you have to do in order to generate the curve).

13  The software tool is called *Cabri-géomètre* and not *Cabri-géométrie*, despite the English version on occasion being called not 'Cabri-geometer' but 'Cabri-geometry' (as if it were a type of geometry). Nevertheless, Laborde here is talking about a different type of geometry.

14  This connects with David Fowler's characterisation of Greek geometric style of proof as *'first* draw the right picture and *then* say the right things about it'. Much of ancient Greek high mathematics offers not so much evidence of a preoccupation with geometric objects as with a ubiquity of geometric language for all of mathematics (as much as ours is algebraic today). The ancient notion of *diknume* proofs, ones evident by direct perception (provided you know how to look at the image), becomes important to contrast with that of calculated proofs. And as Lee and Wheeler's (1989) work on algebraic argument and demonstration has suggested, the conviction produced by algebraic calculation is only slowly acquired. For more on the sheer difference of Greek mathematical ontology from our own, see Fowler (1988) and Fauvel's (1989) review of it.

15  Mathematical tables, too, offer a particular structuring of space, a structured holding of relationships, offering a template not of the numbers themselves in the slots but of the relations among the entries. A spreadsheet offers dynamic relations, but ones still constrained by horizontal and vertical (developing Pascal's triangle can prove a problem). Interestingly, tables seem to be neither geometric nor algebraic.

16      To me, *visualization* seems a term invented by algebraists. Some algebraists think, for example, that the term 'circle' denotes the equation $x^2 + y^2 = r^2$. For them, that lovely curve shaped like the edge of the full moon does not exist by itself, but only to visualize this isotropic quadratic equation.

(Mandelbrot, 1991, p. 4)

17  John Mason (1991) has formulated a view of geometry that claims the most striking thing about geometry is the fact of facts.

18  According to Foucault (1983, p. 36): "Magritte names his paintings in order to focus attention on the very act of naming".

## 4  WHAT COUNTS AS A NUMBER?

1      When I was somewhere between one and nine I brooded over the possibility of finding a new number, an integer between one and nine that had somehow been overlooked. Their names and shapes seemed so arbitrary, ten shapes out of a million trillion thousand hundred and eleventy possible arrays of lines and loops, so how on earth could the adult world, the world no longer in single digits, be so smugly sure it had got them all? This worry has not entirely gone. Like so many people who are good at sums, I turned out to have no aptitude for mathematics: the ciphers continue to haunt me, entering my dreams and my prayers and my obsessions.

(Korn, 1991, p. 16)

The word 'cipher' has a double meaning, that of "numeral", and that of "zero". It is etymologically close to the French word *chiffre*, meaning "digit" or "figure". Rotman (1987, p. 12) tells us that 'cipher' is derived from the Sanskrit word *sunya*, meaning "void", and suggests that it is linked with the empty row on an abacus.

2 There are many more resonances to these words, such as *conter* being the French verb "to tell stories" and *compter* "to count", both deriving from the same Latin root. But *un conte* is also "a tale", and we talk about how many there are 'all-told'. A 'teller' can be one who counts aloud (money, votes), as well as a teller of a tale worth the telling – in other words, a tale that counts. To tell tales is also to reveal secrets. See, also, Love and Tahta (1991, p. 256).

3 A figure is a person, 'seen, but unidentified'. A figure of speech says something other than it seems to. Figurative language is full of metaphors rather than literal, yet figurative (as opposed to abstract) painting is attempting to be literal, to depict accurately what is there. A figure can be a geometric drawing. A figure can also be a number symbol. To figure is to do arithmetic, but also to think. Figures are figments of the imagination. Figures are fictions, contrivances. All f-words come from one Latin root, the verb *fingo*, meaning "to feign or invent".

4 The sense of 'geometer' may also be in the process of shifting, from the one-who-images to the one-who-uses-imaging-software.

5

GIRL: 98 ... Procyon ... 99 ... Aldebaran ... 100 ... Electra.
*(The girl stops skipping and counting. . . .)*

CISSIE 1: What are you doing up so late?
GIRL: I'm counting the stars.
CISSIE 1: Do you really know all their names?
GIRL: Yes I do.
*(There is a long pause.)*
CISSIE 1: How many did you count?
GIRL: A hundred.
CISSIE 1: But there are more than a hundred.
GIRL: I know.
*(There is a longer pause in complete silence.)*
CISSIE 1: Why did you stop?
GIRL: A hundred is enough. Once you have counted one hundred, all other hundreds are the same.

(Greenaway, 1988, p. 4)

6 What is this, 1? And this, 2? And this, 3? (and so on), and this, 9?
Now I want to write ten: how shall I do it?
Put 1 and 0.
But what has ten done to be different from the rest?
Why should it have two signs instead of one like its neighbours? And why does it take signs belonging to its neighbours, instead of having one of its own?
Did ten ask to have two signs? Did it wish to have two? No; then why did we give it two?
I once asked a young friend of mine why he did something in his sum; and he answered: 'My reason is that I was told to do it at school; but I know I ought to have another reason, and I know I haven't.' I thought that was a sensible answer. It applied to most things in arithmetic.

(Mary Boole, in Tahta, 1972, p. 30)

7 It is not the case, however, that all languages embody exactly the same principles. Some languages are more equal than others when it comes to regularity. The first ten Vietnamese number words in order are:

*mot, hai, ba, bon, nam, sau, bai, tam, chin, muoi.*

Eleven is *muoi mot*, fourteen is *muoi bon*, twenty-three is *hai muoi ba* and thirty-seven is *ba muoi bai*.

Translating the Vietnamese number words into English reveals a very transparent structure. Eleven is 'ten one' and twenty-three is 'two ten three'. Knowing this, you could form any number word to ninety-nine. If told that the Vietnamese word for 'hundred' is *tram*, you can now 'count' to nine hundred and ninety-nine.

Counters in English additionally need to know the words 'eleven', 'twelve', 'thirteen', 'fifteen', the '-teen' rule, 'twenty', 'thirty', 'forty', 'fifty' and the '-ty' rule. In passing, the words *eleven* and *twelve* come from Gothic *'ain-lif'* and *'twa-lif'*, meaning "one [or two] left" (after taking away ten, presumably).

8 This is a classical example of a metonymy, in fact, of a synecdoche: substituting the part for the whole. The 'counting' – *one, two, three, four, five* – gets abbreviated into the last word in the counting, *five*.

9 The number thirteen, plausibly through its metonymic link to the Last Supper, is often left out in real-world countings. If a building has a thirteenth floor, one number is commonly skipped and it is called fourteen. It is still the thirteenth floor ordinally, but the unease-provoking association seems to be with the number name itself.

10 John Mason (1980), in his article 'When is a symbol symbolic?', talks of 'seeing through' a symbol.

11 This need not be the case. Sandy Dawson (1991) has produced an account of developing a *written* subtraction algorithm which operates from left to right, arising from observations made when working with Cuisenaire rods.

12 'Working' shows that work has been done and this is an important part of classroom ethos, as well as marking an important boundary, that between work and play (see Walkerdine, 1981).

13 His wonderful practitioner name meaning "of the hand".

14 Is this true at the electrical level with electronic calculators?

15 Apices is the plural of 'apex' (like vertex – vertices), the high point of a triangle. Apices are pointers as well as counters, a physical embodiment of 'a four meaning "four"'. A more familiar example of the apex phenomenon can be seen with the musical stave. Similar blobs that are filled in or not, with attached lines or not, indicate relative duration; the lines are not powers of ten but relative pitch separators, and it is not a calculating device *per se*, merely a means of 'holding' music.

16 There might have come a point where the apparatus was seen to be too clumsy and to be unnecessary. If the symbols were removed from the objects and written down by themselves, then there was a way of computing with reference to these marks alone: that the smile left as the Cheshire cat vanished was sufficient. This transitional story, where the numerals 'substitute' for the apices in quite a real and physical sense, does not match the actual history at all. Nevertheless, calculating with the written notation in the 1200s may still have evoked traces of experience with numbered objects for mediaeval Western users.

17 Something similar happens in Logo when a complex procedure is defined and named: the name can then be used just like any other primitive in the system. In this sense, Logo is a pop-down, rather than a pop-up, language.

18    Almighty and most merciful Father,
      We have erred and strayed from thy ways like lost sheep,
      We have followed too much the devices and desires of our own hearts,
      We have offended against thy holy laws,
      We have left undone those things which we ought to have done,
      And we have done those things that we ought not to have done;
      And there is no health in us.

      A general confession, *The Book of Common Prayer*, p. 4.

19  This section draws on Dick Tahta's (1991) astonishing chapter entitled
    'Understanding and desire', as well as Brian Rotman's (1987) important book
    *Signifying Nothing*. The issues they discuss are at the heart of the murky and
    complex relationships among symbols and meanings in arithmetic in particu-
    lar, and in mathematics in general.

# 5  ALGEBRA TRANSFORMING

1  The word 'algebra' comes from the Arabic term *al-jabr*, particularly associated
   with the title of a work by al-Khwarizmi entitled *Al-kitab al-mukhtasar fi hisab al-
   jabr w'al-muqabalah*. While translations vary, a helpful one is 'The compendious
   book on calculation by completion [*al-jabr*] and opposition [*al-muqabalah*]'. This
   naming indicates that it is the *operations* which are perceived as important
   (naming frequently does that, even if the perceptions underlying the naming
   are no longer current). 'Completion' or 'restoration' refers to adding the same
   thing to both sides of an equation, placing all terms in some standard form.
   'Opposition' or 'balancing' refers to a comparable process of subtraction. For
   my purposes here, it is also of relevance that some of al-Khwarizmi's work was
   primarily concerned with 'manipulating' geometric areas related to what we
   would see as quadratic equations.
2  A colleague, Larry Copes, has told me of a dinner conversation with his
   daughter Lynn (aged ten) and her friend Laurel (sixteen).

   Lynn said, "We're doing algebra in math. Give me an algebra problem.
   But don't use those boring letters like *x* and *y*."
   "OK", replied Larry, "Five alpha plus two is seventeen. What is
   alpha?"
   Laurel, "What's alpha?"
   Larry, "The first Greek letter. It's definitely not boring."

   Lynn thought a while, and then said "Three". After expressing appropriate amazement, Larry asked, "How did you figure it out?"

   Lynn, "Well, I tried alpha as one, then two, then as three, and it finally
   worked."

   Then Laurel said, "There's an easier way. You have the equation five
   alpha plus two equals seventeen. So you subtract two from each side and
   get five alpha equals fifteen. Then you divide both sides by five to get
   alpha equals three."

   Lynn, "I don't understand a word you said. (*Pause*) But I have an idea.
   What if you subtract two from seventeen to get fifteen and then divide
   by three. That's just undoing what you did to alpha to get seventeen."

   Laurel, "That's just what I said."

Lynn, "No it's not. You were talking about equations and doing something to both sides. I didn't understand that."

The doing, the acting, is important – but gets lost. Once again, mathematics becomes static, verbs turn into nouns, 'equating' becomes 'an equation', just as 'moving' becomes 'a motion' in geometry.

3  Martin Hughes (1986) has made extensive comments about the difficulties young children have in representing the process of change.

4  A sixty-minute videotape containing extensive extracts from the lessons and interview is available: see Hewitt (1991). Some of the quotations I cite here are taken from the written notes he produced to accompany this tape.

5  A similar graphic onomatopoeia can be found in James and Mason (1982), where they offer the notion of a balloon or bag grouping the things inside, gradually adapting it to having dotted lines apart from both ends, until finally the brackets are all that is left.

6  It provides a different variant on the 'understanding before doing' story. See Mason *et al.* (1985).

7  Logo is not a computer algebra system, it is a fully fledged, sophisticated computer language. I acknowledge I have done far from justice to the potentiality of Logo in this context. For a much fuller exploration, see Hoyles and Sutherland (1989) and, particularly, Hoyles and Noss (1992).

8  Sutherland writes (1992, p. 37): "Pupils can choose to manipulate the formal Logo procedure or to descend into the geometrical meaning behind the Logo formalism".

9  Talking about a non-Logo environment, Kaput (1989, p. 190) comments:

> This situation will change as symbol manipulation systems specifically designed for educational purposes become available. . . . Some of these new systems will enable the user to perform certain procedures on particular cases (say, solve a particular linear equation), while the system "captures" or records the sequence of actions as a more general procedure to be executed on other linear equations, much as *The Geometric Supposers* (Schwartz and Yerushalmy, 1985) record geometric constructions as procedures to be re-executed on command.

This provides an instance of how increasing software sophistication can result in decreased mathematical challenge.

10  This has not stopped many people exploring their potential educational consequences for schools: see, for instance, the special issue of the ATM journal *Micromath* 9(3), 1993 devoted to computer algebra systems.

11  Some software (e.g. *Math Connections Algebra I* and *II*) actually creates an equivalence: thus, apparently, a table of values can be plotted or *graphed*! The latter option puts a curve through the points, and indeed occasionally 'corrects' table values that have been input if the curve does not exactly fit.

12  What would software look like that did offer forms as forms to be worked on directly? Dave Hewitt has developed a program called GRID Algebra, connected with the rulers lessons described earlier, which provides one response. Details may be obtained from the Centre for Mathematics Education, The Open University, Walton Hall, Milton Keynes, Bucks MK7 6AA, England.

13  A lone voice urging and arguing for caution is that of David Wheeler (1989).

14  A similar situation can be seen with the economic instrument known as the tally stick, which was broken in two as well as doubly graded to show the amount owed. The possessor of the matching counterpart was the person to whom the debt was owed.

15 Curiously, the Latinate root of the word 'object', a term often used as the counterpart to 'symbol', also has the root meaning "throw" (Lat. *jaceo*), while the prefix 'ob' indicates "before": something 'thrown before the mind'.

16 The Frye piece that I have drawn on for this section is called 'The symbol as a medium of exchange'. Money concerns and algebraic concerns are intimately linked, both as explored by Brian Rotman (1987) and by Simone Weil (1952, p. 139): 'Money, mechanisation, algebra. The three monsters of contemporary civilisation. . . . Algebra and money are essentially levellers.' I see Weil's 'levelling' in terms of ignoring difference (whether between labour or dividend as sources of my money, or in algebra in terms of the problem, once algebraicised, disappearing from view and being treated the same irrespective of its source). But it also carries a whiff of 'democracy', of social levelling. And as for commonality across her three monsters, one is that they all involve a loss of action, of will, of agency – an absence or distancing of direct involvement of the human self.

17 That *os* is the Latin word for 'bone' adds an unexpected resonance to *symbolos*. Also, according to Flegg (1983, p. 173), the word *algebra* "came to have the pseudo-medical meaning of 'bone-setter'".

# 6 MAKING REPRESENTATIONS AND INTERPRETATIONS

1 There is a lot of work do be done on the nature of the original in mathematics: what differences are there among 'sphere', 'a sphere' and 'the sphere'? See Benjamin (1969) for a discussion of how the ability to make mechanical reproductions of works of art has altered the notion of 'the original'.

2 This acknowledgement of agency and intent is, for me, some of what gives force to a remark I heard: "My dog stepped on a calculator the other day and drew $\sin(x)$".

3 Virtual reality creates a virtual visual world that is not a reflection, at least not in the 'mirror'-generated sense. It is not a representation either. It offers a scene that is 'virtually' there as far as the eyes perceive, as well as offering an apparently three-dimensional tactile and sonic world.

4 ASA stands for American Standards Association – a metonymy turned into a unit. The numbers used to indicate relative sensitivity to light form a ratio scale, that is a film with an ASA rating of 200 reacts to light twice as fast as a 100-rated film.

5 It is true that light meters are becoming more sophisticated and some now have centre-weighting, to give greater emphasis to the degree of light coming in from whatever is at the centre of the proposed field of view. In 1970, the *Life* magazine photographer Ralph Morse commented about external light meters: "The meter is a great tool, but remember it is just a dumb mechanical instrument. You must use your experience and judgement to interpret it". In the twenty-odd years since that comment was made, light meters have become integral devices in the camera and opportunities for either developing or exercising 'experience and judgement' in interpretation have been curtailed.

# 7 SYMBOLS AND MEASURES

1 Originally from *Baker* Street to Water*loo* Station.

2 Ivins, mentioned in the last chapter, comments that museum art writers, even

when two paintings are in a gallery, will bring photographs of them side by side for comparison, rather than the actual objects, which invites seeing the taking of photographs as a form of measurement, as well as creating a counterpart.

3 Nowhere is this clearer than with computer-generated objects (such as in *Geometer's Sketchpad*) which allows 'measurement' of areas. Since these erstwhile geometric objects are actually specified by arithmetic parameters, there is no sense of error or approximation. The images come from the measurements, rather than conversely.

4 A mathematical example of unit structure comes with scientific notation: $2.67 \times 10^6$ metres. There are two sorts of unit here: an arithmetic scale offered by powers of ten, which is highly *non*-uniform, despite its deceptive appearance, and then a physical unit. See Confrey (1991).

5 The standard English pronunciation of this word, with the second syllable stressed 'kil-*om*-etre', masks this structural link, in a way that the North American first syllable stressed pronunciation 'kil-o-meter' does not.

6 The complexity of economic exchange, the meaning relations among price, money and value, is well explored in Wallace Shawn's play *The Fever*:

> He [Marx] used the example that people say, 'twenty yards of linen are worth two pounds'. People say about every thing that it has a certain value. This is worth that. This coat, this sweater, this cup of coffee: each thing worth some quantity of money, or some number of other things – one coat, worth three sweaters, or so much money – as if that coat, suddenly appearing on the earth, contained somewhere inside itself an amount of value, like an inner soul, as if the coat were a fetish, a physical object that contains a living spirit. But what really determines the value of a coat? What is it that determines the price of a coat? The coat's price comes from its history, the history of all the people who were involved in making it and selling it and all the particular relationships they had. And if we buy the coat, we too form relationships with all of those people, and yet we hide those relationships from our own awareness by pretending we live in a world where coats have no history but just fall down from heaven with prices marked inside. 'I like this coat,' we say, 'it's not expensive,' as if that were a fact about the *coat* itself and not the end of a story about all the people who made it and sold it.
>
> (Shawn, 1991, p. 27)

7 The terms 'minutes' and 'seconds' provide a nice pair of units, in that *minute* derives from its smallness relative to an hour, and *second* comes from "a second order of minuteness". Both of these words have been turned into names of measures: along the way, this status has been confirmed by a shift into nouns and in the first by an altered pronunciation and the second by shedding any sense of ordinality.

8 This has the characteristic of metaphor: first something is assumed to be something else, to enable one result to be determined, then it is believed to be different, in order to compensate for the fact that it is metaphor and not literal description that is involved. See Pimm (1994) for more on this view of metaphor as involving both assertions that it *is* and that it is *not*.

9 "And, according to a now-forgotten etymology, a theorem is above all the object of a vision" (Thom, 1971, p. 697).

10 Ivins, as ever attuned to the particularity of different senses, writes (1969, pp. 53–4) of the centrality of vision in endeavouring to gain knowledge and acquaintance of objects. In particular, he notes a consonance:

This method of symbolization is the making of pictures or images, which, unlike spoken words, are apprehended through the same sense organs which give us the awarenesses we try to symbolize.

He proposes the following criterion.

Thus the more closely we can confine our data for reasoning about things to data that come to us through one and the same sense channel the more apt we are to be correct in our reasoning, even though it be much more restricted in its scope. One of the most interesting things in our modern scientific practice has been the invention and perfection of methods by which the scientists can acquire much of their basic data through one and the same sensuous channel of awareness. I understand that in physics, for example, the scientists are happiest when they can get their data with the aid of some dial or other device which can be read by vision. Thus heat, weight, lengths, and many other things that in ordinary life are apprehended through senses other than vision have become for science matters of visual awareness of the positions of mechanical pointers.

11  Other objects are used besides numbers as measures in higher mathematics. Groups, for instance, are widely used as measures of spaces in algebraic topology. But in each case there is the arithmetic-algebraic displacement which moves from the particular realm of interest into another.

## 8 LIVING IN THE MATERIAL WORLD: SYMBOLS IN CONTEXTS

1  Yves Chevallard (1990, p. 6) writes trenchantly about the *need* of mathematics educators to write in defence of their subject:

Such a study [he is reviewing a special issue of a journal on cultural issues in mathematics education] pertains to the category of *apologetical discourses*. To put it plainly: mathematics "noospherians" – members of the noosphere (reviewer's personal jargon), i.e. members of the mathematics education intelligentsia – have "to put over the goods", to convince society that mathematics, and therefore, mathematics education, are highly *beneficial* to society. However subtly, fighting in defence of mathematics and mathematics teaching is the common lot of the literature on mathematics education.

2  This is not new. My mother recalls being in the army during the Second World War and the officer dividing the new recruits into two groups: those with 'general schools' mathematics over there and the rest over there. Those in the first group were then offered training in a range of technical tasks such as repairing the electrical systems of trucks.

3  See, for instance, d'Ambrosio (1985), but also Wheeler's comments in his review of Marcia Ascher's book on ethnomathematics (1992). As I write, a special issue of *For the Learning of Mathematics*, **14**(2) devoted to this theme has just appeared.

4  For a subtle analysis of some features and effects of various text styles, see Dowling (1991a, 1991b).

5  Lesley Lee has remarked to me how at a recent meeting about the teaching and learning of algebra, she noticed and commented on how every problem in a beginning set of algebra problems was about money. She was told how publishers and hence authors were uneasy about offending some or other

group or section of the population (food was also taboo), thus acting against 'math for all'. Such self-censoring may well result in no people now featuring directly in problems.

She commented, "It seems that one subject of apparent social consensus in the US is money (and the capitalist system), so that if one wants one's textbook to sell to as wide an American market as possible, ... " Swetz' (1987) book *Capitalism and Arithmetic* may yet be rewritten about algebra in the US in the twenty-first century rather than being in part about algebra in fifteenth-century Italy – see Tahta (1990b).

## 9  ON FLUENCY AND UNDERSTANDING

1  "One might say that the project [*Automath*] is a modern version of "Leibniz's Dream" of making a language for all scientific discussion in such a way that all reasoning can be represented by a kind of algebraic manipulation" (de Bruijn, 1986, p. 61).

2  When learning to play the saxophone, one goal was to learn to play the scales fluently. The temptation to which I regularly succumbed was trying to learn to play them fast. I was repeatedly told by my teacher to play them more slowly, evenly and fluently, and that speed would come.

3  In a recent Key Stage 1 SAT (UK national test for seven-year-olds), pupils were to be given two numbers and asked to add them without giving any indication of counting on (e.g. no finger movements). What if they looked up? Were they counting on in their heads?

4  Recall an *automaton* is a thing which can move by itself, apparently at will and therefore seemingly embodies a sense of will.

5  For more on the history and development of primary mathematics textbooks, see Gray (1991).

6

The apt use of a word (in its poetical sense), its repetition, twice, three times, or even more frequently, according to the need of the poem, will not only tend to intensify the internal structure but also bring out unsuspected spiritual properties in the word itself. Further, frequent repetition of a word (a favorite game of children, forgotten in later life) deprives the word of its external reference. Similarly, the symbolic reference of a designated object tends to be forgotten and only the sound is retained.

(Kandinsky, 1947, p. 34)

7  In the story *Franny and Zooey*, Salinger writes of the Jesus Prayer, to be said incessantly: "Enlightenment's supposed to come *with* the prayer, not before it" (1964, p. 113).

8  In 1992, a constitutional referendum was held across Canada with regard to the terms under which anglophones and francophones would agree to Quebec as a formal part of Canada. The slogan of one unificationist group, '*Mon Canada comprend le Québec*', shows both meanings to their full extent. The result of the referendum suggested that parts of Canada did not choose to 'understand' Quebec.

9  A few of the papers include: Skemp (1976), Michener (1978), Sierpinska (1990), Pirie and Kieren (1989, 1992), Davis (1992) and Sfard (1994). Many of the approaches involve dividing up understanding into types: for instance, the distinction between 'relational' and 'instrumental', made by Mellin-Olsen, then extended and promulgated by Skemp. One point here about this particular

distinction is the common identification of 'rote learning' or 'rote teaching methods' with 'instrumental understanding', yet for its delineators, it was a form of *understanding*. Similarly, associations derived from symbolic forms are, for me, a form of meaning.

10 There is a strong analogy with the use of the sense of touch in pottery. Otto Natzler, in his book *Ceramics*, writes:

> When you hold a pot in your hands, when you go over its walls with your fingers, you feel the hands of the potter, his fingermarks, his touch. You may not know who he was or what he looked like, but, handling the pot, be it hundreds or thousands of years old, you can still feel the imprint of his hands. It is this fact about a pot that makes it so endearing, so very personal. It makes the physical handling of a pot such an important part of its appreciation, as important as its visual impact and at times even more so.
>
> (Natzler, 1968, pp. 38–9)

Consider the technology of pottery. First, pots can be completely hand-made, formed without tools, producing something which is particular, idiosyncratic and potentially interesting – there is plenty of room for surprises and actuality turning out differently from intention. The pot is organic and in intimate relation with the maker, down to the point of leaving fingerprints on it – the imprint that personality can impose on form. Then, with pottery thrown on a wheel, the generative motion creates fewer opportunities for spontaneous elements, but can offer more symmetry and also speed. Finally, with slip-casting technology (use of a mould), we have lost all evidence of individual hands and thus the organic connectedness with the person. The result inherits a certain uniformity and smoothness, but also a certain unchangingness from the mould. There is the possibility of exactly repeatable clay statements.

Apart from completely hand-made pots, all pots are created in part by means of some technology which has its own functions that can intervene to shape the end result. More sophisticated tools can expand the imaginative possibilities by allowing things to be done that could not be done by hand alone. As with the example of photography in Chapter 6, in terms of artistry, there is a tension between functioning and automation on the one hand and creativity and human control (and hence variability) on the other. But there are also different experiences of that tension, depending on whether you are more novice or expert.

## 10 ON MANIPULATION

1 There is an odd connection here in that Spencer Brown (1977, p. 93) informs us that the origin of the verb 'to argue' also involves silver. He writes:

> Although *count* rests on *putare* = prune, correct, (and hence) reckon, the word *reason* comes from *reri* = count, calculate, reckon. Thus the reasoning and computing activities of proof were originally considered as one. We may note further that *argue* is based on *arguere* = clarify (literally 'make silver'). We thus find a whole constellation of words to do with the process of *getting it right*.

2 I am grateful to Eric Love for providing me with this information.
3 COBUILD is a research project sponsored by Harper Collins Publishers at the University of Birmingham. The Bank of English consists of 200 million words,

held as a number of corpora from a wide range of language sources. It is possible to search some or all of these corpora for occurrences of particular words and hence, relative to the scope of the database, to get a feel for relative frequency and common co-occurrences of words and expressions. The Collins COBUILD dictionary (1987) was one product of this work.

4 See Pimm (1988) for a discussion of the functioning of creative metaphoric juxtapositions such as this one.

5 There is a tension between symbol for object (metonymy) and symbol as object (metaphor). Fluency and understanding result from different balances among these two always present possibilities. See Tahta (1991) for more detail about the sense of these terms.

# REFERENCES

Ainley, J. (1988a) 'Perceptions of teachers' questioning styles', *Proceedings of the 12th PME Conference*, Veszprem, Hungary, pp. 92–9.

Ainley, J. (1988b) 'Maths in motion', *Child Education*, September, 33–5.

Ainley, J. (1991) 'Is there any mathematics in measurement?', in Pimm, D. and Love, E. (eds) *Teaching and Learning School Mathematics*, London, Hodder and Stoughton, pp. 69–76.

Ainley, J. (1994) 'Building on children's intuitions about line graphs', *Proceedings of the 18th PME Conference*, Lisbon, Portugal, 2, pp. 1–8.

Ainley, J. and Goldstein, R. (1988) *Making Logo Work*, Oxford, Basil Blackwell.

Atiyah, M. (1986) 'Mathematics and the computer revolution', in Churchhouse, R. *et al.* (eds) *The Influence of Computers and Informatics on Mathematics and its Teaching*, (ICMI Study Series), Cambridge, Cambridge University Press, pp. 43–51.

ATM (1985) *Away with Maths*, Derby, Association of Teachers of Mathematics.

ATM (1992) Special Feature on *Cabri-Géomètre*, *Micromath*, 8(2), 22–39.

Balacheff, N. (1988) 'Aspects of proof processes in pupils' practice of school mathematics', in Pimm, D. (ed.) *Mathematics, Teachers and Children*, London, Hodder and Stoughton, pp. 216–35.

Balacheff, N. (1991) 'Construction et analyse d'une situation didactique: le cas de "la somme des angles d'un triangle"', *Journal für Didaktik der Mathematik*, 12 (2/3), 199–264.

Barthes, R. (1984) *Camera Obscura: Reflections on Photography*, London, Fontana.

Beeney, R. *et al.* (1982) *Geometric Images*, Derby, Association of Teachers of Mathematics.

Belenky, M. *et al.* (1986) *Women's Ways of Knowing: The Development of Self, Voice and Mind*, New York, Basic Books.

Benjamin, W. (1969) 'The work of art in the age of mechanical reproduction', in Benjamin, W., *Illuminations*, New York, Schocken Books, pp. 217–51.

Bidwell, S. and Clason, R. (1970) *Readings in the History of Mathematics Education*, Washington, DC, National Council for Teachers of Mathematics.

Bloomfield, A. (1990) *People Maths*, Cheltenham, Stanley Thornes.

Boero, P. (1993) 'About the transformation function of the algebraic code', Working conference on *Algebraic Processes and the Role of Symbolism*, London, Institute of Education.

Boyer, C. (1968) *A History of Mathematics*, New York, Wiley.

Brown, L. (1991) 'Prerequisite', *Mathematics Teaching*, 135, 23.

Brown, S. (1974) 'Musing on multiplication', *Mathematics Teaching*, 69, 26–30.

Bruner, J. (1966) *Toward a Theory of Instruction*, Cambridge, MA, Harvard University Press.

## REFERENCES

Cajori, F. (1916) *William Oughtred: A Great Seventeenth Century Teacher of Mathematics*, Chicago, IL, Open Court.

Calvino, I. (1988) *Six Memos for the Next Millennium*, Cambridge, MA, Harvard University Press.

Carlyle, T. (1836; 1987) *Sartor Resartus*, Oxford, Oxford University Press.

Channell, J. (1994) *Vague Language*, Oxford, Oxford University Press.

Chazan, D. (1993) 'F(x) = G(x)?: an approach to modelling with algebra', *For the Learning of Mathematics*, **13**(3), 22–6.

Chevallard, Y. (1990) 'On mathematics education and culture: critical afterthoughts', *Educational Studies in Mathematics*, **21**(1), 3–27.

Churchhouse, R. *et al.* (eds) (1986) *The Influence of Computers and Informatics on Mathematics and its Teaching*, (ICMI Study Series), Cambridge, Cambridge University Press.

Clement, J. (1989) 'The concept of variation and misconceptions in Cartesian graphing', *Focus on Learning Problems in Mathematics*, **11**(2), 77–87.

COBUILD (1987) *The Collins COBUILD English Language Dictionary*, London, Collins.

Confrey, J. (1991) 'Learning to listen: a student's understanding of powers of ten', in von Glasersfeld, E. (ed.) *Radical Constructivism in Mathematics Education*, Dordrecht, Kluwer, pp. 111–38.

D'Ambrosio, U. (1985) 'Ethnomathematics and its place in the history and pedagogy of mathematics', *For the Learning of Mathematics*, **5**(1), 44–8.

Davenport, G. (1987) *Every Force Evolves a Form*, Berkeley, CA, North Point Press.

Davis, R. (1992) 'Understanding "understanding"', *Journal of Mathematical Behavior*, **11**(3), 225–41.

Davydov, V. and Markova, A. (1983) 'A concept of educational activity for schoolchildren', *Soviet Psychology*, **21**(2), 50–76.

Dawson, S. (1991) 'Learning mathematics *does not (necessarily) mean* constructing the right knowledge', in Pimm, D. and Love, E. (eds) *Teaching and Learning School Mathematics*, London, Hodder and Stoughton, pp. 195–204.

de Bruijn, N. (1986) 'Checking mathematics with the aid of a computer', in Churchhouse, R. *et al.* (eds) *The Influence of Computers and Informatics on Mathematics and its Teaching*, (ICMI Study Series), Cambridge, Cambridge University Press, pp. 61–8.

DES (Department of Education and Science) (1982) *Mathematics Counts* (the Cockcroft report), London, HMSO.

DES/WO (Department of Education and Science/Welsh Office) (1988) *Mathematics for Ages 5 to 16*, London, HMSO.

Dienes, Z. (1963) *An Experimental Study of Mathematics Learning*, London, Hutchinson.

DIME (1985) *Feely Box*, Diss, Norfolk, Tarquin Publications.

Doerfler, R. (1993) *Dead Reckoning: Calculating without Instruments*, Houston, TX, Gulf Publishing Company.

Donaldson, M. (1979) *Children's Minds*, London, Fontana.

Douady, R. (1985) 'The interplay between different settings, tool-object dialectic in the extension of mathematical ability', in Streefland, L. (ed.), *Proceedings of the Ninth International Conference for the Psychology of Learning Mathematics*, State University of Utrecht, OW&OC, pp. 33–52.

Douglas, M. (1978) *Natural Symbols*, Harmondsworth, Penguin.

Douglas, M. (1991) 'Faith, hope and probability', *London Review of Books*, 23 May, 6–8.

Dowling, P. (1991a) 'Gender, class and subjectivity in mathematics: a critique of Humpty Dumpty', *For the Learning of Mathematics*, **11**(1), 2–8.

REFERENCES

Dowling, P. (1991b) 'A touch of class: ability, social class and intertext in SMP 11–16', in Pimm, D. and Love, E. (eds), *Teaching and Learning School Mathematics*, London, Hodder and Stoughton, pp. 137–52.

Dufour-Janvier, B., Bednarz, N., and Belanger, M. (1984) 'Pedagogical considerations concerning the problem of representation', in Janvier, C. (ed.) *Problems of Representation in the Teaching and Learning of Mathematics*, Hillsdale, NJ, Lawrence Erlbaum Associates, pp. 109–22.

Elson, R. (1964) *Guardians of Tradition: American Schoolbooks of the Nineteenth Century*, Lincoln, NE, Nebraska University Press.

Fauvel, J. (1988) *Topics in the History of Mathematics* (MA290), Milton Keynes, The Open University, Unit 3.

Fauvel, J. (1989) 'Academics at the Academy', *Mathematics Teaching*, **128**, 38–40.

Fauvel, J. and Gray, J. (eds) (1987) *The History of Mathematics: A Reader*, London, Macmillan.

Feynman, R. (1988) *What do YOU Care what Other People Think?*, New York, Norton.

Fisch, M. and Bergin, T. (1944) *The Autobiography of Giambattista Vico*, a translation from the Italian original, Ithaca, NY, Cornell University Press.

Flegg, G. (1983) *Numbers: Their History and Meaning*, London, André Deutsch.

Foucault, M. (1983) *This is Not a Pipe*, Berkeley, CA, University of California Press.

Fowler, D. (1988) *The Mathematics of Plato's Academy: A New Reconstruction*, Oxford, Clarendon Press.

Freeman, R. (1960) *Yesterday's School Books*, Watkins Glen, NY, Century House.

Freudenthal, H. (1973) *Mathematics as an Educational Task*, Dordrecht, D. Reidel.

Frye, N. (1987) 'The symbol as a medium of exchange', in Leith, J. (ed.) *Symbols in Life and Art*, Montreal, McGill-Queen's University Press, pp. 3–16.

Garfinkel, H. (1968) 'On the origins of the term "ethnomethodology"', in Hill, R. and Stones Crittenden, K. (eds) *Proceedings of the Purdue Symposium on Ethnomethodology*, Institute Monograph Series No 1, Institute for the Study of Social Change, Purdue University, pp. 5–11.

Gattegno, C. (1963a) *Modern Mathematics with Numbers in Colour*, Reading, Educational Explorers Ltd.

Gattegno, C. (1963b) 'A matter of relationships', *For the Teaching of Mathematics*, volume 3, Reading, Educational Explorers Ltd., pp. 80–4.

Gattegno, C. (1967) 'Functioning as a mathematician', *Mathematics Teaching*, **39**, 6–9. (Reprinted in *A Gattegno Anthology*, Brown, L. *et al.* (eds), Derby, Association of Teachers of Mathematics, pp. 28–9.)

Gattegno, C. (1970) *What We Owe Children*, New York, Outerbridge & Dienstfrey.

Gattegno, C. (1974) *The Common Sense of Teaching Mathematics*, New York, Educational Solutions.

Gattegno, C. (1983) 'On algebra', *Mathematics Teaching*, **105**, 34–5.

Gerdes, P. (1988) 'On culture, geometrical thinking and mathematics education', *Educational Studies in Mathematics*, **19**(2), 137–62.

Gilligan, C. (1982) *In a Different Voice: Psychological Theory and Women's Development*, Cambridge, MA, Harvard University Press.

Goldenberg, E. (1987) 'Believing is seeing', *Proceedings of the Eleventh International Conference for the Psychology of Learning Mathematics*, Montreal, QC, pp. 197–203.

Goldenberg, E. (1988) 'Mathematics, metaphors and human factors: mathematical, technical and pedagogic challenges in the educational use of graphical representations of functions', *Journal of Mathematical Behavior*, **7**, 135–73.

Goldenberg, E. and Feurzeig, W. (1987) *Exploring Language with Logo*, Cambridge, MA, MIT Press.

Gould, S. (1981) *The Mismeasure of Man*, New York, Norton.

# REFERENCES

Goutard, M. (1964) *Mathematics and Children*, Reading, Educational Explorers.

Gray, E. (1991) 'The primary mathematics textbook: intermediary in the cycle of change', in Pimm, D. and Love, E. (eds) *Teaching and Learning School Mathematics*, London, Hodder and Stoughton, pp. 122–36.

Gray, J. (1988) *Topics in the History of Mathematics* (MA290), Milton Keynes, The Open University, Unit 8.

GRE (1993) *Information and Registration Booklet of the Graduate Record Examination*, Princeton, NJ, Educational Testing Service.

Greenaway, P. (1988) *Drowning by Numbers*, London, Faber and Faber.

Halliday, M. (1975) *Learning How to Mean*, London, Edward Arnold.

Harnasz, C. (1993), 'Do you need to know how it works?', in Selinger, M. (ed.) *Teaching Mathematics*, London, Routledge, pp. 137–44.

Hatch, G. and Hewitt, D. (1991) 'On symbolic manipulators', *Mathematics Teaching*, **137**, 16–18.

Hewitt, D. (1991) *Working Mathematically with Symbols in Key Stage 3* (PM647H), Milton Keynes, The Open University.

Higbee, K. and Kunihira, S. (1985) 'Cross-cultural applications of Yodai mnemonics in education', *Educational Psychologist*, **20**, 57–64.

HMI (Her Majesty's Inspectorate) (1979) *Aspects of Secondary Education*, London, HMSO.

HMI (1985) *Mathematics from 5 to 16*, Curriculum Matters 3, London, HMSO.

Hoare, C. (1990) 'The invisible Japanese calculator', *Mathematics Teaching*, **131**, 12–14.

Hoban, R. (1982) *Riddley Walker*, London, Picador.

Hockney, D. (1993) Quoted in 'Sound and Vision', R. Barnes, *The Guardian*, 9 August, **2**, p. 5.

Howson, G. (1982) *A History of Mathematics Education in England*, Cambridge, Cambridge University Press.

Hoyles, C. and Noss, R. (eds) (1992) *Learning Mathematics and Logo*, Cambridge, MA, MIT Press.

Hoyles, C. and Sutherland, R. (1989) *Logo Mathematics in the Classroom*, London, Routledge.

Hughes, M. (1986) *Children and Number*, Oxford, Basil Blackwell.

Huxley, A. (1956) *The Doors of Perception* and *Heaven and Hell*, New York, Harper and Row.

Ignatieff, M. (1993) *Blood and Belonging*, London, Viking Penguin.

Ivins, W. (1946) *Art and Geometry: A Study in Space Intuitions*, New York, Dover.

Ivins, W. (1969) *Prints and Visual Communication*, New York, NY, Da Capo Press.

James, N. and Mason, J. (1982) 'Towards recording', *Visible Language*, **16**(3), 249–58.

Janvier, C (1984) 'Translation processes in mathematics education', in Janvier, C. (ed.) *Problems of Representation in the Teaching and Learning of Mathematics*, Hillsdale, NJ, Lawrence Erlbaum Associates, pp. 27–32.

Jaworski, B. (1985) 'A poster lesson', *Mathematics Teaching*, **113**, 4–5.

Jaworski, B. and Pimm, D. (1986) *Practical Work in the Secondary Classroom* (PM644), Milton Keynes, The Open University.

Kandinsky, W. (1947) *Concerning the Spiritual in Art*, New York, George Wittenborn Inc.

Kaput, J. (1984) 'Representation systems and mathematics', in Janvier, C. (ed.) *Problems of Representation in the Teaching and Learning of Mathematics*, Hillsdale, NJ, Lawrence Erlbaum Associates, pp. 19–26.

Kaput, J. (1989) 'Linking representations in the symbol systems of algebra', in Wagner, S. and Kieran, C. (eds) *Research Issues in the Learning and Teaching of Algebra*, Reston, VA, Lawrence Erlbaum Associates/NCTM, pp. 167–94.

# REFERENCES

Kaput, J. (1994) 'Democratizing access to calculus: new routes using old roots', in Schoenfeld, A. (ed.) *Mathematical Thinking and Problem Solving*, Hillsdale, NJ, Lawrence Erlbaum Associates, pp. 77–156.

Keitel, C. (1989) 'Mathematics education and technology', *For the Learning of Mathematics*, 9(1), 7–13.

Kerslake, D. (1982) 'Talking about mathematics', in Harvey, R. *et al.*, *Mathematics* (Language, Teaching and Learning #6), London, Ward Lock, pp. 41–83.

Kieren, T. (1991) *Investigations into a Recursive Theory of Mathematics Understanding* project, Edmonton, AB, University of Alberta.

Kieren, T. and Pimm, D. (1989) 'Mathematics, Logo and language: two turtles in a hot tub', *Logo Exchange*, 8(3), 26–8.

Klee, P. (1964) *The Thinking Eye*, New York, George Wittenborn Inc.

Korn, E. (1991) 'The meaning of Mngwotngwotiki', *London Review of Books*, 10 January, p. 16.

Laborde. C. (1993) 'Do the pupils learn and what do they learn in a computer based environment? The case of *Cabri-géomètre*', *Proceedings of the Technology in Mathematics Teaching Conference*, Birmingham, University of Birmingham, pp. 39–52.

Lave, J. (1988) *Cognition in Practice*, Cambridge, Cambridge University Press.

Lebowitz, F. (1982) *Social Studies*, London, Arrow.

Lee, L. (1990) 'Radical practice', *Mathematics Teaching*, **133**, 55–8.

Lee, L. and Wheeler, D. (1989) 'The arithmetic connection', *Educational Studies in Mathematics*, **20**(1), 41–54.

Lieberthal, E. (1979) *The Complete Book of Fingermath*, New York, McGraw-Hill.

Lodge, D. (1984) *Small World*, London, Secker & Warburg.

Love, E. (1987) *Working Mathematically on Film with Sixth Formers* (PM647B), Milton Keynes, The Open University.

Love, E. and Mason, J. (1992) *Teaching Mathematics: Action and Awareness*, Milton Keynes, The Open University.

Love, E. and Tahta, D. (1991) 'Reflections on some words used in mathematics education', in Pimm, D. and Love, E. (eds) *Teaching and Learning School Mathematics*, London, Hodder and Stoughton, pp. 252–72.

MA (1934) *The Teaching of Algebra in Schools*, London, G. Bell.

Mandelbrot, B. (1991) Preface, in Peitgen, H.-O., Jürgens, H. and Saupe, D., *Fractals for the Classroom: Part 1*, Berlin, Springer-Verlag, p. 4.

Mason, J. (1980) 'When is a symbol symbolic?', *For the Learning of Mathematics*, 1(2), 8–11.

Mason, J. (1990a) *Shape and Space* (PM649), Milton Keynes, The Open University.

Mason, J. (1990b) 'Geometry: what, why, where and how?', *Mathematics Teaching*, **129**, 40–7.

Mason, J. (1991) 'Questions about geometry', in Pimm, D. and Love, E. (eds) *Teaching and Learning School Mathematics*, London, Hodder and Stoughton, pp. 77–90.

Mason, J. *et al.* (1985) *Routes to / Roots of Algebra* (PM641), Milton Keynes, The Open University.

Maxwell, J. (1985) 'Hidden messages', *Mathematics Teaching*, **111**, 18–19.

Michener, E. (1978) 'Understanding understanding mathematics', *Cognitive Science*, **2**, 361–83.

Morelli, L. (1992) 'A visual approach to algebra concepts', *The Mathematics Teacher*, 85(6), 434–7.

Morse, R. (1970) *The Life Library of Photography Photographer's Handbook*, New York, Time inc., p. 21.

## REFERENCES

Natzler, O. (1968) *Gertrud and Otto Natzler: Ceramics*, Los Angeles, CA, The Los Angeles County Museum of Art.

NCTM (1989) *Curriculum and Evaluation Standards for School Mathematics*, Reston, VA, National Council for Teachers of Mathematics.

NCTM (1993) *Algebra for the Twenty-First Century*, Reston, VA, National Council for Teachers of Mathematics.

Niss, M. (1983) 'Considerations and experiences concerning integrated courses in mathematics and other subjects', in Zweng, M. *et al.* (eds), *Proceedings of the Fourth International Congress on Mathematical Education*, Boston, MA, Birkhäuser, pp. 247–9.

Noss, R. (1985) 'Revealing messages', *Mathematics Teaching*, **112**, 38.

Noss, R. (1986) 'Constructing a conceptual framework for elementary algebra through Logo programming', *Educational Studies in Mathematics*, **17**(4), 335–57.

Noss, R. (1988) 'The computer as a cultural influence in mathematical learning', *Educational Studies in Mathematics*, **19**(3), 251–68.

Noss, R. (1991) 'The social shaping of computing in mathematics education', in Pimm, D. and Love, E. (eds) *Teaching and Learning School Mathematics*, London, Hodder and Stoughton, pp. 205–19.

Noss, R. (1994) 'Structure and ideology in the mathematics curriculum', *For the Learning of Mathematics*, **14**(1), 2–10.

NRC (1989) *Everybody Counts*, Washington, DC, National Academy Press.

Nunokawa, K. (1994) 'Improving diagrams gradually: one approach to using diagrams in problem solving', *For the Learning of Mathematics*, **14**(1), 34–8.

Open University (1989) *Using Mathematical Thinking* (ME234), Milton Keynes, The Open University.

Ortony, A. (1975) 'Why metaphors are necessary and not just nice', *Educational Theory*, **25**, 45–53.

O'Shea, T. (1993) 'The role of manipulatives in mathematics education', *Contemporary Education*, **65**(1), 6–9.

O'Shea, T. (1994) 'Calculator algorithms and the school mathematics curriculum' in Marks, S. (ed.) *Proceedings of the 1994 International Symposium on Mathematics/ Science Education and Technology*, Charlottesville, VA, Association for the Advancement of Computing in Education, pp. 128–32.

Papert, S. (1980) *Mindstorms: Children, Computers and Powerful Ideas*, Brighton, Harvester.

Parsysz, B. (1988) '"Knowing" vs "seeing": problems of plane representation of space geometry figures', *Educational Studies in Mathematics*, **19**(1), 79–92.

Pimm, D. (1987) *Speaking Mathematically: Communication in Mathematics Classrooms*, London, Routledge and Kegan Paul.

Pimm, D. (1988) 'Mathematical metaphor', *For the Learning of Mathematics*, **8**(1), 30–4.

Pimm, D. (1993a) 'The silence of the body', *For the Learning of Mathematics*, **13**(1), 35–8.

Pimm, D. (1993b) 'Just a matter of definition', *Educational Studies in Mathematics*, **25**(3), 261–77.

Pimm, D. (1994) 'Another psychology of mathematics education', in Ernest, P. (ed.) *Constructing Mathematical Knowledge: Epistemology and Mathematics Education*, Brighton, Falmer, pp. 111–24.

Pimm, D. and Love, E. (1991) Introduction, in Pimm, D. and Love, E. (eds) *Teaching and Learning School Mathematics*, London, Hodder and Stoughton, pp. v–x.

Pirie, S. and Kieren, T. (1989) 'A recursive theory of mathematical understanding', *For the Learning of Mathematics*, **9**(3), 7–11.

## REFERENCES

Pirie, S. and Kieren, T. (1992) 'Watching Sandy's understanding grow', *Journal of Mathematical Behavior*, **11**, 243–57.

Powell, A. (1986) 'Economizing learning: the teaching of numeration in Chinese', *For the Learning of Mathematics*, **6**(3), 20–3.

Pratt, D. (1994) 'Active graphing in a computer-rich environment', *Proceedings of the 18th PME Conference*, Lisbon, Portugal, pp. 57–64.

PrIME (1991) *Calculators, Children and Mathematics*, London, Simon and Schuster.

Random House (1979) *The Random House College Dictionary*, New York, Random House.

Reynès, F. (1990) 'Géométrie ou trahison des dessins?', *Petit x*, **26**, 73–5.

Richards, M. (1989, 2nd edition) *Centering*, Middletown, CT, Wesleyan University Press.

Riley, B. (1993) in conversation with E. H. Gombrich, BBC Radio 3, 24th August.

Roth, P. (1985) *My Life as a Man*, Harmondsworth, Penguin.

Rotman, B. (1987) *Signifying Nothing: the Semiotics of Zero*, London, Macmillan Press.

Salinger, J. (1964) *Franny and Zooey*, Montreal, Bantam.

Schmidt, R. (1986) 'On the signification of mathematical symbols', Preface to Bonasoni, P. (trans. Schmidt) *Algebra Geometrica*, Annapolis, MD, Golden Hind Press, pp. 1–12.

Second World Conference (1980) *Recommendations of the Second World Conference on Muslim Education*, Islamabad, King Abdulaziz University and Quaid-i-Azam University.

Serres, M. (1982) *Hermes: Literature, Science, Philosophy*, Baltimore, MD, Johns Hopkins University Press.

Sfard, A. (1994) 'Reification as the birth of metaphor', *For the Learning of Mathematics*, **14**(1), 44–55.

Shawn, W. (1991) *The Fever*, London, Faber and Faber.

Sierpinska, A. (1990) 'Some remarks on understanding in mathematics', *For the Learning of Mathematics*, **10**(3), 24–36.

Skemp, R. (1976) 'Relational and instrumental understanding', *Mathematics Teaching*, **77**, 20–6.

Skovsmose, O. (1985) 'Mathematical education versus critical education', *Educational Studies in Mathematics*, **16**(4), 337–54.

Skovsmose, O. (1990) 'Mathematical education and democracy', *Educational Studies in Mathematics*, **21**(2), 109–28.

Skovsmose, O. (1992) 'Democratic competence and reflective knowing in mathematics', *For the Learning of Mathematics*, **12**(2), 2–11.

Souriau, P. (1881) *Théorie de l'Invention*, Paris, Hachette et Cie; cited in Hadamard, J. (1945), *An Essay on the Psychology of Invention in the Mathematical Field*, Princeton, NJ, Dover, p. 64.

Spencer Brown, G. (1977) *Laws of Form*, New York, The Julian Press.

Stevens, W. (1967) *The Collected Poems of Wallace Stevens*, New York, Alfred A. Knopf.

Sträßer, R. (1991) 'Dessin et figure: géométrie et dessin technique à l'aide de l'ordinateur', Occasional paper no 128, Bielefeld, Germany, Institut für Didaktik der Mathematik der Universität Bielefeld.

Sutherland, R. (1992) 'What is algebraic about programming in Logo?', in Hoyles, C. and Noss, R. (eds) *Learning Mathematics and Logo*, Cambridge, MA, MIT Press, pp. 37–54.

Swan, M. (1982) *The Meaning and Use of Decimals*, Nottingham, Shell Centre for Mathematical Education.

Swetz, F. (1987) *Capitalism and Arithmetic*, London, Open Court.

REFERENCES

Tahta, D. (ed.) (1972) *A Boolean Anthology*, Derby, Association of Teachers of Mathematics.

Tahta, D. (1981a) 'About geometry', *For the Learning of Mathematics*, 1(1), 2–9.

Tahta, D. (1981b) 'Some thoughts arising from the new Nicolet films', *Mathematics Teaching*, 94, 25–9.

Tahta, D. (1985) 'On notation', *Mathematics Teaching*, 112, 49–51.

Tahta, D. (1988) 'Lucas turns in his grave', in Pimm, D. (ed.) *Mathematics, Teachers and Children*, London, Hodder and Stoughton, pp. 306–12.

Tahta, D. (1990a) 'Is there a geometrical imperative?', *Mathematics Teaching*, 129, 20–9.

Tahta, D. (1990b) 'Gratifying usefulness', *Mathematics Teaching*, 132, 57–8.

Tahta, D. (1991) 'Understanding and desire', in Pimm, D. and Love, E. (eds) *Teaching and Learning School Mathematics*, London, Hodder and Stoughton, pp. 221–46.

Tahta, D. (1992) 'Curricular configurations', *Micromath*, 8(2), 37–9.

Thom, R. (1971) '"Modern" mathematics: an educational and philosophical error?', *American Scientist*, 59, November–December, 695–9.

Thom, R. (1973) 'Modern mathematics: does it exist?', in Howson, G. (ed.) *Developments in Mathematical Education*, Cambridge, Cambridge University Press, pp. 194–209.

Thorndike, E. (1973) 'Measurement', in Ennis, R. and Krimmerman, L. (eds) *Philosophy of Educational Research*, New York, Wiley, pp. 17–24.

van den Brink, J. (1984) 'Acoustic counting and quantity counting', *For the Learning of Mathematics*, 4(2), 2–12.

Walkerdine, V. (1981) *Reading the Signs of Mathematics*, London, Report of the Leverhulme Trust.

Walkerdine, V. (1982) 'From context to text – a psychosemiotic approach to abstract thought', in Beveridge, M. (ed.) *Children Thinking Through Language*, London, Edward Arnold, pp. 129–55.

Walkerdine, V. (1988) *The Mastery of Reason*, London, Routledge.

Walsh, A. (1991) 'The calculator as a tool for learning', in Pimm, D. and Love, E. (eds) *Teaching and Learning School Mathematics*, London, Hodder and Stoughton, pp. 61–8.

Watson, A. (1991) 'Getting in touch', *Mathematics Teaching*, 135, 26–7.

Weil, S. (1952) *Gravity and Grace*, London, Routledge and Kegan Paul.

Weizenbaum, J. (1984) *Computer Power and Human Reason: From Judgement to Calculation*, Harmondsworth, Pelican.

Weldon, F. (1989) *Sacred Cows*, London, Chatto and Windus.

Weldon, F. (1991) *Letters to Alice*, London, Coronet.

Wheatley, G. (1992) 'The role of reflection in mathematics learning', *Educational Studies in Mathematics*, 23(5), 529–42.

Wheeler, D. (1989) 'Contexts for research on the teaching and learning of algebra', in Wagner, S. and Kieran, C. (eds) *Research Issues in the Learning and Teaching of Algebra*, Reston, VA, Lawrence Erlbaum Associates/NCTM, pp. 278–87.

Wheeler, D. (1992) 'Review of *Ethnomathematics: a multicultural view of mathematical ideas*, by Marcia Ascher', *The Mathematical Intelligencer*, 14(4), 64–5.

Whitehead, A. (1925) *Science in the Modern World*, New York, Macmillan.

Whitehead, A. (1947) *Essays in Science and Philosophy*, New York, Philosophical Library.

Whitney, H. (1973) 'Are we off the track in teaching mathematical concepts?', in Howson, G. (ed.), *Developments in Mathematical Education*, Cambridge, Cambridge University Press, pp. 283–96.

Wittgenstein, L. (1958) *The Blue and Brown Books*, Oxford, Basil Blackwell.

# NAME INDEX

# SUBJECT INDEX